Here's How

Write
Term Papers
and Reports

Here's How

Write Term Papers and Reports

L. Sue Baugh

NTC LearningWorks

NTC/Contemporary Publishing Group

Library of Congress Cataloging-in-Publication Data
is available from the United States Library of Congress.

Acknowledgments
This book has benefited greatly from the comments, suggestions, and criticism of many people. Chief among them, I would like to thank Verlin Fraser of Glenbrook North High School, Northbrook, Illinois, for her expertise and guidance; May Brottman, also of Glenbrook North High School; Robert J. Hamper of Rosary College; the editors of NTC/Contemporary Publishing Group, for their patience and many valuable suggestions; and Ann-Marie Sargent, for careful attention to detail in copyediting the text.

Originally published as *How to Write Term Papers and Reports*, Second Edition
Cover illustrations by Art Glazer

Published by NTC LearningWorks
A division of NTC/Contemporary Publishing Group, Inc.
4255 West Touhy Avenue, Lincolnwood (Chicago), Illinois 60646-1975 U.S.A.
Printed in the United States of America
International Standard Book Number: 0-8442-2608-4

99 00 01 02 03 04 ML 19 18 17 16 15 14 13 12 11 10 9 8 7 6 5 4 3 2 1

CONTENTS

Part 2
FROM FIRST DRAFT TO FINAL PAPER

CHAPTER 6
Works Cited and Works Consulted Lists

Part 3
FINAL TOUCHES

INTRODUCTION

Eight Keys to a First-Rate Paper

Your paper is due next month, next week, in three days. You need to find a topic, research it, and write the paper. How do you meet your deadline and still do a first-rate job?

This book is designed to help you at every step of the research and writing process. Whether you need help with a specific problem or with the process in general, by learning the eight keys to a first-rate paper, you can create a term paper or report that reflects your best abilities. Once you master these keys, you can apply them to any paper assigned in any course throughout your academic career.

First Key: Select and Focus Your Topic

What type of paper do you need to write—argumentative, descriptive, position, or literary? How do you choose an appropriate topic and make sure it's not too broad or too narrow? The decisions you make at this step affect your entire research and writing process. Students often need the most help at this first stage.

Chapter 1 provides essential guidelines on how to choose the best topic to fit your assignment, how to focus the topic, and how to make sure enough information is available to complete a research paper.

Second Key: Set Up a Research Strategy

Because your papers are usually written under tight deadlines, you need to know how to find information quickly and efficiently in any library. Chapter 1 presents a step-by-step strategy for conducting preliminary research on your topic. The strategy begins with general references and takes you through various research materials to books, periodicals, and special documents.

Third Key: Develop a Preliminary Thesis Statement

The thesis statement establishes what you want to say or prove in your paper. By following the guidelines in Chapter 2, you can quickly create a thesis statement based on your focused topic that sets the stage for your in-depth research. This statement acts like a general map guiding your research efforts.

Fourth Key: Conduct In-Depth Research

Also in Chapter 2, you learn the six key steps of research that will save you hours of effort—for example, how to set up key words and index terms for computer searches. Checklists for each type of paper help you determine what you really need to research about your subject.

The chapter also reviews the major resources found in a library, shows you how to retrieve hard-to-find information, and provides guidelines for evaluating the resources you uncover. Information is only as valuable as it is useful for your paper.

Fifth Key: Take Good Notes

Learn how to skim material for key words and concepts, then take notes on only the information pertinent to your topic. Chapter 2 shows you how to paraphrase, summarize, outline, and quote material on your note cards and how to establish a note-taking system that will be invaluable in developing an outline and writing your first draft.

Sixth Key: Choose the Best Structure— Create an Outline

Once you know the basic structure of any term paper or report, and the particular arrangement of information for each type of paper, creating an outline is relatively painless. A good outline makes writing the first draft considerably easier. Chapter 3 provides detailed guidelines on how to tailor your outline for the structure of an argumentative, descriptive, position, or literary term paper or report.

Eight Keys to a First-Rate Paper

First Key

> **Select and Focus Your Topic**
> - Choose general subject area
> - Narrow the topic
> - Select focused topic from general subject area
> - Verify topic with instructor

Second Key

> **Set Up Research Strategy**
> - Research available information—is there enough?
> - Start research

Third Key

> **Develop Preliminary Thesis Statement**

Fourth Key

> **Conduct In-Depth Research**
> - Set up key terms and searches
> - Locate sources
> - Retrieve, evaluate sources
> - Create bibliography cards

Fifth Key

> **Take Good Notes**
> - Set up system
> - Paraphrase, summarize, outline, quote

Sixth Key

> **Choose the Best Structure—Create an Outline**
> - Insert source numbers
> - Select illustrations

Seventh Key

> **Complete the First Draft**
> - Insert source references
> - Select illustrations

Eighth Key

> **Revise Your First Draft**
> - Create Works Cited / Works Consulted List
> - Check logical flow
> - Revise introductory, middle, concluding paragraphs
> - Prepare final illustrations

Seventh Key: Complete the First Draft

If you suffer from fear of the blank page—relax. The key to writing the first draft is to set your critical mind aside and simply write until you have completed the paper. Begin at the beginning if you can. If you can't, start in the middle or at the end. Don't worry about elegant phrasing, paragraph structure, or grammatical mistakes at this stage. Use your outline as a guide and keep on writing until you finish. Save any criticisms or judgments for the final step.

Eighth Key: Revise Your First Draft

Revision can turn a mediocre or flawed first draft into a first-rate work. Chapter 4 presents five secrets for revising your first draft that can speed up the revision process. Whether you have one night or several days to work on your draft, these five secrets can help you to improve the logic, flow, and impact of your paper. If you are going to put time and effort into a term paper or report, why not make it the best one possible?

Special Features of This Book

In addition to the eight keys above, several special features of this book can help you develop a first-rate paper.

- *Grammar and style tips.* Chapter 5 provides a quick, easy reference for the grammar and style questions that often prove the most troublesome to students. This chapter helps you improve your writing style and correct any grammatical mistakes.

- *Guidelines for typing and proofreading the paper.* Chapter 6 shows you how to prepare the Works Cited list. Chapter 8 provides guidelines for typing the title page, body, and special pages of your paper either on a typewriter or a word processor. A step-by-step proofreading system shows you how to check your paper for errors before handing it in.

- *How to use illustrations.* The right chart, map, or table can enhance the impact of your words. Chapter 7 discusses not only when to use illustrations but how to choose the best ones for your topic.

- *How to give an oral presentation.* Is part of your assignment an oral report based on your paper? Chapter 9 presents the four R's—respond, restructure, rehearse, relax—to help you create and deliver an effective oral presentation. You might even enjoy the process!

- *List of books on topics, research, and writing.* Appendix A contains a list of recommended books that can help you choose a topic, find the best resources quickly, and improve your writing style.

- *Sample term papers and reports.* Appendix B provides sample papers to show you how the principles and guidelines discussed in this book apply to the finished paper.

Whether you have to write a five-page report or a twenty-page term paper, the principles and guidelines provided in this book can make your next paper your best one.

PART 1
Preparing to Write

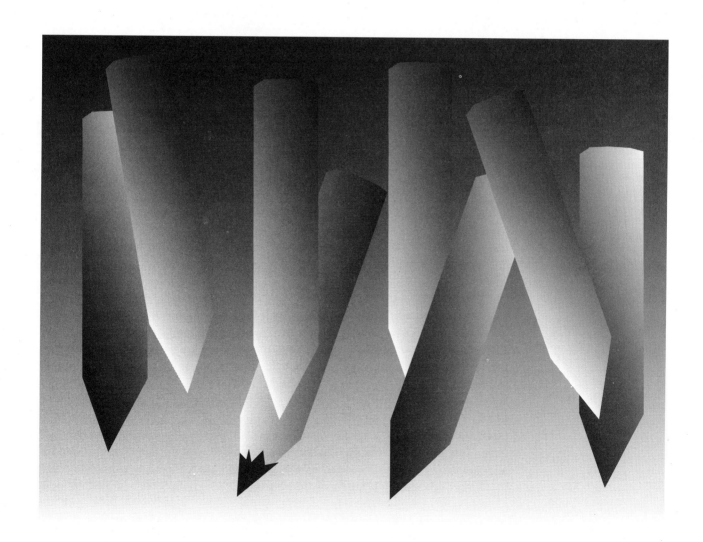

CHAPTER 1
Choosing and Focusing Your Topic

You've just been assigned a paper to write. If it's a report, you may have only a week or two to complete the assignment. If it's a term paper, you may have up to two or three months. One look at your class load, however, and you know you'd better get started right away.

Your immediate problem is a practical one: What do you write about? Whether you are assigned a topic or must choose one yourself, the task is roughly the same. You must take a general topic, do preliminary research to narrow it down, and determine if there is enough information to complete a paper. From that point on, you can conduct your research, develop a thesis statement, create an outline, and start writing.

The task of selecting and focusing a topic is not a matter of trial and error but a process anyone can learn. You can use it for any paper you write in any humanities course from English to social studies to history.

This chapter offers several strategies to help you determine the subject of your paper. Once you have the topic clearly defined, you are halfway home. Figure 1.1 outlines the steps you need to take to develop a usable topic from selection to preliminary research.

FIGURE 1.1   Key Steps in Choosing a Topic for Literary, Argumentative, Position, or Descriptive Papers

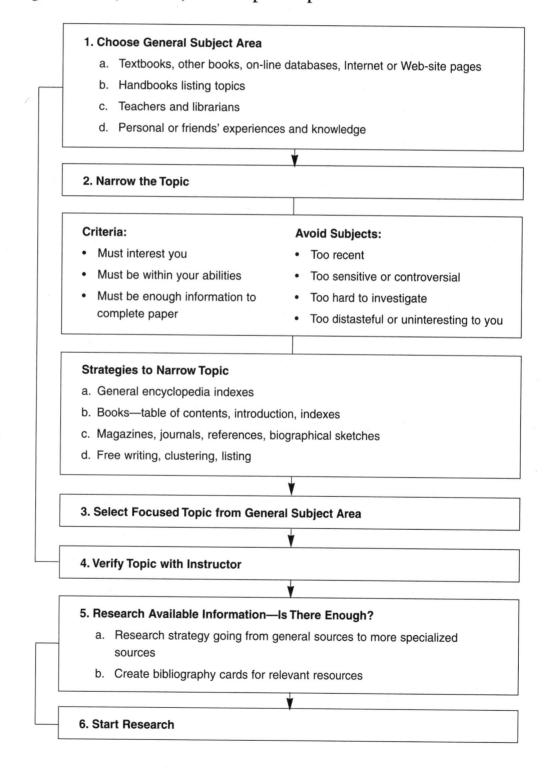

First Key

Select and Focus Your Topic

Second Key

Set Up Research Strategy

1. Choose General Subject Area

   a. Textbooks, other books, on-line databases, Internet or Web-site pages

   b. Handbooks listing topics

   c. Teachers and librarians

   d. Personal or friends' experiences and knowledge

2. Narrow the Topic

Criteria:

• Must interest you

• Must be within your abilities

• Must be enough information to complete paper

Avoid Subjects:

• Too recent

• Too sensitive or controversial

• Too hard to investigate

• Too distasteful or uninteresting to you

Strategies to Narrow Topic

a. General encyclopedia indexes

b. Books—table of contents, introduction, indexes

c. Magazines, journals, references, biographical sketches

d. Free writing, clustering, listing

3. Select Focused Topic from General Subject Area

4. Verify Topic with Instructor

5. Research Available Information—Is There Enough?

   a. Research strategy going from general sources to more specialized sources

   b. Create bibliography cards for relevant resources

6. Start Research

☞ 1 Select and Focus Your Topic

Topics and Types of Papers

Your topic is largely determined by the type and length of the paper you are to write. In most cases you will be asked to write a literary, an argumentative, a position, or a descriptive paper. The length may vary from five to twenty-five typed pages, depending on whether it is a brief report or term paper.

- *Literary paper.* For this paper, you must select an author and analyze his or her works. You can either compare and contrast them or analyze a specific element within the works—for example, the author's use of imagery, theme, setting, character, or plot. You need to support your comparison and contrast or analysis using the opinions of critics and other writers you find through your research.

- *Argumentative paper.* In this type of paper, your topic must have two opposing points of view—for example, the United States should or should not destroy all of its nuclear weapons. You choose one point of view, discuss the pros and cons, and then build a logical argument for the position you have taken, backed up by your research.

- *Position paper.* The topic of this paper may have two opposing views, but you need to discuss only the side that supports your position. You do not have to argue against the opposing view, only mention it at the beginning.

- *Descriptive paper (or report).* For this paper, you simply discuss a topic that interests you—for example, the oldest trees in the world. You are not trying to argue for or against anything; you are merely reporting on a topic.

In addition to the type of paper, the length of the paper will also determine the topic you choose and the amount of research you conduct. Naturally, a short paper will have a more limited focus and require fewer resources than will a longer paper. Before starting a search for a topic, make sure you understand the type and length of paper you are assigned.

"What Should I Write About?"— How to Select Your Topic

At the beginning of this process, you may feel as if you've entered a strange territory without a map. You need guidelines for choosing your topic if you must select your own or for narrowing a general topic assigned to you. This section shows you how to get ideas for topics and what subjects are best to avoid.

Three Criteria for a Topic

Whether you write a literary, argumentative, position, or descriptive paper, the subject you select must meet three important criteria.

1. The topic should interest you.

2. It should be within your abilities.

3. There should be enough information available on it to complete a paper.

The first criterion is the most important. Something besides fear of failure has to sustain you through all the hours it takes to research, write, and revise a report or term paper. Make the paper a process of discovery for yourself— something you want to know or say about a topic. That desire will help to see you through to the end of the project.

The second criterion is also essential. You may be interested in a topic but not have the background or ability to handle it in a paper. Say, for example, you are interested in the flights of *Voyagers 1* and *2*. You want to do a report on some of the computer programs that send commands to the small spacecrafts. The scientific journals are filled with complex diagrams and explanations, but you find none of it makes any sense to you. You have no background in computer programming and no ability to translate technical information into plain English.

You will either have to find a book or an article that translates the material for you or find another topic—perhaps what *Voyager 2* revealed about the rings of Uranus or the surprises the spacecraft uncovered as it passed by the outer planets. Although the topic about the computer programs fulfills two of the three criteria—it interests you and there is plenty of information—if it is beyond your abilities, you will not be able to complete a paper successfully.

Finally, make sure enough information is readily available for you to develop your paper. For instance, you may have heard about rock-and-roll bands springing up in Tibet. The subject intrigues you, and you feel you have enough musical background to write about it. But your preliminary research turns up only a half-page article in a weekly news magazine. Obviously, you are not going to be able to build a ten- or fifteen-page report on one short article. A better topic may be the rise of rock bands in China and Japan, a phenomenon covered in the U.S. and international press.

Finding a General Area of Interest

Suppose you must choose the topic of a paper yourself. Although this task might seem somewhat overwhelming at first, it can be broken down into manageable steps, as shown in Figure 1.1. The first step is knowing where to go for ideas about general or broad subject areas.

There are several major sources for topic ideas: textbooks; reference books that list term paper or report topics; teachers and librarians; your own or your friends' interests and experiences; and on-line databases, Internet, and Web sites. If you must do a term paper for a history course, for example, skim through your history textbook to find a broad subject area that interests you. Perhaps you find the European voyages of discovery appealing. Or your interest may be piqued by the medical practices of the Middle Ages or the complex politics of the Balkans in the mid-1990s.

If your textbooks do not provide a topic of interest, investigate the reference section of any bookstore or library. You are likely to find books that list hundreds of term paper or report topics under all subject areas—history, literature, art, social science, political science, and psychology. One of these topics may appeal to you.

Teachers and librarians are also good sources for ideas. They can help you to pinpoint an area of interest or can suggest topics that you haven't considered. It is a good idea to get to know your reference librarian, and this can be one way to introduce yourself. Good reference librarians are invaluable guides through the maze of research and reference sources. Their expertise can save you hours of effort.

If none of these sources yields any results, you can fall back on yourself or on your friends. Think about the movies, magazines, books, or activities that interest you: science fiction, sports, the war on drugs, international relations, music, the environment, psychic phenomena.

What would you like to know about these topics? What opinions do you have about them? Do you think drugs should be legalized? Do you feel that the government should do more or less to help protect the environment? In your opinion, have science fiction movies or TV series had any impact on shaping our current world? Should professional athletes be allowed to play in the Olympic games? Are psychic phenomena real or imaginary?

One of these four sources—textbooks, reference books, teachers and librarians, your own or your friends' interests—will give you a general topic area for your paper.

Subject Areas to Avoid

Part of the process of choosing a topic is knowing which subjects *not* to use. In your search for a topic, keep in mind these guidelines for subjects to avoid.

- *Subjects that are too recent.* If a new law has just been passed, for example, there will not be enough information about its impact to serve as the subject of a paper.

- *Subjects that are too sensitive or controversial.* Some issues, such as the firing of a popular principal or a recent racial incident in school, are highly emotional and likely to provoke strong reactions on all sides. It is often difficult to find objective information to present a fair treatment of the topic.

- *Subjects that are hard to investigate.* This can include subjects that are too narrow or specialized to have much information, too technical for your own and the readers' background, or for which information is too difficult to acquire. For example, the information may be in specialized libraries closed to the public, in international institutions, or written in a language you cannot read.

- *Subjects that are distasteful or uninteresting to you.* You may be tempted to accept any topic just to have something to write about. However, material that is unappealing to you at the beginning will tend to become more so as you work on it. If you dislike the subject of your paper, it's a good bet your readers won't like the way you write about it. Your own distaste or boredom will come across in your writing.

Remember the three criteria mentioned previously as you search for a usable topic: It must interest you, it must be within your abilities, and there must be enough information readily available on the topic to complete a paper.

"I've Got a Subject, Now What?"— How to Focus Your Topic

Once you have selected, or been assigned, a broad subject area, your next task is to narrow the topic for your paper. For instance, you may have a strong desire to write on mid-1990s Balkan politics. Obviously, you can't cover such a broad subject in a five- to ten-page paper. You will have to come up with a more manageable topic.

From Wide-Angle to Close-Up

When you narrow a subject, you are choosing to discuss only a portion of all the things that can be said about that topic. It is like moving from a wide-angle perspective to a close-up shot. The larger circle in Figure 1.2 represents everything known about the general subject (modern Balkan politics). The smaller circle focuses only on one part of that subject—perhaps the conflict between Bosnia and Croatia. Everything outside that circle is outside the scope of your paper. Your objective in narrowing the topic is to decide what should be included solely in that small circle.

You may have to take two steps to narrow your topic. For example, you may find the Bosnia-Croatia issue is still too broad a topic. You may want to narrow the focus further to the peace process or the role of the United Nations in the conflict. In that case, you would draw a smaller circle inside the Bosnia-Croatia conflict circle, as in Figure 1.3. Now you have a subject that can serve as the focus of your paper.

FIGURE 1.2   Narrowing Your Topic—First Stage

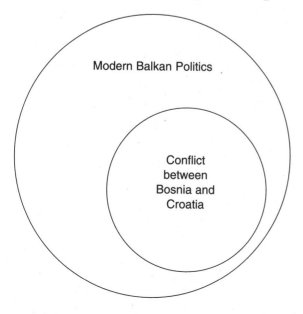

FIGURE 1.3   Narrowing Your Topic—Second Stage

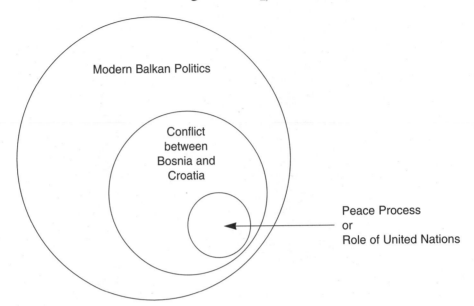

Strategies to Narrow Topics

As outlined in Figure 1.1, several methods can help you narrow your topic: conducting preliminary research, free-writing, clustering, and listing. You may want to use a combination of these techniques to take full advantage of both your analytical and creative abilities.

Preliminary Research.   Sources for preliminary research include encyclopedias, books, magazine articles, and various readers' guides and indexes.

To begin, look up your general topic in the index of a detailed encyclopedia such as Encyclopaedia Britannica, Encyclopedia Americana, or Colliers Encyclopedia. For example, the index listings under "Egyptians" might include "burial practices" or "magic rituals." You would then read the article to see if narrowing the topic to "magic rituals" is something that would interest you. You might find that you want to narrow "magic rituals" further to cover only the rituals that apply to weddings. The article in the encyclopedia will give you an overview of the important divisions of your topic.

If your topic is not covered adequately in the encyclopedia, then look through the library card catalog or computer catalog to locate a book about the general subject. Study the book's table of contents, introduction, or index to see if some part of the larger subject catches your interest. For example, a book on the greenhouse effect might have chapters on how human health will be affected, suspected causes of the effect, or what steps people can take now to lessen its impact. Another book might have a chapter arguing that the alarm over the greenhouse effect is exaggerated and that natural weather cycles are responsible for worldwide temperature increases. Any of these chapters might suggest a narrower focus for the general topic of greenhouse effect.

If there is no book on your general subject, search for magazine, journal, or newspaper articles in the *Readers' Guide to Periodical Literature,* in computer databases such as INFOTRAC, Dialog, Internet or Web-site sources, or in specialized indexes compiled on various topics. Ask the librarian to help you locate these sources.

Freewriting, Clustering, and Listing. If your preliminary research has not helped you narrow your topic or if your focused topic is still too broad, you can use freewriting, clustering, and listing to help choose a suitable focus.

These techniques make use of your mind's natural ability to organize information and store it in logical form. People are often pleasantly surprised by how much more they know about a subject than they realized or by the thought-provoking questions they find themselves asking. Such questions can serve to focus the topic and start you off on your research.

- *Freewriting.* This strategy involves writing continuously about the general topic for a specified time—usually ten minutes. It is essential to keep writing without lifting your pen or pencil from the paper. Keep going no matter how unrelated, silly, or odd the writing may seem. Write what you think and feel about the topic, questions that occur to you, images that arise, statements you've heard others make, whatever comes in the allotted time.

  For example, your subject might be censorship in the schools. Your freewriting might include statements such as these: "Censorship only makes the books censored more popular, trying to suppress ideas doesn't work; on the other hand, maybe some books harmful, maybe some ideas distorting, giving kids the wrong picture." You may ask questions like, "Is censorship based on values or fear? Fear of what? If values, what are we trying to exclude and why? Whose taste, whose reality, whose definitions? Is censorship ever justified? Is it necessary in education to censor certain books?"

  When the time is up, reread what you have written. Highlight any statements or questions, that strike you as particularly interesting, something you would like to investigate, such as the criteria used to decide which books are censored. List all the topics you have developed through freewriting and choose the one that interests you the most. Conduct your preliminary research to make sure there is enough information on the selected topic to complete a paper.

- *Clustering.* For this technique, take a sheet of paper at least 8 1/2 by 11 inches or larger. In the center write a word or short phrase that represents the general topic—for instance, "Violence on TV" or "Illegal aliens." Draw a circle around the word or phrase, Then write down each word that comes to mind when you think about the topic. Branch these words off the main circle until you begin to form a cluster pattern like the one in Figure 1.4. When you have finished, reread your cluster. Are there any branches that suggest suitable topics? Choose the one that interests you the most.

- *Listing.* This technique involves listing all the topics you can think of that fall under your general subject. Then cross out the ones that are too broad or inappropriate and check those that might be a good starting point for your preliminary research (see Table 1.1). Select the one that you find the most interesting.

FIGURE 1.4 Clustering Strategy

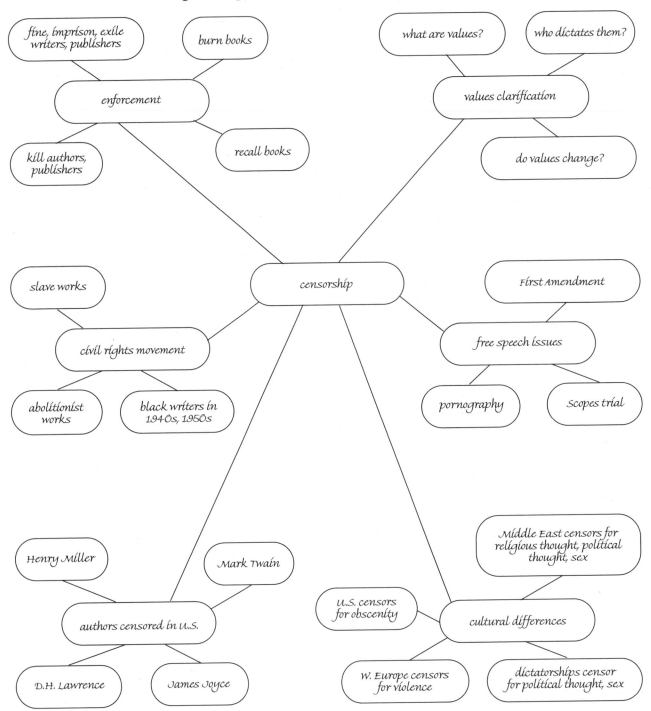

Topic: Criteria for censorship are determined by cultural context and not by objective standards.

1. Western Europe censors material for violence.
2. U.S. censors material for obscenity.
3. Dictatorships censor for political thought, sex, some religious ideas.
4. Middle Eastern countries censor mainly religious ideas, political thought, sex.

TABLE 1.1 Listing Strategy

General Topic: Censorship

~~1. First Amendment rights~~ *(too broad)*

~~2. Role of free thought in democracy~~ *(too broad)*

~~3. Criteria for censorship—who sets them, do they change with the times?~~
(not interesting to me)

~~4. Censorship and education~~ *(too broad)*

✓ 5. Enforcing censorship—can it be done? *(mildly interesting)*

✓ 6. Censorship as free publicity for groups, books, material *(interesting)*

✓ 7. Self-censorship on part of the press—what do they agree not to print and
why? *(research this one)*

       1—government secrets?

       2—misconduct of officials?

       3—foreign affairs blunders?

       4—military errors

       5—misconduct of certain groups?

Once you have narrowed your topic, check with your instructor to make
sure the topic is acceptable and that it meets the requirements of the assignment. This simple step is often overlooked by students. You don't want to
spend two or three weeks researching a topic that fails to fulfill the assignment. Once you have verified your topic with the instructor, the next step is
to make sure there is enough information available on the topic to complete
your paper.

➭ 2 Set Up Research Strategy

"Is There Enough Information?"— Research Strategy

The research strategy outlined in Figure 1.5 is similar to the steps you took
to focus your topic. (This strategy is based on the work of May Brottman,
Glenbrook North High School, Northbrook, Illinois.) In this stage, however, you are searching for books, articles, reviews, essays, and other information specifically related to the topic you have selected.

The principal advantage in such a strategy is to help you find information
quickly without having to do too much reading. You move from general reference sources that provide an overview of the topic, such as encyclopedias,
to more specialized, detailed sources, such as articles and books. Although
many instructors do not allow you to cite an encyclopedia as a reference,
encyclopedia articles often list books and periodicals that provide information
on your topic. These references can be cited in your paper.

FIGURE 1.5   Research Strategy for Locating Information

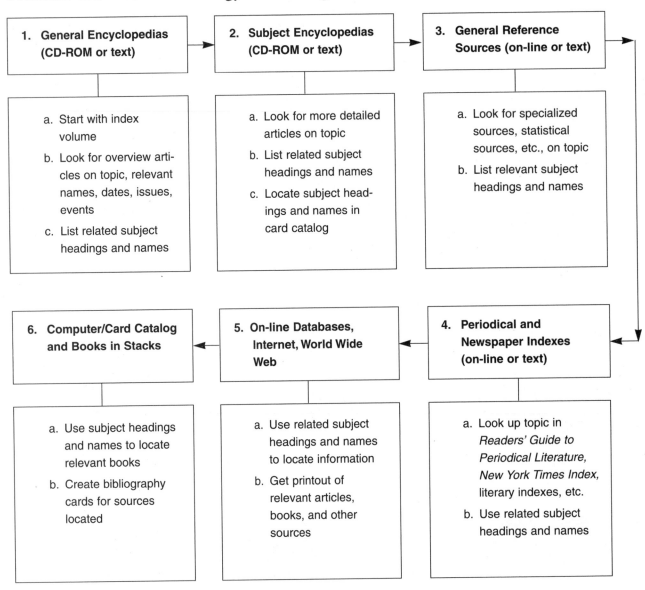

Also, the general encyclopedia index often lists entries for related topics and the names of people associated with your selected topic. These entries can provide subject headings for further research in readers' guides, subject indexes, on-line databases, CD-ROMs, and other computer information sources, and the computer card catalog. General references will show you what gaps in information you need to fill with articles, books, or interviews.

Finally, look at the bibliography or reference section found in many articles and books. They will often be a source of other references—books, articles, essays. This step can help to cut down on your research time and give you a rough idea of the number of sources on your topic.

Bibliography Cards and Idea Sheets

As you locate suitable research materials, make a bibliography card for each reference you might use for your paper. In this way, you accomplish three goals during your preliminary research.

1. You verify that you have sufficient information available to research the subject.

2. You are able to locate a source when you need it.

3. You create a list of titles for your Works Cited list (what used to be known as a bibliography) when you write the final draft of your paper.

Format for Bibliography Cards

In most cases, your references will be either books or articles. The basic format for bibliography cards has been developed by the Modern Language Association and presented in the *MLA Handbook for Writers of Research Papers* by Joseph Gibaldi and Walter S. Achtert. Consult this handbook to find the correct format for any reference—films, musical works, art works, collections, reprinted books, newspapers, and audiocassettes. Use either 3 × 5 or 6 × 8 notecards for your sources. You can also create a working bibliography file on your computer.

Bibliography cards or files for books must contain the author's name (last name first), the full title of the book (underlined), place of publication, a shortened version of the publisher's name, copyright date, and library call number or other source of the book. Specific page numbers are included only if a particular chapter of the book is used. Number each card in the upper righthand corner or number each file entry. You may also want to write a brief note about the book's contents to remind yourself why you selected this source. Figure 1.6 shows how the information for books is arranged on a card or in a computer file. There are software programs that will create Works Cited lists from reference entries. These programs automatically put entries into MLA style and arrange them alphabetically.

Bibliography cards or computer file entries for magazine and journal articles contain the following information: author name, if listed (last name first); title of the article (in quotation marks); title of the magazine or journal (underlined); date (day, month, year or month and year); page numbers followed by a period. Number each source card in the upper righthand corner. Figure 1.7 shows how information for articles is arranged.

See Chapter 6, Works Cited and Works Consulted Lists, for more detailed bibliography formats for books and periodicals, or consult the latest edition of the *MLA Handbook.*

Idea Sheets

In addition to bibliography cards, create an idea sheet as you conduct your preliminary research. On this sheet, note any questions, comments, or ideas that occur to you on your topic. At a later stage, your idea sheet can help you formulate a thesis statement and create an outline.

FIGURE 1.6   Bibliography Card and Computer File Entry for a Book

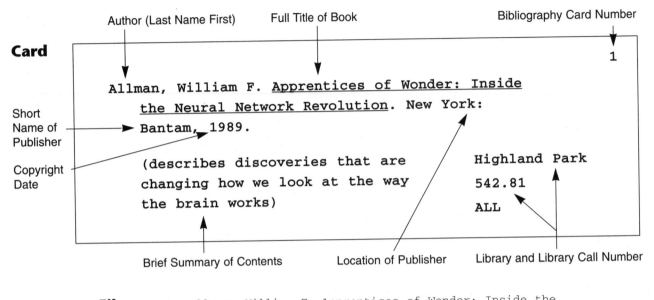

Computer File

1. Allman, William F. <u>Apprentices of Wonder: Inside the Neural Network Revolution</u>. New York: Bantam, 1989. (Highland Park Library 542.81 ALL). Describes discoveries that are changing how we look at the way the brain works

Source Information in Parentheses

FIGURE 1.7   Bibliography Card and Computer File Entry for an Article

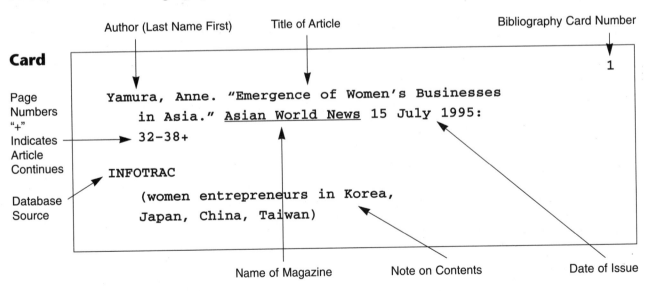

Computer File

2. Yamura, Anne. "Emergence of Women's Businesses in Asia." <u>Asian World News</u> 15 July 1995: 32–38+ (INFOTRAC) Women entrepreneurs in Korea, Japan, China, Taiwan

Database Source in Parentheses

The idea sheet can be adapted for each type of paper. For an argumentative paper, for example, divide the sheet into "Pro" and "Con" and jot down arguments or questions on both sides.

If you are writing a descriptive paper—on Mount St. Helens, for instance—list the questions you need answered. What caused the volcano to become active again? How powerful was the explosion that rocked the mountain? What damage did the blast do? How quickly has the area recovered? Will such an explosion happen again? If your preliminary research provokes other questions, write those down on your idea sheet.

For a position paper, note arguments that support your stand and the examples or reasoning that justify your position. Finally, for a literary paper, list the authors' major works and try to see common themes or elements that run through them. Write down your impressions, questions, or ideas about the author and the works that may provide fruitful lines of research.

Chapter 2 takes you through the next steps in the process: how to develop a preliminary thesis statement, conduct in-depth research, and take notes for your paper.

CHAPTER 2
Researching Your Topic

Once you have narrowed your topic, conducted a preliminary survey of reference material, and generated an idea sheet, you are ready for the next steps: formulating a rough thesis statement, conducting in-depth research, and taking notes. At this stage of the process, you have an opportunity to develop the skills of a good investigative reporter. Like a reporter, you'll be answering who, what, where, when, why, and how about your topic through research and note taking. Figure 2.1 summarizes the key steps in researching your topic.

FIGURE 2.1   Key Steps in Researching a Topic

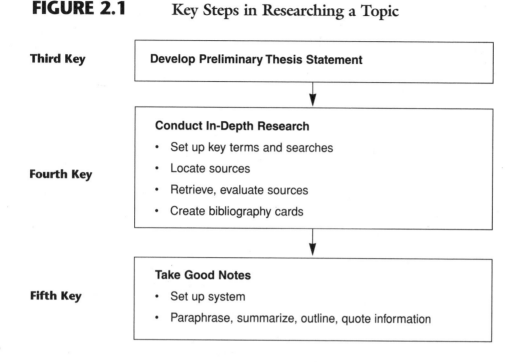

Third Key

Develop Preliminary Thesis Statement

Fourth Key

Conduct In-Depth Research
- Set up key terms and searches
- Locate sources
- Retrieve, evaluate sources
- Create bibliography cards

Fifth Key

Take Good Notes
- Set up system
- Paraphrase, summarize, outline, quote information

☞ 3 Formulate Preliminary Thesis

Preliminary Thesis Statement

The thesis statement is like a rough map that helps you find your way through the unfamiliar territory of your topic. The details are filled in as you conduct your research. A thesis statement is one or two sentences that state your goal and the main idea of your paper. Why are you writing about this subject and what do you intend to describe, prove, or analyze?

The statement should be related to the type of paper you are writing—literary, argumentative, position, or descriptive. The main idea must be one that can be developed through research. Remember, this is still a rough version of your statement. As you conduct your research, you may find that you want to modify it.

All your research and every paragraph in your paper must relate to the thesis statement. As you can see, a good statement can save you a great deal of time by further narrowing your focus and by concentrating your research on information that supports or proves your main idea.

Developing Your Thesis Statement

No one claims that writing a thesis statement is easy. However, you can use more than one strategy to develop your statement. If you have written notes, comments, or reactions during your preliminary research, this "idea sheet" can serve as a starting point. The techniques—laundry list, free-writing, and clustering—that served to narrow your topic can also be used to develop a thesis statement.

Laundry List. Make a list of all the ideas you have regarding your topic. In the Bosnia-Croatia example from Chapter 1, for instance, you may have narrowed the topic down to the role of the United Nations in the conflict. What is it you want to say about the topic? Are you taking a position, describing an event, arguing a point, or examining the impact of the event on Balkan children?

Select one or two ideas that most closely fit the type of paper you are going to write. Try to put your ideas into one or two sentences. Can the idea be researched?

Freewriting. Look over your idea sheet or simply start writing for ten minutes on your topic. For example, suppose you are writing a paper on superstitions in modern culture and have narrowed the topic down to the superstitions of famous sports figures.

Again, select one or two ideas that seem to capture what you want to say about the subject and that fit the type of paper you are writing.

Clustering. If neither of these two techniques work, you might try clustering to develop a thesis statement. Perhaps you are working on a literary paper about Isaac Asimov's *Foundation* trilogy. You have narrowed the topic down to a discussion of Asimov's psychohistory theory of cultural development. Write the term "psychohistory theory" in the center of a piece of paper and begin to branch out from the center, jotting down ideas as fast as they occur to you.

Select one or two branches and determine which one can serve as a thesis statement for your paper. Develop the statement in one or two sentences and make sure it can be researched.

Table 2.1 shows examples of preliminary thesis statements and their relationship to the type of paper being written. Look over these statements and notice how they give a sharper focus to the research that must be done.

What Do You Need to Know?

Now that you have developed a rough thesis statement and know more clearly the purpose of your paper, the next step is to ask yourself what information you need to complete your work. A little planning at this point can save you considerable time later on. A series of questions can help to guide your research.

1. Am I researching
   - an event? (Wall Street Crash of 1929)
   - an object? (*Voyager 2*)
   - a practice? (superstitions of sports figures)
   - a person? (author, scientist, politician)
   - a location? (country, town, geological feature)
   - an idea? (free speech versus censorship)

TABLE 2.1   Examples of Preliminary Thesis Statements

Topic	Type of Paper	Thesis Statement
Role of the United Nations in the Bosnia-Croatia conflict	descriptive	The Bosnia-Croatia conflict placed the United Nations in the difficult position of trying to maintain the peace without having either the troops or the authority to stop the conflict.
Legalization of illegal drugs in the U.S.	argumentative	The "war on drugs" will do far more to help control and eliminate illegal drug use in the U.S. than will legalization of drugs.
Superstitions among leading sports figures	position	Although many people believe superstitions are a thing of the past, it has been shown that superstitious rituals and beliefs can actually improve the performance of many leading sports figures.
The psychohistory theory in Asimov's *Foundation* trilogy	literary	Asimov uses his psychohistory theory to show the dangers of overreliance on scientific formulas when it comes to guiding human affairs.

2. What do I already know about the subject? If it is a practice, for example, what was or is its purpose? How did it arise and why is it continued? What does it involve? Who carries it out? What effect does it have?

3. What more do I need to know about the topic? For an event, when and where did it happen? What events led up to it? Who were the main characters involved? What happened at the event itself? What were the short-range consequences? What were the long-range consequences? How are things different because of this event?

4. What information should I collect for the type of paper I am writing? Each type of paper has its own research requirements.

Literary

- Biographical information about the author
- Titles of major works and when they were published
- Story lines and major themes of each work
- Common or contrasting themes, images, story lines, characters among various works
- Other writers' and critics' analyses of the works
- Reviews of works in journals, newspapers, books, etc.
- Views of writers or critics that support your topic

Argumentative

- Overview or description of the topic
- Background information showing the development of the issue

- Articles and books about the issue, for and against
- Views that support your position, reasons writers give for the stand they take
- Information on the opposing view

Position
- Background information about topic, events leading up to it
- Description of topic for benefit of reader
- Important ideas and people related to topic
- Information supporting your position
- Information on opposing or alternative views

Descriptive
- Background information on topic, events leading up to the main occurrence
- Description of topic for benefit of reader
- Important ideas and people related to topic
- Historical development of subject
- Experts' and other writers' ideas, opinions, research, conclusions about subject

5. Where am I likely to find information on this topic? Your preliminary research will give you some idea what your main sources of information might include: general reference, special collections, magazine or newspaper articles, books, government documents, S.I.R.S., computer databases.

6. How should I conduct my in-depth research? The research strategy outlined in Chapter 1 is still the basic pattern to follow. This question is covered later in this chapter in the section "In-Depth Research: Locating Sources."

☞ 4 Find the Right Information

In-Depth Research: Preliminary Steps

Whether you conduct a manual or computer search, the basic principles are the same. You must complete six steps.

1. Identify subject headings or key words (also called "designators") for your search.

2. Use these headings and key terms to search various general and specialized indexes, card catalogs, or computer databases to locate books, articles, and documents on your topics.

3. Select the sources most relevant to your thesis statement.

4. Retrieve the sources—obtain books, copies of articles, copies of microfiche or microfilm data.

5. Evaluate information for its accuracy and objectivity, coverage of the topic, and usefulness to your paper.

6. Create bibliography cards or computer file entries for each source, and take notes on the material selected.

No matter what subject or type of paper you are writing, these six steps are the same.

Identifying Subject Headings, Key Words, or Designators

To conduct in-depth research, you must be able to determine under what key words—also known as designators—the information has been categorized. Knowing how to set up the correct terms can mean the difference between finding information and having to choose another topic.

Suppose, for example, you are researching the superstitions of sports figures. You have found only one book on the subject and decide to use INFO-TRAC, a computerized database, to locate articles from magazines and major newspapers. You type in the heading "superstitions." To your dismay, only one entry, with no subheadings, appears:

```
Superstitious Mind, book review
```

You are almost ready to pick another topic when a rare moment of inspiration strikes. You start over and type in "superstition"—singular! The computer responds:

```
        Superstition

            see also

                    Amulets

                    Demonology

                    Ordeal

                    Talismans

                    Vampires

                    Voodooism

                    Werewolves

        —analysis

        —anecdotes, facetiae, satire, etc.

        —business applications

        —economic aspects

        —history

        —psychological aspects

        —public opinion

        —social aspects

        —sports use

        —theater traditions
```

Only one letter difference and, like a magic key, your subject heading opens the computer database and reveals its knowledge. You then highlight "sports use" and the computer search turns up numerous articles on your focused topic.

Many students make the mistake of giving up too soon if they fail to find information on the first try. Identifying key words requires some ingenuity, a little detective work, and some help from the reference librarian. Use these guidelines to help you select key words to open databases and card catalogs to you.

1. Locate key words in general indexes, indexes in books, *Library of Congress Subject Headings,* and subject guides to computer databases. The subject headings in these sources can provide you with key terms to use in your search.

2. Check your key word for obvious errors. Make sure you have spelled the item correctly and have the correct full name of a location, event, or person. Is it Peter*son* or Peter*sen*? *Mt.* St. Helens or *Mount* St. Helens? Gettys*berg* or Gettys*burg*? Battle of *Manassas* or Battle of *Bull Run* (both names refer to the same battle)? Check with the reference librarian if you are in doubt.

3. Try alternative forms of the key word or subcategories under the key word. Use the singular form if the plural form draws a blank and vice versa. Or try words derived from the key word. If physics does not give you the information you need, try physicists or different branches of physics such as quantum mechanics or subatomic particles. It may be that your original key word is too broad.

4. If your topic does not appear in the index of any encyclopedia, book, or database, widen your search to the historical period in which the topic occurs. If you are researching a key battle in ancient Rome, for example, you might look up Rome, Ancient in a classical history encyclopedia and see if your battle is mentioned in the article. Perhaps you can research it under the name of the Roman commander who led the attack. At the very least, you will be gaining background information about your topic.

5. If you find yourself running into one dead end after another, consult with your instructor or the reference librarian. It may be that there simply isn't enough information on your narrowed topic. You may have to go back to your original subject and choose another focus.

Surveying the Library

Before heading straight for the reference section in your library, take time to learn the layout of the entire building. Libraries arrange their resources according to various subject categories and specialized services. These include art, film, and music rooms; books on various subjects classified by Dewey decimal or Library of Congress method; a reference room with computer search terminals; magazine and newspaper collections with microfilm or microfiche machines; and special subject rooms (poetry, business, science, government documents, special collections).

Figure 2.2 shows the layout of one library. Although the layout of each library will differ, the basic arrangement of its materials is roughly the same from one library to the next. Each library you visit should be able to provide

FIGURE 2.2   Layout of a Library

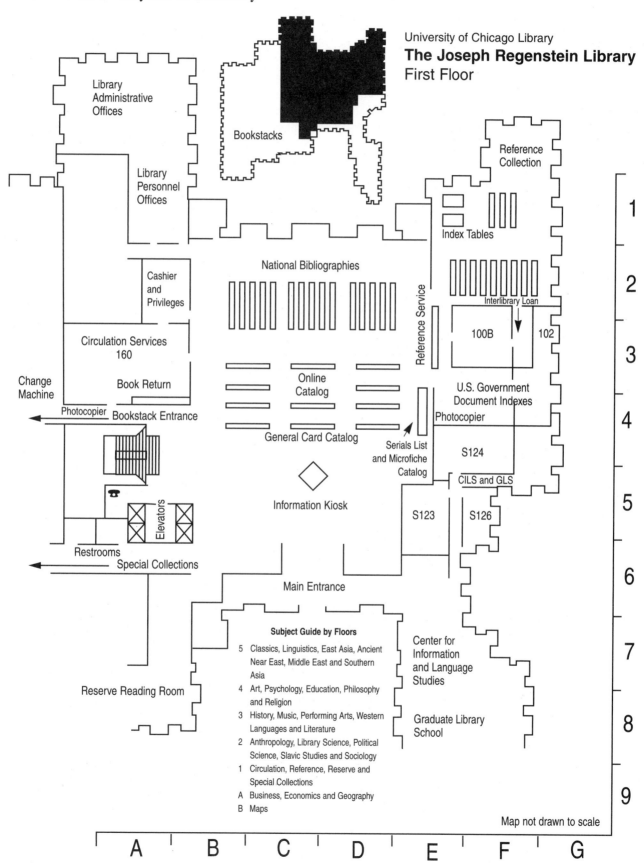

you with a printed layout showing you how and where its materials are arranged. You can obtain a copy at the library's information desk.

This initial scouting survey can save you considerable time later on when you need to locate specific references quickly. Also, you may discover references you never knew existed that could provide key information for your paper.

One student, for example, had trouble finding information on the mythology of Northeastern Indian tribes. During her survey of the library, she discovered—in a specialized reference room—a fourteen-volume edition of Indian myths published in 1918. One entire volume was devoted to the mythology of Northeastern tribes.

Dewey Decimal versus Library of Congress Classification

It is also a wise practice to become familiar with both the Dewey decimal and Library of Congress methods of classification. Most high schools and many public libraries use the Dewey decimal system to organize and arrange books or other items. However, many college and university libraries and a growing number of public libraries are using the Library of Congress method. This method provides greater flexibility and a more detailed breakdown of categories. The main classes of each system are as follows.

Dewey Decimal

000	General Works
100	Philosophy and Psychology
200	Religion
300	Social Sciences
400	Language
500	Pure Science
600	Technology (Applied)
700	The Arts
800	Literature
900	General Geography, History

Library of Congress

A	General Works
B	Philosophy, Religion, Psychology
C	History: Auxiliary Sciences
D	History: General and Old World
E–F	History: American
G	Geography, Anthropology, Folklore, Sports, Recreation
H	Social Sciences
J	Political Science
K	Law
L	Education
M	Music
N	Fine Arts
P	Language and Literature
Q	Science and Mathematics
R	Medicine

S   Agriculture
T   Technology
U   Military Science
V   Naval Science
Z   Bibliography and Library Science

The Library of Congress system uses both letters and arabic numbers. From a base of twenty-one letters (I, O, W, X, Y are not used), the system can be expanded to more divisions than can the Dewey decimal system. The number-and-letter combinations serve as a class number and author number for the book. For example, P86.Y15 tells you that the book is in the language and literature section and that the author's name begins with a "Y."

Another advantage of learning the Library of Congress system is that many databases take their subject headings from this system's index. If you know how the Library of Congress classifies information, it will be easier to formulate key words or designators for your searches.

In-Depth Research: Locating Sources

Once you know the general layout of the library, you can use the research strategy summarized in Figure 2.3. The object of in-depth research is to collect final sources to use for taking notes and constructing your paper. You are not going to use every reference you find, only those that relate specifically to your topic. Along the way, you will be creating bibliography cards for your Works Cited pages.

The following sections give you a brief summary of the sources available to you for your research. Many of these sources are now available on CD-ROM as well as text. Ask the reference librarian for help.

Library Reference Section

The amount of information contained in even a modest-sized library reference section is truly astonishing. You have already used some of the references in your preliminary research to determine if enough material exists on your chosen topic. Now you will be searching through reference material for sources you can use for your paper.

Encyclopedias. At this stage in your research, you may want to consult some of the specialized and technical encyclopedias to help you find key words, names, books, and other sources. Some of these encyclopedias include *Grzimek's Animal Life Encyclopedia; The McGraw-Hill Encyclopedia of World Drama; Cyclopedia of Biblical, Theological, and Ecclesiastical Literature;* and *The Modern Encyclopedia of Basketball.*

Encyclopedias exist for nearly every topic, including film, television, pop and rock music, medicine, law, business, history, military affairs, economics, political issues, and literature. Consult the reference card catalog or computer catalog to locate the volumes on your subject.

Current Affairs. Because current social and political affairs change rapidly, the reference section contains several works updated weekly, monthly, or annually. These include the following.

FIGURE 2.3 Summary of In-Depth Research Strategy

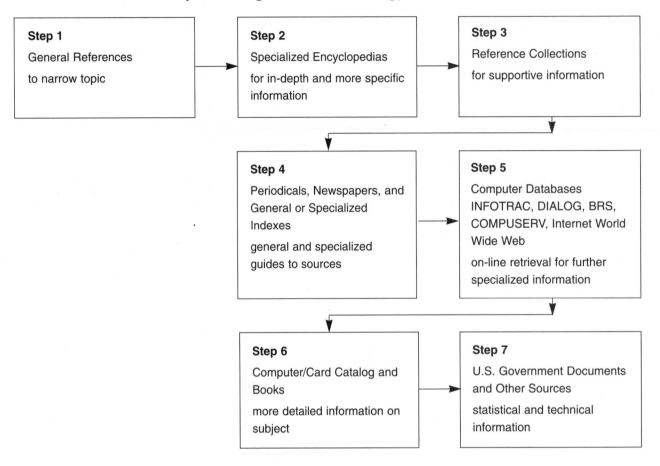

- *Facts on File.* Offers weekly reviews of domestic and world affairs.
- *Editorial Research Reports.* Published four times a month; each issue is devoted to a single current affairs subject.
- *S.I.R.S. (Social Issues Resource Series).* A multivolume set that addresses a different social issue with each volume. Kept in three-ring binders, these indexed volumes contain articles from newspapers, magazines, and journals.
- *Pamphlet files.* These are files containing pamphlets, brochures, or articles clipped from newspapers, magazines, documents, and other sources and placed in file folders in cabinets. They are arranged alphabetically according to subjects.
- *Great Contemporary Issues Series.* This series is similar to S.I.R.S. Each of its twenty volumes addresses a different social topic and contains *New York Times* reprints.

Biographical References. Biographical information can be found in a wide range of sources. Some of the most important include the following.

- *The New York Times Biographical Service.* A listing of past and current figures in all fields. It is published monthly and provides in-depth knowledge about each biographee.

- *Webster's Biographical Dictionary; Chamber's Biographical Dictionary.* These two volumes contain over 65,000 historical listings. They provide thumbnail sketches of each entry.

- *Dictionary of Scientific Biography.* Brief biographies of those who have made significant contributions in all areas of science, listing their major achievements, awards, and publications.

- *American Writers; Contemporary Authors; Dictionary of Literary Biography;* and others. Provide biographies of writers, including a list of the authors' major works with their publication dates.

- *Who's Who editions.* These editions can be found in nearly every field—who's who in art and music, banking and finance, corporate business, education, engineering, film and theater, history, law, literature, medicine, politics, religion, and so on. Some volumes are arranged by geographic regions, ethnic or racial origin, gender, or nationality. The oldest and most reliable of these volumes is published by Marquis company.

  The one drawback of these volumes is that the biographees write their own entries. You should double-check vital information with a second or third source to ensure accuracy. Few people may be able to resist the temptation to embellish their lives!

Almanacs and Yearbooks. Almanacs are a ready source of world information on a wide range of topics. If you need to know what world records were set in swimming events in the 1988 Olympics, the almanac for that year will tell you. What about world wheat harvests, the number of shoes manufactured in Italy, or the top money-making U.S. film of the year? It's all in the almanac. The two most authoritative and complete volumes are the *World Almanac and Book of Facts* and the *Information Please Almanac.*

Yearbooks appear either as year-in-review summaries of specific subjects, such as *McGraw-Hill Yearbook of Science and Technology,* or as general yearly updates for encyclopedias. These updates cover world events and technological advances for the preceding year.

Statistical Material. The right use of statistics can enrich your term paper or report. You may need to know the rate of increase of the Hispanic population in certain states, or the amount of consumer debt incurred by Americans in the 1980s. The most accessible statistical volumes include the following.

- *World Almanac and Book of Facts; Information Please Almanac.* These volumes present statistics covering business and economics, education, population, politics, meteorology, cities, states, countries, and many other categories.

- *Statistical Abstract of the United States.* Published by the Census Bureau in Washington, DC, this reference contains statistical information on nearly every aspect of American culture from how many hamburgers a year we consume to how many tons of garbage we throw away.

- *Census of Population and Housing.* Published by the Census Bureau every ten years, it provides a state-by-state breakdown of population and housing.

Other major statistical references include Gallup Poll survey results, *The East European and Soviet Data Handbook* covering Eastern bloc nations, *The Statistical History of the United States from Colonial Times to Present,* and *European Historical Statistics.* Consult your reference librarian to find out what range of statistical material your library carries.

Maps, Atlases, and Gazetteers. These references are found in abundance in any library and provide excellent current and historical maps of countries, wars, populations, and the like. Volumes such as *The Times Index-Gazetteer* lists offer 345,000 geographical entries describing towns, cities, rivers, states, mountain ranges, and other features.

Some of these works, particularly *Maps on File,* allow you to photocopy maps at no charge for research purposes. The right map can provide the perfect illustration for your paper.

The references discussed above are only a few of the volumes found in any library reference section. It may be well worth your time to explore this section and learn the range of sources the library contains. Who knows what you might find?

Periodicals

Periodicals include magazines, specialized journals, and newspapers. The size of your library determines to a large extent how many periodicals it will carry. These references and their indexes are often expensive, require considerable space to house back issues, and are perfect targets for thieves. In many cases you must show your library card to order back issues or even be allowed into the periodicals room.

Your first, and often best, source to consult for magazines is the *Readers' Guide to Periodical Literature,* published twice a month. This old standby is still one of a researcher's single most valuable tools. Articles are arranged by Library of Congress subject heading, author, and title. Magazine titles are followed by volume number, page, and date, as shown below. Once you understand the system, you will have no trouble identifying the source you need.

LENSES, PHOTOGRAPHIC
So you thought zoom lenses always stay in focus as
you zoom? Well, they don't! H. Keppler, il *Popular
Photography* 96: 38–9 + Jl '89

Headings are cross-referenced to more detailed information about a topic. For example, suppose you are researching the question "Should illegal drugs be legalized?" The first heading you look up is "Drug Control." You see the following entry.

DRUG CONTROL   *See* Narcotics laws and regulations

You turn to the new heading and see exactly the subject you need.

NARCOTICS LAWS AND REGULATIONS
See also
Airplanes in narcotics regulation
Drug paraphernalia—Laws and regulations
Legalization of narcotics

The heading "Legalization of narcotics" yields the following articles published from January through November 1989.

LEGALIZATION OF NARCOTICS
Accepting the presence of drugs. A. S. Trebach. il *New
   Perspectives Quarterly* 6:40–4 Summ '89
The enemy within. M. B. Zuckerman, il *U. S. News &
   World Report* 107:91 S 11 '89
A war for the Surgeon General, not the Attorney
   General. K. Schmoke. il *New Perspectives Quarterly*
   6:12–15 Summ '89
                    Netherlands
The Dutch model. E. Engelsman. *New Perspectives
   Quarterly* 6:44–5 Summ '89
                    Western Europe
A Common Market of crack? C. Dickey. il *Newsweek*
   114:37 S 18 '89

Unfortunately, no comparable reference exists for technical, medical, and other specialized journal articles. Journal indexes are arranged by field of study and often contain abstracts, or summaries, of the articles. *Social Sciences Index, Biological Abstracts, Psychological Abstracts,* and *America: History and Life* are good examples of these indexes.

Newspaper articles offer fresh, factual information unencumbered by historical analysis. The major indexes for newspapers include *The New York Times Index, The Wall Street Journal Index, Christian Science Monitor Index,* and *The Newspaper Index* (covering the *Chicago Sun-Times, Chicago Tribune, Denver Post, Detroit Chronicle, Los Angeles Times, Washington Post*). In addition, most large newspapers such as the *Boston Globe* maintain their own indexes. You can call the paper's library to see if they will help you find articles on your topic.

Most libraries carry microfilm versions of back issues of newspapers. One microfilm spool can store two weeks to one month of a major newspaper's daily editions. Once you locate the articles you need, you can view the microfilm on machines called readers and either print out a copy or take notes as you read.

The computer database INFOTRAC will enable you to search hundreds of magazines and major newspaper indexes at one sitting. You can select either a magazine or newspaper index for your searches. Figure 2.4 shows what INFOTRAC's main menu looks like. The computer will use your key word to search through the index looking for articles related to your topic.

FIGURE 2.4   INFOTRAC's Main Menu

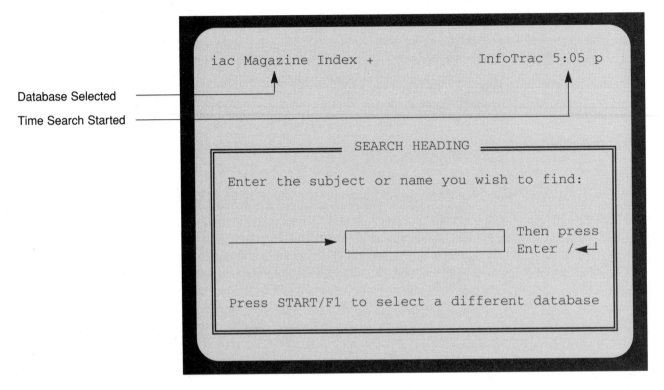

Database Selected

Time Search Started

Computer Databases

One of the marvels of modern technology—and a great boon to student researchers—has been the creation of computer databases. Through these databases, you can conduct a search of thousands of publications and articles from around the world in a matter of minutes.

In many schools, database searches are free to students and faculty. However, a fee may be charged for specialized database searches. Check with the reference librarian before you start your search.

Public libraries generally offer INFOTRAC searches free of charge, but do charge a fee for computer searches of other databases. Again, check with the reference librarian at your library. Fees are generally minimal, ranging from $5 to $15 for an average search of twenty to sixty entries.

Computer versus Manual Search. Although there are advantages to both manual and computer searches, on-line searches are best in the following circumstances.

- *When you want an exhaustive examination of the literature on a particular topic.* For example, a computer would enable you to search for all articles published on the Polish labor union Solidarity from 1980 to the present.

- *When you need to search more than one index.* INFOTRAC, for instance, allows you to search magazine and newspaper indexes. Other databases include periodicals along with books, proceedings, annual reports, and other documents.

- *When you need abstracts or brief summaries of social science, science, or other specialized articles.* The medical database MEDLINE, for example, provides abstracts of each article. Abstracts can help you to decide which articles to use for your paper.

- *When you need to do several searches at once, using variations or alternative terms.* The speed and flexibility of computer searching allows you to change key words and search for articles or books quickly.

Setting Up the Search. The secret to success in using any database is to set up your key words or designators before beginning your search. The computer will recognize only those headings programmed into its system and will ignore everything else. If you are searching for "Diet and immune system" and the database lists the topic under "*Nutrition* and immune system," you will have no success in your search.

While many databases use Library of Congress subject headings, others have their own vocabulary. These headings are usually published in a guidebook to the database. Most libraries have a special reference librarian who can help you set up your computer search.

Types of Databases. Databases are grouped according to three categories. *Bibliographic* or reference databases offer merely standard bibliographies and indexes, such as *Books in Print,* in electronic form.

Numeric (or source) databases provide numeric data in raw form: for example, corporate earnings, stock market quotations, manufacturing statistics.

Full text databases include the complete text of books, magazine, journal, and newspaper articles, wire services, and the like. You can request a printout of an entire article. In the past few years, these databases have also begun offering computerized versions of major encyclopedias.

Each database is categorized according to one of these three classifications. A complete list of online services can be found in the *Directory of Online Databases,* available at most libraries. The most commonly used vendors include the following.

- *Bibliographic Retrieval Service (BRS).* Founded in 1976, BRS contains more than eighty databases, concentrating on the sciences, education, and business. Databases available from this service include ABI/INFORM (business index and abstracts), BIOSIS Previews (life-science literature), Books in Print, ERIC (Educational Resources Information Center), MEDLINE/MEDLARS (medical sciences), PsycINFO (psychology journal abstracts).

- *CompuServ.* A division of H & R Block, this service provides Associated Press newswire and business news, *Grolier's Encyclopedia,* and Standard and Poors' General Information File.

- *DIALOG Information Services, Inc.* One of the largest and best vendors, DIALOG offers over 200 databases covering all major sectors of knowledge. In addition to the databases offered by BRS, DIALOG provides information on economics, history, philosophy, math, biography, world affairs, and technology.

CD-ROM References. Many encyclopedias and other general or special references are now stored on laser disks called CD-ROMs (**compact disk—read only memory**). "Read only" means you cannot write on the disk or change any of the information—you can only read it. The disks contain the same information printed in book versions of the encyclopedia or other resource. These programs often come with special features such as key word searches to help you find information on your topic, animated pictures illustrating some of the data, and color graphics. CD-ROMs can be used in your personal computer (if you have enough memory to run the programs) and do not require a subscription to an electronic database or service. Ask your reference librarian for catalogs listing CD-ROMs that might be available from libraries, government offices, or other low-cost institutions.

Card/Computer Catalogs and the Stacks

The "stacks" refer to the shelves in a library containing books that may be checked out by the public. Books are classified according to the Dewey decimal system or Library of Congress system. Each volume in the library is represented by at least three cards in the card or computer catalog system—main entry or author card, title card, and subject card, as shown in Figure 2.5.

Main Entry or Author Card. This card or entry lists the book by its author's last name. Where the book has more than one author, each author has his or her own card. The same rule applies when only an editor is listed.

Title Card. All titles are alphabetized by the first letter of the word, except for *A, An, The.* The title card is particularly helpful if you don't know the author's name or if the book had no author or editor.

FIGURE 2.5 Sample Author, Title, Subject Cards

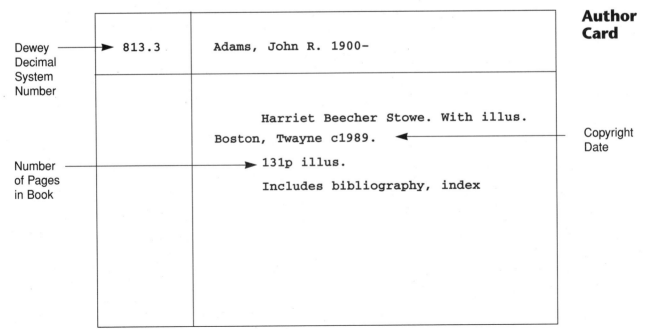

FIGURE 2.5   Sample Author, Title, Subject Cards (Continued)

**Title
Card**

813.3	Harriet Beecher Stowe c1989.
	Adams, John R.

**Subject
Card**

813.3	Stowe, Harriet Beecher, Criticism and Interpretation
	Adams, John R. 1900- Harriet Beecher Stowe. With illus. Boston, Twayne c1989 131p illus. Includes bibliography, index.

Subject Card. If you have no author and no book title, but want to find resources on your topic, you can conduct a search under a subject heading. A subject card lists not only a major subject but subcategories under that main heading. For example, "United States—Economics" or "United States—History—World War II." You might also want to look under "World War II" to find further entries.

The only problem with subject cards is that you need to know how the library categorizes headings. Computer catalog systems such as LUIS (Library User Information System) use Library of Congress headings, but many smaller libraries may have their own systems. Check with the reference librarian before you start your search.

"See Also" Card. These cards, usually found only in paper card catalogs, refer you to related topics. "Psychoanalysis," for example, might have the following "see also" references.

	Psychoanalysis	see also
	Adler, Alfred Freud, Sigmund Jung, Carl Psychiatry	

"See also" listings for computer catalogs are usually contained in the subject heading index to the system.

Before the advent of computers, these cards were always actual pieces of paper stored in file drawers near the stacks. Today in many libraries, "cards" have become "entries" in computerized catalog systems such as LUIS. You can search under "Author," "Title," and "Subject" headings, just as in the manual system, but only one "card" appears for all three categories, as shown in Figure 2.6

Consult the *Library of Congress Subject Headings* for key words to use in conducting a search for books on your topic. (See Figure 2.7.) For example, suppose you are writing a paper on Israeli-Arab conflicts before the West Bank uprising. The entries in the index can tell you what additional subject headings to use in your search and which headings are not used in the system.

While the computerized catalog system allows you to search for books more quickly, it has a major disadvantage. Should the computer go off-line for any reason, no one can search for anything. Card catalogs never suffer from this drawback.

U.S. Government Documents

U.S. Government publishes an astounding quantity and range of materials each year. These government-sponsored pamphlets, books, monographs,

FIGURE 2.6 Computerized Catalog Entry (LUIS System)

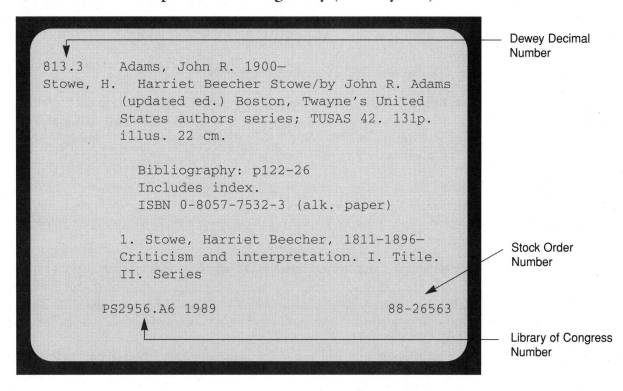

FIGURE 2.7 Library of Congress Subject Headings Entry

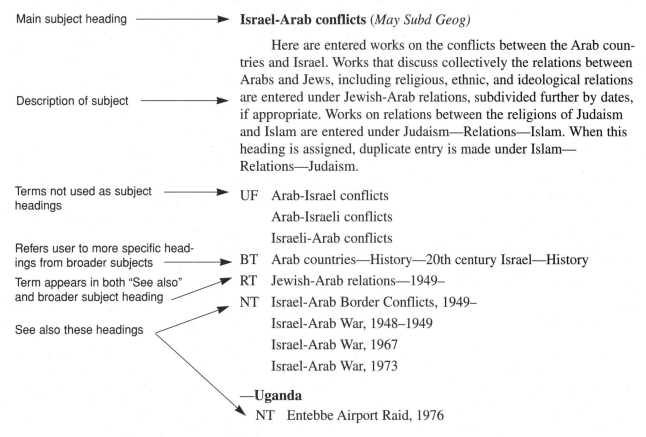

articles, and journals cover virtually every imaginable topic from alpha particles, bee keeping, Congressional hearings, parapsychology, and special sub-committees, to weather, xerography, yurts, and zircon.

Most of these publications are packed full of first-rate information, are highly readable, and are free or relatively inexpensive. The trick is finding what you need in this avalanche of material.

Libraries. Fifty libraries, one in each state, act as Regional Depository Libraries and receive almost all of the most popular and requested government publications. Other libraries take whatever government publications are useful or whatever they can store.

In some instances, government material is kept in the reference section; in others, it is housed in a special collection with its own separate room. *The Directory of Government Document Collections and Libraries* lists all libraries containing government information by state, then indexes them by library name and type of collection.

Superintendent of Documents and Other Agencies. One of the best ways to research government publications is through the *Monthly Catalog of United States Government Publications*. This volume lists about 2000 new government publications in each issue. It is available in all libraries that receive government materials.

Publications can be ordered either directly from the Government Printing Office, Superintendent of Documents, Washington, DC 20402, or from individual agencies listed after each entry. Ask the librarian for help in filling out the order form. You'll need to include the stock number and correct money amount with each order.

One word of caution, however. It often takes two to four weeks for the government to process your order. If you want to use government publications for your research, order them far enough ahead of time that they arrive before you finish your paper.

Consumer Information. All consumer information is handled by the government's Consumer Information Center (CIC) in Pueblo, CO 81009. The CIC publishes a quarterly *Consumer Information Catalog,* free to the public. Subjects covered include careers and education, financial planning, food, health, children, small business, and travel and hobbies.

Technical Information. This information is available from the National Technical Information Service (NTIS), Department of Commerce, 5285 Port Royal Rd., Springfield, VA 22161. NTIS handles all government-sponsored science and technology projects available for inspection by the general public.

Government Bookstores. The federal government has established bookstores in twenty-five states for distributing its materials. Although the inventories of these stores are often small, many of the most popular and requested titles are on hand. Your local library should have a listing of these bookstores by state. The obvious advantage of a walk-in store is the time saved versus waiting for your mail order to be processed.

Films, Videotapes, Art Prints, Music

Most libraries have special rooms for music, film, and artworks. Ask the librarian to show you the film, music, and art card/computer catalogs. In some instances you may be able to check out music scores as well as recordings. See the *MLA Handbook for Writers of Research Papers* for the correct bibliographic form to create your source cards for musical recordings, films and videotapes, and artworks.

Major references in these areas include the following.

New York Times Film Reviews
International Directory of Film and Filmmakers (volumes are grouped by film, directors/filmmakers, actors/actresses, writers and production artists)
The Film Encyclopedia
Complete Guide to Videocassette Movies
Film and Video Finder
Art Index (guide to art periodicals)
Variety International Showbusiness Reference
Index to Record and Tape Reviews (guide to periodicals)
CD Review Digest Annual
The World's Encyclopedia of Recorded Music
Orchestral Music in Print
Various biographical reference works in the arts

Retrieving Information

You've located thirteen magazine articles and six books on your subject, and you're ready to retrieve the information. In most cases, you simply request back copies of the magazines from the periodicals room and locate the books in the stacks.

To your dismay, however, three of the key articles are in magazines your library doesn't carry. Not only that, but the one book out of the six that focuses exclusively on your topic was checked out last November and hasn't been seen since. As part of developing good research skills, you need to know strategies for tracking down and retrieving information that is not readily available.

Magazines, Journals, Newspapers

The strategy for locating hard-to-find periodicals is roughly the same for magazines, journals, or newspapers.

- *Double-check your library's index of the periodicals it carries.* You may have misspelled the periodical's name or looked under the wrong heading.

- *Ask the reference librarian if the periodical can be located through interlibrary loan.* This service enables several libraries in an area to loan materials to each other. In some instances you may be able to have a photocopy of the article sent to you from another library.

- *Order a copy of the periodical or a reprint of the article from the periodical's editorial offices.* The addresses and telephone numbers for most magazines, journals, and newspapers can be found in reference volumes such as *Gale Directory of Publications and Broadcast Media, The Working Press of the Nation* (separate directories for magazines and newspapers), *Standard Periodical Directory, Ulrich's International Periodicals Directory, Magazine Industry Market Place,* and *Editor and Publisher Yearbook.* Call or write the editorial offices and explain what you need. They can send you either the volume in which the article appears or a reprint of the article itself. Be aware that this process may take time, so be sure to call well in advance of the date your term paper or report is due.

Books

If you can't locate the book you want in your library, follow these steps.

- *If the book is listed in your library card catalog, double-check the stacks to make sure the book has not been misplaced on the shelf.* Ask the librarians to verify that the book is missing and not merely overdue.
- *Ask if the book can be ordered through interlibrary loan.* You will need to fill out a request form stating the author, title, publisher, and publication date of the book. The only drawback to this strategy is that it may take anywhere from two to six weeks to obtain the book you want. In some cases the book may be a reference volume that cannot be lent.
- *Check the local bookstores to see if a copy is available.* If the book has been published recently or is a standard reference work, your local bookstore may have a copy in stock.
- *If you really need the book, order a copy directly from the publisher.* This is an option only if the book is in print and is not prohibitively expensive. Don't order through the library or local bookstore; such orders can take over a month or longer to fill. Find the publisher's address and telephone number in the reference volume *Literary Market Place.* Most publishers will ship the book to you via United Parcel Service or Federal Express if you need it in a hurry.

Government, Institution, Corporate Documents

There are several techniques for getting your hands on hard-to-find documents.

- *Ask the reference librarian if the document you want can be ordered through interlibrary loan.* Some libraries maintain more extensive collections of such documents than others.
- *Check to see if there are specialty libraries in your area.* Some libraries carry only business, government, or institution materials; their collections may be more extensive than a general library's.
- *Order the material directly from the individual agency, institution, or company.* Ask the reference librarian to help you locate the address and telephone number of the specific government agency, private or public institution, or company that published the document.

Evaluating Information

Once you have begun to assemble your sources, you need some way to evaluate their usefulness to your paper. Not every source will be appropriate or suitable. You may wonder how you—no expert in the field you are researching—can evaluate the work of supposed authorities and experts. The following questions will serve as good guidelines for separating the wheat from the chaff in your materials.

Is the Publication Useful to You?

After three days of persistent research, you have finally obtained a copy of *Logistics of the Army of Alexander the Great*. You want to find out how Alexander kept his troops supplied as they marched over 5000 miles of rugged terrain.

You open the book and find page after page of statistical tables badly labeled and confusing to read. The book contains no maps, no illustrations, few headings, and worst of all, no index. Finding what you want to know will be a nightmare. Although the book may be valuable to specialists in military history, it is useless for your paper on Alexander's abilities as a commander.

Check through your sources for similar problems. Can you understand the material? Is it too theoretical, too general, too specific? Does it contain illustrative material to clarify information? Can you use it as a source for your notes?

Is the Material a Primary or a Secondary Source?

Primary sources are classified as eyewitness accounts of events (Chuck Yeager's account of breaking the sound barrier) or as an original document or manuscript (Susan B. Anthony's speech "On Woman's Right to the Suffrage"). A secondary source is a work based on primary sources (Tom Wolfe's account of Yeager breaking the sound barrier or Gertrude Stein's opera based on Anthony's life, *The Mother of Us All*).

One source is not necessarily better than the other. Biases and errors can creep into both kinds of works. Overall, the best way to evaluate these sources is to include a balance of primary and secondary materials in your paper. In that way, you can cross-check information and gain some idea as to the usefulness and accuracy of primary and secondary work.

How Recent Is the Source?

Check the publication date of your books, articles, and other sources. Make sure you have the latest information on your topic. Even ancient history is constantly being updated and revised as new archeological evidence is uncovered or old evidence is reevaluated. Current information is even more critical when it comes to technological subjects, where the knowledge base changes from month to month.

Be especially careful if the book is a reprint. Look at the original publication date, then check the introduction or preface. Has the book been updated or revised for the new printing?

Is the Writer an Authority or Reliable Scholar in the Field?

Look up the author's credentials in biographical sources. Does he or she have the necessary expertise, training, or experience to write competently about the subject? What do colleagues or others in the field think about this author's work? Find reviews of your source that give you an idea of the writer's ability to report on the topic accurately and fairly. Journals and newsletters in an author's field are good sources of such reviews.

Does the Writer Cite Sources?

Where did the author get the information that forms the basis of the book? Does he or she cite primary and secondary sources in footnotes, end notes, or a bibliography? What experts or other references does the author cite?

Notice not only the *number* of sources listed but the *quality* of those sources. For example, if the author cites mainly popular magazines or poorly documented research, the material cannot be considered highly reliable.

Does the Writer Have Biases or Prejudices?

Most writers have some slant or opinion about their subject. But does that bias distort the accuracy or credibility of the writer's work? For example, during the Korean War, President Truman fired general Douglas MacArthur as commander of U.S. forces. These two men are likely to have widely different opinions on what led up to this event. You need to keep this fact in mind when reading either man's version of the story.

Notice also when the author lived—is he or she too close to an event to have an objective view of it? Someone writing in 1920 about Germany's actions in World War I may have his or her views colored by the freshness of the conflict. Another author writing twenty or thirty years later may offer a more balanced, objective view.

Ask yourself, does the writer have some personal motive for writing for or against a topic? Is the language filled with emotional adjectives and adverbs that color the facts? Are the facts loaded on one side or another of an issue? Does the author present both sides accurately, and are the facts substantiated by other sources? What is the opinion of other writers or scholars about the work?

Has the Writer Defined Terms and Major Concepts?

The question of defining terms and concepts is particularly important when a writer is presenting an argument or opinion piece. What exactly do writers mean by *free market, socialism, obscenity, excellence in education,* or any other terms they use? Are the definitions too personal or too vague to be useful? Do not accept an author's definitions at face value. Check with other sources to determine if the way the author uses terms or concepts appears valid.

Take time to sift through your sources to be sure you have the best quality information available to you.

☞ 5 Take Good Notes

Taking Notes

Note taking has three important objectives: First, to record the main ideas that will form the backbone of your report; second, to gather specific evidence to support your main ideas; and third, to record the exact wording of sources you may want to quote in your paper.

Despite its importance, this stage of research is generally one that most students like the least. They consider note taking a tedious, thankless job: scribbling on small index cards for hours until their eyes blur and their fingers cramp.

Yet like everything else in research, there is a trick to taking good notes. The secret is twofold.

1. Develop a system and stick to it.

2. Know what *not* to take notes on as well as what to write down.

Note-Taking System

Although several systems exist for collecting notes, the one described here is among the simplest and most efficient to use.

1. Once you have all your bibliography or source cards filled out, arrange them alphabetically and number them in the upper righthand corner.

2. Use 3×5 or 6×8 note cards for your note taking, either lined or blank.

3. Place the number of the source you are using in the upper righthand corner of each card. Number each of the cards containing notes from the source like this: 1–1, 1–2, 1–3, and so on. The first number stands for the source, the second number for the note card.

   This system will be invaluable when you create your final outline. You can simply write in the number of the card or cards that contain information on each point. In the rough draft, you can note in the margin which cards served as the source of your information to indicate where you need to document your facts.

4. In some cases, you may need to write the author's name or a shortened title of the work to the immediate left of the source and notecard number. In other instances, the source number alone will be adequate.

5. Write the main idea of the card as a heading at the top. This is called a *slug line* and gives you an idea of the subject of each card. *Write only one idea per card and on only one side of the card.* When it comes time to write your report, you will have no trouble arranging your cards by main point.

6. After the body of the note, write the page number from which you obtained the material on the lower righthand corner of the card.

Figure 2.8 shows how note cards and bibliography cards work together. Once you have established your note taking, stick to it! Don't be tempted

FIGURE 2.8 Sample Bibliography Card and Note Card

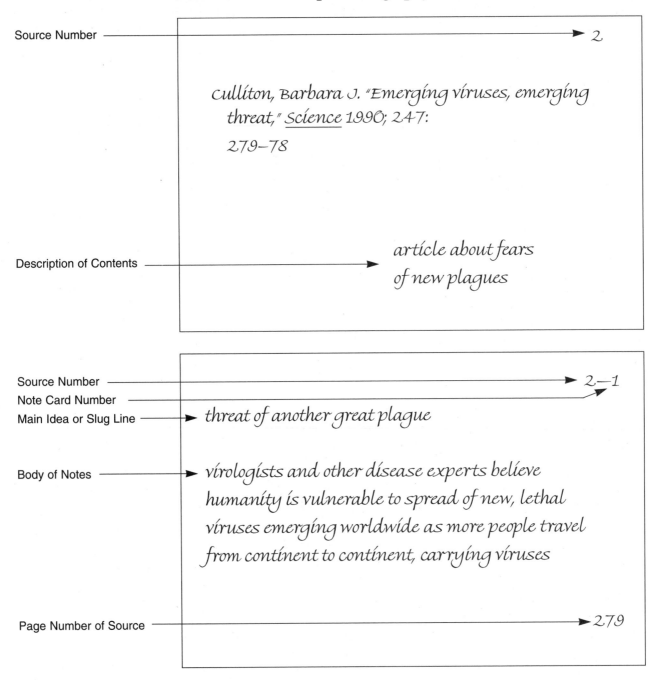

by laziness, fatigue, or deadline pressure to stop writing slug lines, to leave off source and note card numbers, to fail to write down page numbers, or to put two or three ideas on the same card. While such tactics may save time in the short run, you will spend hours later trying to find the source for important quotations, the exact page number of key facts, or under which main idea to group the card.

The more pressured you are, the more valuable this system can be if you stick with it.

A Word about Computer Note Taking

As more students acquire laptop and notebook computers, they will use them not only to write the paper but to take notes. If you use a computer to take notes, be sure to establish a similar system of note taking as you would for cards. For each note, identify the reference source and the page numbers. Later, as you write your draft, you can incorporate your notes into your text by cutting and pasting them electronically.

The drawbacks of computer note taking are that you cannot see all of your notes at the same time without printing them out, you must take your computer with you whenever you do your research, and you risk losing your notes if the computer's memory fails or the files crash. These drawbacks aside, computer note taking can be a time-saving way to do your research.

A word of caution: computer note taking can make it easier to inadvertently plagiarize an author's work, that is, using his or her exact words as your own. You may copy the author's words simply because it's faster and more convenient than rephrasing them in your own words. If you use these notes in your paper, you may not remember that you copied them exactly from the author's text, and you will be guilty of plagiarism. Always take time to paraphrase, summarize, or quote an author's work in your computer notes.

Previewing, Skimming, Reading

Many students make the mistake of trying to take notes the first time they begin reading a book or article. If you do so, you run the risk of taking notes on material you probably won't need. It is much more efficient if you preview, skim, then read the article.

To *preview* a source, size up the content before you begin to read. If the source is a book, read through the table of contents, introduction or preface, and index. Get an idea of how much material on your topic the book contains. If the source is an article, read the abstract, summary, or first and last paragraphs to discover the tone, approach, and basic coverage of the article.

Skim the material by looking through it for key words that relate to your topic. Read the first few sentences of each paragraph—authors usually describe what the paragraph contains in the first one or two sentences. If you are writing on how viruses are transmitted from one population to another, for example, look for words such as *infection, airborne or waterborne contamination, transmission, incubation, epidemic.* Look for concluding statements that interpret, summarize, or highlight the main points of the paragraph

Finally, *read* the material carefully with an eye to taking notes. By this time you will know more clearly what information is important to your topic and what data is not essential. Try to grasp the main points of the material so that you can put the information into your own words.

Guidelines for Taking Notes

Regardless of the material you are researching, follow these few tips for taking effective notes.

- *Use phrases instead of complete sentences.* This not only saves space on the card, but will help guarantee that you do not copy the author's words exactly.
- *Avoid using unusual abbreviations as a form of shorthand in note taking.* When you reread your notes, you may not understand them.
- *Identify facts and opinions as you take notes.* For opinions, use phrases such as "according to author," or "author believes."
- *Facts of common knowledge such as the bombing of Pearl Harbor do not have to be documented.* Unusual or little-known facts, such as how many civilians were killed in the surprise attack, do need to be documented. Make sure you include your source on the note card.
- *When copying quotations, use ellipses if you omit a few words.* Otherwise, you may not remember that you condensed the quoted material.
- *Keep all your note cards until your paper has been graded.* Your instructor may ask to see your notes or may have questions about a fact in your work.

Taking Only the Notes You Need

Your notes paraphrase, summarize, comment on, or directly quote material. The more of your own words, thoughts, and insights you can put into your notes, the more original your work is likely to be. Also, the less likely you will inadvertently copy someone else's work.

Paraphrasing. In this type of note, you express another person's ideas in your own words. A good paraphrase generally condenses the original text to the essential meaning. The act of putting a difficult concept into your own words forces you to think about and understand the idea more completely than if you simply recopy it word for word. Look over the example below.

Original

One is forcibly struck by the fact of how well superstition provides at least the subjective feeling of predictability and control. It may thus serve the function of reducing anxiety; and as intense anxiety is liable to inhibit effective action in dangerous situations, there is a distinct possibility that superstition may have positive survival value in certain circumstances.

Paraphrase

superstition as survival aid   *3–2*

superstition gives subjective sense of control which reduces anxiety. such feelings of control can help people act more effectively in dangerous situations and increase chances of survival

134–135

Remember, paraphrasing is not simply changing a word here and there in a sentence. It is rewriting the author's material in your own words.

Summarizing. In this note, you write down the main idea with details supporting it. Perhaps you are listing the places an author visited on a journey or the main characters in a story who reflect certain values. Like paraphrasing, you are putting the original material into your own words, as shown in the example below.

Original

Alice Walker's substantial body of writing, though it varies, is characterized by specific recurrent motifs. Most obvious is Walker's attention to the black woman as creator, and to how her attempt to be whole relates to the health of her community. This theme is certainly focal to Walker's two collections of short stories, *In Love and Trouble* and *You Can't Keep a Good Woman Down,* to her classic essay, "In Search of Our Mothers' Gardens," and to *Meridian* and *The Color Purple.*

Another recurrent motif in Walker's work is her insistence on probing the relationship between struggle and change, a probing that encompasses the pain of black people's lives, against which the writer protests but which she will not ignore. Paradoxically, such pain sometimes results in growth.

Summary

```
recurrent motifs–walker                              1–3

walker's motifs highlight strengths of black people:

    1   black woman as creator—her struggles to
        be whole affect community's health
    2   relationship between struggle and
        change—pain of struggle sometimes
        produces growth

                                                    39–40
```

Direct Quote. At times you want to preserve the exact words of your source material. For this kind of card, copy information directly from the source, even if it contains grammatical mistakes, misspellings, or errors in fact. If you wish to note the error for the reader, follow it with the word [*sic*] (note brackets), which means the mistake was contained in the original. If you need to add explanatory words to the quotes, enclose such words in brackets.

Original

The French General Henri Navarre was given command of the French troops in Vietnam near the end of the French–Indochina war. At a time when the Viet Minh were soundly defeating his forces, General Navarre uttered a phrase that Americans would hear over and over again on the way to their own defeat in Southeast Asia. "Now we can see it clearly—like light at the end of the tunnel."

Direct Quote

French General Navarre's quote   *4–5*

Phrase that came to haunt Americans in their Viet Nam war first uttered by General Henri Navarre:

"Now we see it [victory] clearly—like light at the end of the tunnel."

                                                                          79

Original Comments and Insights. For this card, the major focus is your own comments and thoughts on what you have read. You may jot down the main idea from the source material on the card, but the rest of the notes should be your own ideas. These cards will often serve as the heart of your paragraphs because they reflect what you think about the topic, not just the facts and figures gathered from your research.

Original

The drug trade is a fine specimen of unrestricted competition which brings down prices and pushes up consumption. Governments refuse to limit the trade by regulation. Instead, they try to prohibit it. In 1980, the U.S. spent just under $1 billion trying to keep heroin, cocaine, and marijuana out of its domestic market. By 1988, it was spending almost $4 billion. Yet the reatil price of drugs dropped faster than the cost of policing them rose.

Your Comments and Opinions

Prohibition encourages drug trade   *4–2*

Prohibition throws drug trade wide open to competition and sets up a vicious cycle—competition brings down price, which makes drugs more affordable, which encourages consumption. More people enter drug trade, costs government more to fight greater number of dealers

                                                                     27–28

A Word about Plagiarism

Plagiarism is the act of copying someone else's exact words and using them as your own, or using someone's published illustrations or ideas without giving credit. The penalty for plagiarism in most schools is an automatic failure for the student.

For example, suppose you are doing a paper on Harriet Beecher Stowe, author of *Uncle Tom's Cabin*. You come across what you believe is a key insight into her character by the author of a critical study on Stowe: "The essence of Harriet Beecher's early life can be expressed in the word *subservience* to the males who dominated the household and all social institutions." Since this is the author's evaluation, you must give credit for using the idea. Your paper may say, "According to author John Adams, Harriet Beecher's early life was characterized by subservience to the men in her household and in her society."

Your best protection against plagiarism is to write your notes in your own words and to give proper credit when you have used someone else's ideas. Compare the two examples below. One is a plagiarized passage while the other is a paraphrase of the same material.

Original

Few people know that during the Battle of Waterloo, a twelve-foot ditch proved to be the best ally of the English troops. As the French cavalry charged across the field, the front ranks tumbled into the ditch, which had been concealed in the tall grass. So great was the press of the charge, that men and horses continued to fall until the ditch was filled with bodies. Only then did the remaining forces ride over their solid mass toward the English. The delay had been enough, however, to allow the English to maneuver their artillery into position. Their savage cannon fire shattered the French cavalry charge.

Plagiarized Version

```
The French took the field first and charged the English
position. But the front ranks tumbled into a ditch which had
been concealed in the tall grass. So great was the press of the
charge that men and horses continued to fall until the ditch
was filled with bodies. Only then did the remaining forces ride
over their solid mass toward the English (no credit is given).
```

Paraphrased Version

```
The French took the field first and charged the English
position. Less than halfway across the field, the front ranks
fell into a concealed ditch. The horses and riders behind them
were unable to stop and tumbled in after, quickly filling the
ditch with bodies. This grisly bridge enabled the rest of the
cavalry to rush across toward the English (Fuller, 60-61).
```

Be sure to rephrase another author's work in your own words and give the proper credit for his or her ideas. Always cite your sources for direct quotes.

PART 2
From First Draft to Final Paper

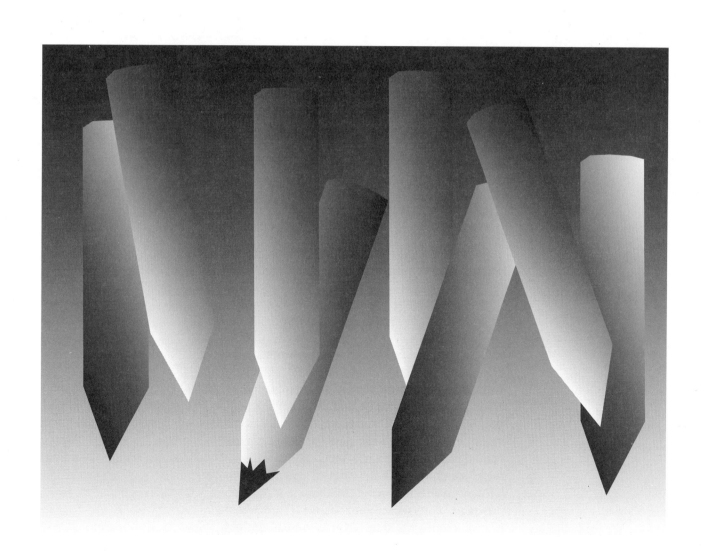

CHAPTER 3
Creating the First Draft

After several days or weeks of conscientious research, you finally assemble your completed research notes, bibliography cards, preliminary thesis, and idea sheet. It is at this stage that your attention to detail in research and note taking pays the biggest dividends. Although you may need to revise your thesis statement in light of your research, you have at hand the basic material to outline, organize, and write your paper. The actual process from this stage on may be easier than you think. Figure 3.1 summarizes the key steps in completing your paper.

FIGURE 3.1 Key Steps in Completing Your Paper

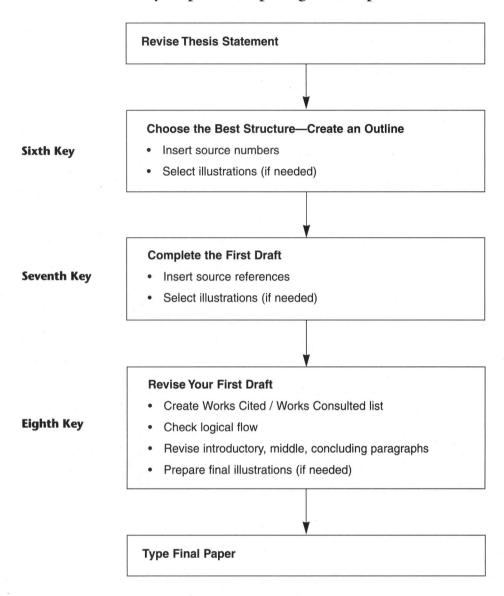

Revise Your Thesis Statement

The preliminary thesis statement served merely to guide and focus your research. As you investigated your topic, you may have changed your mind about your thesis in light of the information you uncovered. For example, instead of a descriptive paper about the role of the United Nations in the Bosnia-Croatia conflict, you may want to write an argumentative paper either supporting or criticizing the U.N.'s actions.

On the other hand, suppose during your research you discover that your topic is too narrow. The thesis statement about the superstitions of sports figures, for example, may need to be expanded to include the superstitions of people in the entertainment business. You might revise your thesis statement as in the following example.

Original

```
Although many people believe superstitions are a thing of the
past, it has been shown that superstitious rituals and beliefs
can actually improve the performance of many leading sports
figures.
```

Revised

```
Although many people believe superstitions are outmoded, it has
been shown that superstitious rituals and beliefs actually
improve the performance of many leading sports and entertain-
ment figures.
```

Remember, the thesis statement presents your goal and the main idea of your paper. What are you trying to prove, show, describe, or evaluate? What do you want the reader to believe, accept, or know after reading your paper? The revised thesis statement should give the reader a clear idea of your paper's purpose and content. This statement serves as the starting point for outlining your paper.

☞ 6 Choose the Best Structure— Create an Outline

Know Basic Structure and Format

Before you begin creating your outline, you need to give some thought to your audience and know something about the basic structure for reports and term papers. Information is generally arranged differently for an argumentative, position, descriptive, or literary paper. You can then tailor your outline to the type of paper you are writing. Why waste time developing an outline that may not fit your paper?

Who Is Your Audience?

Of course your instructor is the one who will read the paper, but think beyond just one person. Imagine that your report or term paper might be published in a magazine or journal. Will your audience be familiar with your topic? Will they know all the key terms you use? Can they follow your argument or analysis easily?

Try to see your material not just through your own eyes but through the eyes of an imaginary reader as well. In an argumentative paper, for example, have you established the basic issues clearly enough that the reader will understand (and might even be persuaded by) your logical argument? For a scientific paper, have you stated the problem or results clearly so the reader can grasp your main point? Have you described your method of research or reasoning in enough detail?

Considering the needs of your audience can help you to choose the best structure to outline and organize your paper.

Three-Part Structure of Reports and Terms Papers

The basic structure of reports and term papers is easy to learn. Visualize it as three fundamental steps to get you into the topic, through each point, and to the final summary. The formal names for these steps are the *introduction, middle* (or *body*), and *conclusion*.

The introductory paragraph or paragraphs begin with a broad, general statement about your topic. From that point, like a funnel, the introduction narrows from the broad statement to your main arguments or points and ends with your thesis.

The body of the paper builds your analysis, argument, or exposition. In humanities papers, you begin with less important points and end with your most important points. For scientific papers, you begin with the most important results or findings and work from most important to least important information describing your methods or procedures. Because most term papers and reports are written for humanities classes, this book focuses on developing these papers. Often science and social sciences instructors have their own format they wish students to follow.

The concluding paragraph or paragraphs are like a pyramid leading you from a restatement of the thesis, to a summary of your main points, and ending with a broad, general statement on the topic again. If you diagrammed the structure, it would look like Figure 3.2.

This basic structure is the same whether your report is five or twenty-five pages long. Within this framework, however, you can exercise considerable variety depending on the type of paper you are writing. Each paper presents information in slightly different ways within the basic structure to accomplish its specific purposes.

Argumentative Paper

Depending on the paper's length and the topic, argumentative papers can be written using two basic arrangements. The first is as follows.

```
Thesis statement—introduction

   I. Background of topic

  II. Arguments against the writer's position

      A. First argument, with evidence, examples

      B. Second argument, with evidence, examples

      C. Etc.

 III. Arguments for the writer's position

      A. First argument, with evidence, examples
```

       B. Second argument, with evidence, examples

    C. Etc.

 IV. Conclusion restating writer's arguments and main points

In this arrangement, all arguments against the writer's position are placed up front. The rest of the paper is devoted to arguments and supporting evidence *for* the writer's position in an effort to convince the reader. The concluding paragraphs are like the closing remarks of a lawyer to the jury. They are meant to underscore the evidence and restate the writer's main point. This arrangement works well for shorter papers, enabling you to dispense with the con arguments quickly.

FIGURE 3.2   Basic Structure of a Term Paper

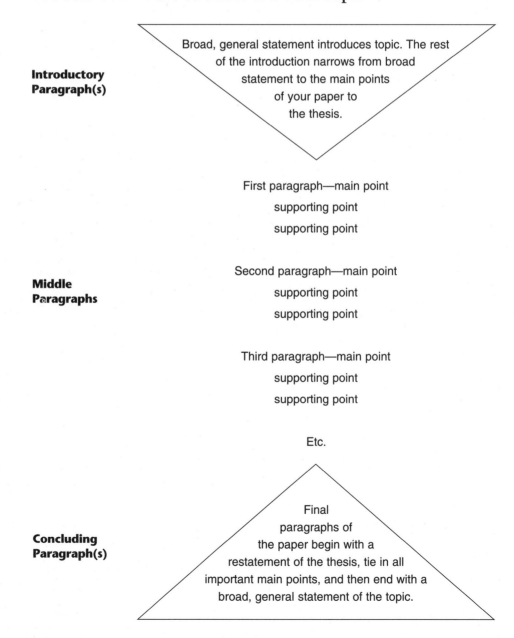

Introductory Paragraph(s)

Broad, general statement introduces topic. The rest of the introduction narrows from broad statement to the main points of your paper to the thesis.

First paragraph—main point
supporting point
supporting point

Second paragraph—main point
supporting point
supporting point

Middle Paragraphs

Third paragraph—main point
supporting point
supporting point

Etc.

Concluding Paragraph(s)

Final paragraphs of the paper begin with a restatement of the thesis, tie in all important main points, and then end with a broad, general statement of the topic.

The second arrangement accomplishes its purpose in a slightly different way.

```
Thesis statement—introduction
    I. Background information
   II. Argument against writer's position, argument for writer's
       position
  III. Argument against writer's position, argument for writer's
       position, etc.
   IV. Arguments for writer's position
       A. First point, with supporting evidence, examples
       B. Second point, with supporting evidence, examples
       C. Etc.
    V. Conclusion restating writer's arguments and main points
```

This format alternates the main pro and con arguments instead of putting all the con arguments up front. In this way, the writer can debate each point individually, demolishing the opposition step by step, then go on to develop a solid case for his or her position.

This arrangement works well for longer papers; otherwise, if all the con arguments are placed up front, the reader may forget them by the fourth or fifth page. By alternating pro and con arguments, you can set the stage to present your strongest, most convincing arguments at the end, having handily disposed of your opposition along the way.

Position Paper

The position paper does not require you to present opposing arguments in any detail or provide background information. You mention the opposing viewpoint at the beginning, but devote the remainder of your paper to your own position and the evidence or reasoning that supports it. This format gives you the perfect opportunity to sound off on a subject, provided your position is backed up by supporting evidence or examples. The basic arrangement looks like the following.

```
Thesis statement—introduction
    I. Background information (if appropriate)
   II. Mention of opposing viewpoint
  III. Points that support your position
       A. First point, with supporting evidence, reasons
       B. Second point, with supporting evidence, reasons
       C. Etc.
   IV. Conclusion restating your main position
```

This arrangement is typical of many editorials found in newspapers and magazines. The editor is expressing a point of view, not debating an opponent. The position format is appropriate for short or long papers.

Descriptive Paper

The descriptive paper or report does not present an argument or position but provides information about a topic—whether a person, place, event, idea, or object. For example, an argumentative paper on Pearl Harbor might attempt to prove that President Roosevelt knew about the attack before it happened yet did nothing because he wanted the U.S. to enter the war. On the other hand, a descriptive paper would simply present the sequence of events in the attack.

The most common formats used for a descriptive paper are chronological, cause and effect, or question and answer. The chronological arrangement simply follows the development of events as they occurred. In the Pearl Harbor example, for instance, a chronological format might look like the following.

```
Thesis statement—introduction

    I. Background of events leading to attack

   II. Events of the attack

         A. Airfield

         B. Battleships

         C. Other areas hit

         D. U.S. military response

  III. Mistakes made by Japanese

   IV. Response to news of attack in United States

    V. U.S. enters World War II

   VI. Conclusion
```

Cause and effect format, on the other hand, attempts to do some analysis of events—describing not only *what* happened but *why*. Remember, you are not building an argument, only putting forth explanations from an objective point of view. In general, after the first main point, each following main point serves as the *effect* of the point before it and the *cause* of the point after it. A cause and effect arrangement might look like this.

```
Thesis statement—introduction

    I. Background explaining Japanese strategic position,
       attitudes toward U.S. (cause)

   II. Explanation of decision to attack Pearl Harbor (effect of
       previous point, cause of next point)

  III. Basic events of the attack (effect of previous point, cause
       of next point)

   IV. War declared on Japan, mobilization of U.S. industry
       (effect of previous point, cause of next point)

    V. Eventual defeat of Japanese, U.S. occupation of Japan

   VI. Conclusion
```

The question and answer arrangement is similar to the cause and effect format in that it is used to provide an objective analysis of a topic. Generally, the format sets up a series of questions to be answered in the paper. For the Pearl Harbor example, the questions might be the following.

```
Thesis statement—introduction

    I. Why did the attack occur?

   II. Could it have been avoided?

  III. What were its effects?

   IV. Would the U.S. have entered the war without the attack?

    V. What have been the lasting effects on the public mind in
       the United States?

   VI. Could such a surprise attack ever happen again?

  VII. Conclusion
```

Any one of these arrangements can be used to complete the descriptive paper assignment, depending on the topic. Check with your instructor before choosing one of these three to be sure the selected approach is suitable for your topic.

Literary Paper

The literary paper is generally either an analysis of literary works or a comparison/contrast of such works. In the analysis format, you are examining one or more literary works to support your thesis statement. The format might look like this.

```
Thesis statement—introduction

    I. Biographical information about the author(s) (if
       appropriate to thesis statement and analysis)

   II. Analysis of first work to support thesis statement

  III. Analysis of second work

   IV. Analysis of third work, etc.

    V. Conclusion
```

For Analysis of Single Work

```
Thesis statement—introduction

    I. Plot summary of literary work

   II. First main point
       examples supporting main point

  III. Second main point
       examples supporting main point

   IV. Etc.

    V. Conclusion
```

The comparison/contrast arrangement can be set up two ways. You may either compare or contrast two or more literary works separately—presenting first one and then the other—or compare or contrast them together.

```
Thesis statement-introduction

    I. Discussion of first point using first work

   II. Comparison or contrast using second work

  III. Discussion of second point using first work

   IV. Comparison or contrast using second work

    V. Etc.

   VI. Conclusion
```

Or

```
Thesis statement-introduction

    I. Discussion of first point comparing or contrasting both
       works

   II. Discussion of second point comparing or contrasting both
       works

  III. Etc.

   IV. Conclusion
```

Either method fulfills the requirements of a literary paper and would be appropriate for a long or short assignment.

Develop Your Outline

Once you have the thesis statement refined and understand which format is best for your paper, the next step is to create a working outline to help you write the first draft. The purposes of an outline are:

1. To organize the information you have collected.
2. To detect any gaps in data you may have overlooked or missed during your research.

Most experienced writers rely on outlines to help them sort through the jumble of information and ideas their research has generated.

While the thesis functioned as a rough guide for your research, the outline is like a detailed map to help you chart your way from beginning to end of the first draft. To create an outline, you will draw on three main sources: your thesis statement, completed notecards, and idea sheet. Using these sources, you will select the main points of your paper, support each point with evidence or examples, and develop a concluding point.

Although this takes some thought, the good news is that once the outline is completed, you have basically written your paper. All you have left to do is to fill in the words for each main point, one paragraph at a time.

Determining Main Points

Many students experience a moment of despair at this point. How do you decide which are the main points for your paper? A good place to begin is with the thesis statement. Remember that each part of the paper you develop—thesis statement, idea sheet, notecards, outline—helps you move on to the next step.

Suppose you are writing a literary paper, for example. Your thesis statement is:

```
In his science fiction trilogy, Foundation, Isaac Asimov shows
how the psychohistory theory of social development must be used
in partnership with human creativity and imagination to guide
human affairs properly.
```

You have several clues to your main points embedded in this statement.

1. The reader will need to know what the trilogy is about. Your first main point will be a brief summary of the plot.

2. What is the psychohistory theory—who developed it and for what purpose? An explanation of the theory and a description of its inventor provides your second main point.

3. How has the theory been used to guide human affairs? The third main point will explain how Asimov used the theory to guide his fictitious second empire.

4. What are the dangers of over-reliance on the theory? Your fourth main point will explain the limitations of the theory and the dangers of relying on it too completely. It cannot accommodate the unexpected, and people lose their ability to respond creatively to novel situations.

5. If the theory cannot be relied on so completely, how do people handle their affairs, and what do they use to guide human development? This main point will explain how individual characters respond to unexpected challenges by using their own wits and imagination.

6. Finally, what is Asimov saying about human nature through his story? The final main point will present your views on Asimov's beliefs about human nature as reflected in his trilogy—how much can science be used to predict and shape human affairs, and what role do human imagination and creativity play in guiding human development and destiny?

Your note cards and idea sheet can also help you select main points. Which of your slug lines echo the questions provoked by your thesis statement? You may have written at the top of your notecards "Summary of trilogy plot," "Description of psychohistory theory," "Examples of over-reliance on theory," "Current theories of social development" and so on. These cards can be used either as main points or as supporting points.

You can also use the laundry list and clustering techniques to help you develop your main points. In the laundry list method, you simply write down all the main ideas generated by your research, then select those points you feel are the most important in light of your thesis statement. When creating the outline, you arrange these points in their most logical order, using the structure of your particular paper as a guide.

Clustering can be especially helpful if you draw a complete blank about how to arrange your research material. This technique takes advantage of the brain's natural ability to organize information. As you give your mind a visual pattern to work with, you may be surprised at how quickly you can generate main points from the wealth of material you have absorbed during your research. Even if your conscious mind cannot make order out of apparent chaos, your subconscious mind often does so automatically. You can number the branches of your cluster in the order they will be arranged in the outline. Figure 3.3 illustrates a cluster for a literary paper about Isaac Asimov's *Foundation* series.

Selecting Supporting Evidence and Examples

Each main point, particularly in the argumentative and position papers, must be supported by sound evidence, reasoning, or examples. If you state that superstitions can improve sports players' performances, list evidence or examples that prove your point. For instance, you may report that tennis star John McEnroe never stepped on the lines of the tennis court when he walked on to serve in a competitive game. Or Lisa Bonder, another tennis star, wore her "lucky" earrings and ate the same food every day she was in a match. Both stars believed such superstitions helped them to play better. These and other examples can be listed to help prove your point.

As you develop your supporting points, next to each one write the numbers of the notecards that served as the source of those statements. If you find that you do not have enough information for points you wish to include, go back to your sources and fill in the gaps. This technique of writing in the numbers of notecards in your outline will prove invaluable when you write the first draft and need to cite facts, opinions, or quotes in the text. You will know exactly which references to cite and the page numbers where information is found.

Creating the Outline

The outline can be written either in topic or sentence form. Both forms use roman numerals for main topics and letters and arabic numbers for supporting points. The difference between the two forms is that topic outlines list only brief phrases for the main points. Sentence outlines use complete sentences for the main points. Your instructor may have a preference for one form over the other. Whichever form you decide to use, be consistent throughout the outline. Don't switch from topic to sentence in midstream.

Remember to begin with the least important or most general points first and end the outline with your strongest points, particularly when writing an argumentative or position paper. Your introductory paragraph should touch on your main position, and each point thereafter will construct your case step by step. The paper should build to a solid, convincing conclusion.

Your completed literary paper outline, following an analysis structure, might look like the one shown on page 66.

FIGURE 3.3   Clustering Technique—Developing Main Points for Outline

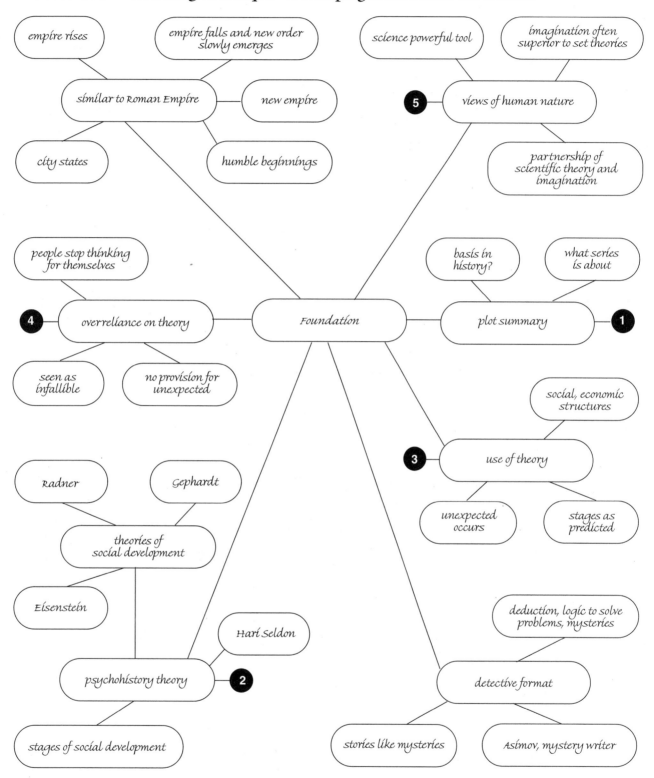

Numbered branches are used to create the outline because they are closely related to the thesis statement. Unnumbered branches are discarded.

Literary Paper (Topic Outline)

Thesis Statement: In his science fiction trilogy, <u>Foundation</u>, Isaac Asimov shows how the psychohistory theory of social development must be used in partnership with human creativity and imagination to guide human affairs properly.

  I. Summary of trilogy plot

    A. Fall of previous empire

    B. Creation of second empire and foundation

    C. Development of second empire--second foundation kept secret

    D. Based on rise and fall of historical cultures

 II. Explanation of psychohistory theory

    A. Hari Seldon creator of theory

    B. Plotted out stages of social development

       1. Religious order in control

       2. Merchant princes and city states

       3. Civil war

       4. Larger nation states formed

       5. Rise of dictator and war against him

       6. Eventual creation of galactic foundation

    C. Theory grounded in current knowledge of human social development

       1. Radner's theory of social development

       2. Gephardt's theory of cultural development

       3. Eisenstein's theory of social stages

III. Second empire uses theory to guide development

    A. Basis for economy and social structure

       1. Wilson's analysis of theory's use

       2. Ellison's comments

    B. Stages conforming to theory's predictions

       1. Ferris's comments on credibility

       2. Jacob's analysis

 IV. Dangers of overreliance on theory

    A. People view theory as infallible, immutable

    B. Substitute Hari Seldon's knowledge for their own thinking

    C. When unexpected occurs, people panic

        1. Appearance of the Mule

        2. No precedent, no guidance in Seldon's theory

        3. Confidence in theory collapses

  V. Response of people when theory fails

    A. Most people fall into despair

    B. Some individuals use wits and imagination to meet
       challenge of Mule

    C. Solutions found to problems Seldon doesn't predict

    D. Larger society also thrown back on its own resources
       eventually

 VI. Asimov's views of human nature

    A. Human efforts to eliminate unknown, unpredictable from
       life via science doomed to failure

    B. Science can help guide human affairs but cannot
       supersede human imagination, creativity

    C. Unknown, unpredictable stimulate human imagination,
       creativity--unique quality of being human

    D. Science and imagination should be in partnership, not
       one superior over the other

Notice that each main point has at least two subpoints supporting it. As a rule of thumb, when you have an *A* subpoint, you must also have at least a *B.* This is because when you divide a main point, you must end up with at least two parts. If you have only one subpoint, it's not really a division of a main idea but should be included in the main point.

Also, notice that all elements in the outline have essentially the same grammatical structure. This means that all roman numerals are either phrases or clauses, and all subpoints have basically the same structure. By forcing yourself to think in parallel structure, you will find it easier to write your paragraphs in the first draft. In most cases, the main points will serve as topic sentences.

The following sentence outline organizes an argumentative paper. The writer has chosen to list all con arguments at the beginning rather than to debate them one by one. The writer has also included notecard references and marked where illustrations are needed.

Argumentative Paper (Sentence Outline)

Thesis Statement: The "war on drugs" will do far more to
control and eliminate illegal drug use in the United States
than will legalization of drugs.

maybe graphic charts ⟶

con arguments ⟶

pro arguments ⟶

pro arguments ⟶

map showing major state programs ⟶

table showing age group of users?

conclusion ⟶

I. The drug problem in the United States has reached epidemic proportions in the last decade, prompting a major effort to address the problem at all levels of society.

   A. President's "war on drugs" calls for three-pronged effort--enforcement, education, treatment (1-3, 1-4, 1-5)

   B. Legalization also proposed by many as solution

II. Those who argue for legalization as the way to control drugs appear to have several valid points.

   A. Legalization takes away criminal element

   B. Government can control drug quality, quantity

   C. More money for prevention, education programs

III. The arguments against legalization, however, are based on a more realistic assessment of the problem.

   A. Legalization violates moral, ethical principles of country

   B. Makes drugs permanent fixture in society

   C. Encourages greater drug use by wider spectrum of users

   D. Subsidizes addiction with public money

   E. Does not address causes of drug addiction in individuals

IV. The three-pronged war on drugs addresses not only the drug supply but also drug abuse prevention and treatment programs.

   A. Coordinated effort among law enforcement agencies at federal, state, and local levels

   B. Development of antidrug education programs and treatment centers at state and local level

   C. Attention directed to factors encouraging drug dealing and addiction

      1. Poverty and lack of education, jobs

      2. Low self-esteem, lack of hope

      3. Lack of community involvement with youth

V. The drug crisis in the United States can be dealt with far more effectively using a three-pronged attack of law enforcement, education, and treatment than through legalizing drugs.

   A. War on drugs a long-range solution

      `B. Addresses major factors underlying drug abuse and`

          `addiction`

      `C. Consistent with our ideals and principles`

      `D. Eventually end widespread drug use`

When you have completed your outline, look at it critically. If possible, wait a few days, then read it over with a fresh eye. Is your thesis statement fully supported by your outline? Do the ideas flow logically? Have you stated your most important points last? Do your main points have enough support and examples to convince the reader? Have you developed a sound concluding point?

Revise the outline as necessary to create a logical flow of ideas from beginning to end. You want to make sure you arrive at your destination by the most logical route possible.

Drafting on the Computer

Some computer word-processing programs have outlining features that offer automatic lettering and numbering. Insert reference numbers just as you would in an outline created by hand or on the typewriter. Once you create a draft outline, you can save it as "Outline 1." When you are ready to revise, you can copy the outline to another file "Outline 2" and make the necessary alterations. Do not discard the original versions of your outline—you may decide that your second or third revision doesn't work and want to go back to an earlier version. Even if you accidentally misnumber an outline, your computer directory will tell you the time and date of each version, enabling you to determine which outline was created before or after the others.

Selecting Illustrations

The outline stage is also the best time to start thinking about any illustrations you might want to use in your paper. The paper against legalization of illicit drugs, for example, might need a graph showing the increase in drug treatment centers since the war on drugs began or a chart depicting the decline in drug use among teenagers over the past five years. See Chapter 7, "Illustrating Your Paper," for valuable guidelines on selecting the right illustration for your topic.

☞ 7 Complete the First Draft

Start Writing!

Your completed outline should inspire you to start writing your first draft. Remember, the purpose of a first draft is not to end up with a polished final product but simply to get down on paper a complete version of your topic.

At this stage, don't worry about the finer points of paragraph development, sentence structure, or correct grammar. Concentrate instead on three elements: (1) consider the needs of your audience, (2) establish an objective point of view, and (3) insert note card numbers to mark your sources.

Remember Your Audience

As you begin writing your first draft, keep your audience in mind. In a literary paper, for example, the reader needs to know something about the author's background or a plot summary of a work you are analyzing or comparing and contrasting. For an argumentative paper, readers need background information on the issues you are debating. The position paper must make it clear to the readers what stand you are taking on an issue and why. Finally, a descriptive paper must orient the reader in time and place and describe events in their logical order. By considering the readers' needs as you write, you will have less revising to do later on.

Maintain an Objective Point of View

Many beginning writers are tempted to express everything from a personal point of view—"*I think* gun control is impractical . . ." "*I believe* pro sports are getting more violent . . ." and so on. Or they try to disguise themselves behind such references as "this writer" or "in this writer's opinion."

Although personal references are fine for essays on your summer vacation, for research reports and term papers you need to project a sense of objectivity and authority. Compare these sentences:

PERSONAL: I think censorship violates Constitutional law.

OBJECTIVE: Censorship violates Constitutional law.

PERSONAL: In this writer's opinion Watergate stands as a symbol of government corruption.

OBJECTIVE: Watergate stands as a symbol of government corruption.

Notice how the sentences without personal references state the opinion more forcefully and authoritatively. Your task in the paper is then to prove the validity of the stated opinion by a carefully reasoned and supported argument or exposition. The use of personal pronouns or references sounds apologetic. You think or feel something, but are you sure? You convey to the reader that you don't have enough confidence to simply state an opinion and support it.

Beware, also, of sneaking the personal pronouns and references in the back door by using "one" or "you" or "people" or any other vague reference that dilutes your words. You can rephrase your sentences to eliminate these unnecessary references.

PERSONAL: When Mount St. Helens exploded, you could hear the sound 100 miles away.

OBJECTIVE: When Mount St. Helens exploded, the sound of the blast carried for 100 miles.

PERSONAL: One can debate endlessly the statement "guns don't kill people, people kill people."

OBJECTIVE: The debate over "guns don't kill people, people kill people" distracts from the real issue.

In the second example, not only has "one" been eliminated, but the entire focus of the sentence is much clearer. The debate is not the focus—its use as a distraction from the real issues is the main point the writer wants to make.

Keep in mind as you write your first draft that you have the right to express your opinions without apologizing or diluting the impact of your words. The objective voice can be a powerful tool in your reports and term papers.

Mark Your Sources

Remember to insert the numbers of source note cards after facts, quotes, and other people's ideas or opinions that you use in your paper. Most of these numbers you will have written beside the main and supporting points on your outline. As you write each point, copy the notecard numbers to mark the reference you used. When you revise your paper, you will replace these numbers with author or title names and page numbers, as shown in Chapter 4, "Preparing the Final Paper."

By inserting note card numbers in your rough draft, you will find it easier to construct your Works Cited list for the final paper. You will know which sources you actually used in your paper and which ones can be listed in a Works consulted reference page.

Keep Writing until the End

Although you must consider your audience and maintain an objective point of view, your primary mission at this stage is *to keep writing until you complete the first draft.* For this part of the process, set aside your critical inner voice and allow yourself to write freely. Don't worry about elegant phrasing or smooth transitions. Your writing is likely to sound rough and your flow of ideas within a paragraph to be less than logical—that's one reason this version is called a "rough" draft. A first draft paragraph might look like the following.

```
    Antidrug education programs in elementary schools and
high schools emphasize how to "Just say no" (13-1). They   ◄————— Note card reference
give information on drug abuse, how using drugs becomes a
destructive way of life. Costs a lot to maintain habit, so
they must find a way to make money quickly to buy drugs. Also
help students look at how they see themselves--lack of
self-esteem makes them want to be accepted or use drugs to
block out painful reality (14-3, 14-4). Programs offer
alternatives to despair. They show kids how to feel good about
themselves, how to succeed at something, what to do in place of
```

```
drugs when they are feeling troubled or depressed (13-2, 13-3,

13-4). These education programs are pro-people, not just

antidrugs.
```

Nor should you worry about where to start. Some people can begin at the beginning and write straight to the end of the paper. Others find they need to write the final paragraph or the middle paragraphs first, then tackle the introduction. One writer could never start a paper until he had written the last, concluding line. If you find yourself unable to begin at the beginning, start anywhere in the paper that catches your interest. You can come back and pick up the first points later.

Above all, use your outline as your guide and keep writing until you finish the first version of your paper. The next chapter focuses on revising your rough draft into a finished paper. You'll learn how to document your sources, check your paper for logical development, create effective paragraphs and sentences, and write smooth transitions from one section to another.

CHAPTER 4
Preparing the Final Paper

If you have time, let your rough draft cool off before you start revising and polishing it. Set it aside for a day or two, then come back to the draft with a fresh eye. You may be able to spot lapses in logic, missing references, or other problems more easily.

Your goals in converting the rough draft to a final paper are to correct errors in logic, fill in missing information and references, document your sources, and polish your language.

Your completed report or term paper will consist of the following.

1. Title page (optional)
2. Table of contents (optional) or outline (if requested by instructor)
3. Body of the report or term paper
4. Works Cited (and Works Consulted if required by instructor)
5. Note cards (if requested by instructor)

The revision process actually works from the last point to the first. If you are required to turn in your note cards, arrange them in the order in which you used them for your paper. This will make it easier for your instructor to match note cards to the text to check facts or references. Next, create a Works Cited list based on the references cited in the draft. Then revise the body of your paper, and finally, if needed, create a table of contents and title page.

Works Cited List

Prepare the Works Cited list before revising your final draft. In the final paper, you will be replacing your note card numbers with author or article titles and page numbers. You can use the list as a reference to make sure you insert the proper citations in your text. *Include only those references you actually used in your paper.* Books, articles, or documents that served as background material or additional sources can be placed in a Works Consulted list.

At this point, you are ready to insert the names of your sources for the note card numbers you put in your rough draft. For example, if you have listed one of your sources in the rough draft as 1–2, 1–3, substitute the name of that source and appropriate page numbers to document your facts, quotes, or other information. Look over the following example.

Rough Draft

According to some critics, Faulkner is one of the few American writers who has exploited the unusual flexibility of the

Note card references ⟶ English language (1-3, 1-4). As one critic stated, "Faulkner catches the rhythms of Southern speech in a manner that echoes the Elizabethan prose of Shakespeare" (2-1, 2-2).

Works Cited

Bibliography reference #1 ⟶ Bartel, Arthur. <u>Southern Writers Since 1930</u>. New York: Morrow, 1978.

Bibliography reference #2 ⟶ Martin, Julia C. "Why doesn't Anyone Write Like Shakespeare?" <u>MLA Bulletin</u>, 13 March 1982, 34+.

Final Paper

According to some critics, Faulkner is one of the few American writers who has exploited the unusual flexibility of the

Replaces note card reference ⟶ English language (Martin 34-35). As one critic stated, "Faulkner catches the rhythms of Southern speech in a manner that echoes the Elizabethan prose of Shakespeare" (Bartel 26).

Once you have completed your Works Cited list, go back to your rough draft and read it over carefully. Have you included all the references you need? Are there any you want to add or delete? Chapter 6, "Works Cited and Works Consulted Lists" describes the correct format for these lists and how to type the pages.

Citations in the Text

Today, most schools have adopted the Modern Language Association method of placing citations within the text instead of using footnotes or endnotes. Citations enable the reader to locate full bibliographic information for each reference in the Works Cited list. Citations are used to document:

- Ideas or concepts developed by author(s) and used in your paper

- Facts and statistics not common knowledge

- Direct quotations, whether only a few words or an extended excerpt taken from a published work

As the writer, you are responsible for providing your reader with enough information to locate the correct source. The contents of each citation will vary according to the way you present your information. Follow these guidelines for documenting your sources.

1. *When you use an idea or concept of an author and do not mention the author's name in the text, give a full citation at the end of the paraphrase or quote.* Write the author's name or, if there is no author, a shortened title of the book or article and the page number(s) in parentheses *followed by a period.* The citation is considered part of the sentence in which it appears. If the citation follows a quote, place it after the final quotation marks but before the period.

```
Watergate precipitated the greatest executive branch crisis
since the impeachment of Johnson following the Civil War
(Afferty 334).
```

```
According to one political observer, "Watergate precipitated
the greatest executive branch crisis since the impeachment
of Johnson following the Civil War" (Afferty 334).
```

2. *If you use the author's name or author's name and title of the work in the text, write only the page number of the source in the citation.* In this case, you have cited the author's name or title of the work in the text, and the reader will be able to look up the reference in the Works Cited. You need to add only the page number(s) in parentheses.

```
According to A. C. Afferty, Watergate represented the great-
est crisis to affect the executive branch since the impeach-
ment of Johnson following the Civil War (334).
```

As A. C. Afferty states in his book <u>America in Turmoil</u>, Watergate represented the greatest crisis to affect the executive branch since the impeachment of Johnson following the Civil War (334).

3. *If you summarize a work and mention the author and title, you do not need a citation.* A summary refers to an entire work, therefore page numbers are not needed. Also, since you have already referred to the author and title, you don't need to mention them in a citation.

Few books have documented the Hitler era in Germany as thoroughly as William L. Shirer's <u>The Rise and Fall of the Third Reich</u>. This massive volume uses actual Nazi documents to trace Hitler's rise to power and Germany's ultimate defeat in World War II.

4. *If you use two or more of an author's works as sources, use a shortened title of each work along with the author's name and page numbers in the citation.* The shortened name, enclosed in quote marks, tells the reader which of the author's works served as your source.

As deep-sea research has shown, the environment is being degraded by pollution even at depths of several thousand feet (Cousteau "Dying Sea" 45-48).

5. *The citation for a single volume of a multivolume work must include the volume number.* If you are using a single volume in a multi-volume series, list the volume number after the author's name. Use a colon to separate the volume number and page number(s).

The violence in Flannery O'Connor's work differs radically from the violence in Norman Mailer's novels. O'Connor's stories have an Old Testament flavor to them in which her characters struggle against demonic forces within and outside themselves (Curtis 4:356).

6. *For a citation with no author, use a shortened version of the title and the page number(s), if appropriate.* In some cases, a book or magazine article will not list an author. If the title is more than two or three words long, use the first two or three words, omitting any articles (a, an, the).

Works Cited

"An African Nation Enters the 21st Century." <u>World Opinion</u> 5 May 1988, 76-82.

```
Genetic engineering has saved over 50 endangered species

from extinction in this remote section of Africa ("African

Nation" 76-82).
```

7. *When documenting facts, place the citation as close to the data as possible.* If you mention a figure or statistic in the middle of a sentence or paragraph, place the citation after the data and not at the end of the sentence or paragraph—unless the reference covers then entire sentence or paragraph as well.

```
One state spent only $40,000 on AIDS research for the entire    ◄── The citation refers only
                                                                    to the money amount.
year (Whitney 45), which seems hardly believable given all

the publicity the disease has received in the press.
```

```
New York spent $40,000 on AIDS research in one month,      ◄── The citation refers to
                                                               the whole sentence, not
which represented a 30 percent increase over the amount         just to the money
                                                               amount.
spent on this research for the entire previous year (Whitney

47).
```

Remember, if you have not stated an author's name or a source title in the text of your paper, you must include them in the citation along with the appropriate page numbers. Consult the *MLA Handbook* if you need more detailed information on documenting your sources.

℅ 8 Revise Your First Draft

Five Secrets of Revising Your Paper

Many students fail to revise their first draft either because they don't know where to start or they feel there's no time before the paper is due (tomorrow—or even sooner). Yet revision is often the key to turning a mediocre paper into a first-rate work.

Once you know the secrets of revising your paper, you can often accomplish the task in fairly short order.

- Check for logical development of your ideas.

- Know how to create well-developed paragraphs.

- Begin at the true beginning.

- Get smoothly from one point to another.

- End with a bang, not a whimper.

Checking for Logical Development

"Logical development" means not only the flow of main points throughout the paper, but the development of each main idea within each paragraph. Many students toss the reader a collection of facts or ideas gathered from their research and assume they have fulfilled the assignment. The reader has no idea what many of the facts or ideas mean or how they relate either to the main topic or to one another. As the author, your job is not only to cite the facts or do the analysis but to tell the reader *what it all means*.

Flow of Main Points

Your first step is to make sure your main points follow logically from your thesis statement and build on one another to the final conclusion. You may discover in writing your paper that your outline is not so logical after all. Suppose you are arguing that the holes found in the ozone layer are caused by chemical pollution and that all industrialized nations must act to preserve this layer. Your outline sets up the main points as follows.

```
Thesis statement--introduction

  I. Some scientists argue threat to ozone layer minimal, holes
     discovered caused by natural phenomena

 II. Holes discovered in ozone layer due to chemical pollution
     not natural causes

III. United action required to ban all chemicals harmful to ozone
     layer

 IV. Ozone layer the main protective shield against lethal dose
     of ultraviolet radiation

  V. World science community must search for substitute
     chemicals not harmful to ozone layer

 VI. Conclusion
```

You begin writing your rough draft:

```
Thesis statement: Chemical pollution is degrading the ozone
layer that protects life on earth, and the world community must
act to curb the use of chemicals harmful to this layer.

     At first some scientists claimed that the holes in the
ozone layer discovered over both poles were due to natural
causes. Intensive chemical analysis of the atmosphere, however,
revealed the true culprit--chemical pollution. Synthetic
chemicals such as chlorofluorocarbons, used in aerosol sprays,
were combining with molecules in the atmosphere and slowly
degrading the ozone layer.
```

```
     One nation alone cannot stop this slow destruction; all

industrialized nations must act together and ban chemicals that

degrade the ozone layer. Without a united effort, the damage to

this layer will continue, threatening all life on earth.

     The importance of the ozone layer has been recognized only

within this century as technical developments enabled us to

study the composition and layers of the atmosphere. The ozone

layer is a protective shield surrounding the earth that

prevents the sun's ultraviolet radiation from reaching the

earth in lethal doses. Without this shield, life as we know it

would not be possible on earth. Therefore, anything that

threatens this protective layer is a direct threat to us all

and must be addressed by the entire world community.
```

Looking over what you have written, you see some problems in logical development of your main points. You explain what is happening to the ozone layer before you explain what the ozone layer is and does. If the readers know at the beginning how important the ozone layer is, then the rest of your argument will carry more weight. You will have captured your readers' attention and inspired them to keep reading.

In the argumentative structure outlined in Chapter 3, background information is presented before the main pro and con arguments are introduced. Otherwise, the reader does not know enough about the issue to judge whether your position is a plausible one.

The original arrangement of information in the sample outline above is typical of many beginning writers' work. They are so concerned with telling *how* and *why* something is happening, they forget the reader may not know *what* is being discussed. They fail to give the reader background information about their topic before launching into an analysis or giving an opinion on the subject.

In general, when you are checking for logical development of the main points in your paper, use the following rules of thumb.

- Background information *comes before* analysis or opinion.

- Minor points *come before* major points.

- Explanation *comes before* discussion of consequences.

- Arguments and reasons *come before* conclusions.

The revised outline about the ozone layer would look like the following.

```
Thesis statement--introduction

    I. Ozone layer the main protective shield against lethal dose

       of ultraviolet radiation. Damage to it threatens life on

       earth.
```

```
 II. Some scientists argue threat to ozone layer minimal, holes
     discovered caused by natural phenomena
III. Holes discovered in ozone layer due to chemical pollution
     not natural causes
 IV. United action by all nations required to ban chemicals
     harmful to ozone layer
  V. World science community must search for substitute
     chemicals not harmful to ozone layer
 VI. Conclusion
```

The paper now proceeds from background information to con and pro arguments, minor to major points, and finally to the conclusion.

The second step in checking for logical development is to make sure you have proven your points or fully explained your ideas within each paragraph. This step is one of the most critical in revising your rough draft into a polished final paper.

The Well-Developed Paragraph

At its most basic level, a term paper or report is nothing more than a series of connected paragraphs. This fact is one reason why knowing how to write well-tuned paragraphs can speed up the revision process of your rough draft. Only a few basic elements make up an effective, convincing paragraph.

1. Each paragraph discusses only *one main point*.

2. Each paragraph contains *a topic sentence* that introduces or summarizes the main point.

3. Each paragraph provides *examples* proving or illustrating the main point.

With these three principles in mind, you should be able to analyze your rough draft and quickly spot areas that need revision. Remember, the purpose of a paragraph is to discuss one idea, present a brief explanation with examples or illustrations, and stop. If you find yourself writing page-long paragraphs or no paragraphs at all, follow these guidelines when revising your rough draft.

1. *To determine where paragraph breaks should occur, notice how sentences group around your ideas.* Look at the ideas you discuss in your rough draft paragraphs. Notice how sentences tend to fall into a natural grouping around these ideas. For example, look over the rough draft paragraph from Chapter 3.

Note card reference ———→
```
     Antidrug education programs in elementary schools and
high schools emphasize how to "Just say no" (13-1). They
give information on drug abuse, how using drugs becomes a
destructive way of life. Costs a lot to maintain habit, so
```

```
they must find a way to make money quickly to buy drugs.

Also help students look at how they see themselves--lack of

self-esteem makes them want to be accepted or use drugs to

block out painful reality (14-3, 14-4). Programs offer

alternatives to despair. They show kids how to feel good

about themselves, how to succeed at something, what to do in

place of drugs when they are feeling troubled or depressed

(13-2, 13-3, 13-4). These education programs are pro-people,

not just antidrugs.
```

The writer has several main points in this paragraph: mentioning information on drug abuse in antidrug education programs, describing how drug use affects individual lives, looking at some of the causes prompting students to turn to drugs, and presenting the pro-people aspect of drug education programs.

2. *Use each main point to begin a new paragraph, introduced or summarized by a topic sentence.* Each of the main points listed above should have its own paragraph. Key sentences—called topic sentences—let the reader know what subject or argument the paragraph will discuss.

1ST MAIN POINT
```
Antidrug programs in elementary schools and
high schools emphasize not only saying "no"
to drugs but how to build a healthy, creative
life. . . .
```

2ND MAIN POINT
```
First, these programs help students understand
the effects of drugs and drug addiction on
their lives. . . .
```

3RD MAIN POINT
```
Second, the programs emphasize reasons, such
as poor self-esteem, that prompt many students
to turn to drugs. . . .
```

4TH MAIN POINT
```
Finally, the best antidrug programs are
pro-people, offering alternatives to despair
and addressing some of the underlying causes
of drug abuse in students.
```

How long should a paragraph be? Take a second look at any paragraphs that run over six or seven sentences. They may contain too many ideas; you may need to split them up. On the other hand, in formal writing, such as reports and term papers, one-sentence paragraphs are not allowed. You will need to expand on your idea or incorporate the sentence into another paragraph.

3. *Each main point must be supported by specific examples or illustrations.* As the writer, you can say or argue anything you like. But you must be prepared to back up your statements with evidence, examples, or illustrations to prove that your points are valid. Thus, even someone who disagrees with your position or analysis will be forced to acknowledge that you support it well.

Look at the third point in the example above. "The programs emphasize reasons, such as poor self-esteem, that prompt many students to turn to drugs." What evidence supports this statement? How does poor self-esteem encourage drug use? Is everyone with poor self-esteem at risk? What other reasons may cause someone to become addicted to drugs? This statement cries out for supporting evidence.

Look over your own rough draft paragraphs. What statements have you made that need logical support, examples, illustrations? Ask yourself the following questions after each argument, analysis, or opinion.

- What proof do I have for this statement?
- What specific details support it?
- What does my statement mean?

It may help to imagine that you are talking about your subject with a highly skeptical friend. After each opinion or argument, the friend challenges you to prove or show that you have some basis for what you say. If during revision you find you don't have enough evidence or examples to support your main points, go back to your sources and fill in the missing information.

A fully developed paragraph on the third main point in the antidrug program example might look like the following.

```
     Second, the programs emphasize reasons, such as poor
self-esteem, that prompt many students to turn to drugs.
For example, psychologists have found that students who
experience chronic depression, a sense of hopelessness
about life, or a lack of self-worth are in considerable
psychological pain and may take drugs to get relief from
their symptoms (Adlemere 23-27). Still other students may
go along with taking drugs because they desperately want
to be accepted as "part of the crowd" (Worthington 34-35).
Thus, antidrug programs show students that when they
are psychologically troubled, they may be particularly
vulnerable to drug addiction.
```

Once you know the basics of writing well-developed paragraphs, it will be easier for you to write the introductory, middle, and concluding paragraphs in your paper. You can adapt your skills to the specific purposes of these three parts and spot immediately when these paragraphs fail to achieve their purposes.

Introductory Paragraphs— Begin at the Beginning

The purpose of the introductory paragraphs is to:

1. Introduce your subject.
2. Preview the organization of the paper by presenting the major points in the order they will appear.
3. Come to the point of your paper or report.

These paragraphs contain your thesis statement, generally as the concluding sentence leading into the body of the paper.

In many ways, the introduction is different from any other section in your paper because its function differs. As shown in Chapter 3, introductory paragraphs are like a funnel that begins with a broad general statement about your topic and narrows to the thesis statement.

Generally, beginning writers have two problems in creating the introductory paragraph: They start from too broad or too narrow a perspective, or they try for the clever opening.

False versus Real Beginnings

Suppose that you want to write about the issue of whether animals are used unnecessarily in laboratory experiments and testing. You talk to a friend about it, but instead of stating what your opinion is, you begin with a broad general statement about the historical use of animals. Your friend is bewildered. "What's your point?" she wants to know. If you were writing such an introduction, your opening general statements might look like the following.

```
      The domestication of animals marked a turning point in
human history. Researchers believe that the first animals
domesticated were the dog, oxen, horses, and other beasts of
burden. Their use enabled humanity to cultivate vast tracts of
land, travel long distances, raise cattle and other animals
for food and hides, and perform many other tasks that human
strength alone could not accomplish. This partnership between
humans and animals has existed for thousands of years, even
though machines have assumed many of the tasks that animals
used to perform.

      The past few years have witnessed a growing movement of
"animal rights" activists who maintain that most if not all
product testing procedures using animals are inhumane and
unnecessary.
```

The reader is one paragraph into the paper and still finds no mention of the animal rights issue. Although domestication is an interesting subject, it is not the topic of your paper. The real beginning of your introduction is the second paragraph, which starts with a broad statement on the subject of the paper.

The other extreme is bringing in the thesis statement too soon without setting the stage. Suppose, in talking to your friend, you simply blurted out, "Medical laboratories are abusing animals for no reason!" Your friend might be equally bewildered by this opening. She will naturally ask, "What are you talking about? What's the problem?" You need to set the stage before stating your opinion. Don't lead with your thesis sentence or main argument. Orient your readers by giving them some idea what the issues are before presenting your position.

Other writers may try for the clever opening. They take their cue from advertising or news tabloids where flashy, hard-hitting words and pictures reach out and grab readers' attention.

> Animal rights advocates clash with medical students! Dogs kept chained in dark cages for weeks! Evidence of abuse brings research to a halt! Such headlines scream at a public outraged by abuses in science labs around the country. What can be done to end this nightmare?

Or

> Little Caryl Wade, victim of a rare blood disease, stares forlornly out the window at her friends who are healthy enough to play. In another city, a young researcher pores over his animal experimentation data with growing excitement. Using specially bred mice, he has isolated a cure for victims like little Caryl. Because of his work, hundreds of children will live to run and play again. Do animal rights advocates ever consider this side of research when they scream for an end to all animal testing?

Such statements generally make poor openings—they substitute glitter and effects for real content. Your reader may distrust your motives and arguments, since writers who use emotion to manipulate readers generally have little hard evidence or proof to support their positions.

If you begin at the true beginning—with a general statement of your topic—you are far more likely to win the reader's trust and to set up the structure of your paper. An introductory paragraph that begins at the true beginning—with neither too broad nor narrow a focus—might look like the following.

> The past few years have witnessed a growing movement of "animal rights" activists who maintain that most if not all product testing procedures using animals are inhumane and unnecessary.

```
    Although many researchers argue that such work cannot be

done without animal models, procedures for testing cosmetics

and drugs can be accomplished in other ways. The use of animals

for testing commercial products should be banned and other

types of testing procedures employed instead.
```

This paragraph makes a general statement to introduce the topic but stays focused on the subject as stated in the thesis. Each succeeding sentence after the general statement establishes how you will proceed in your paper—setting up the opposition's argument about the use of animals in product testing, countering with your own arguments, and ending with your thesis statement.

How to Find the Real Beginning

Many students start out on the wrong foot with their introductory paragraph because they don't know the correct one. How do you decide which general opening statement is the best one to make? To begin, look to your thesis statement for clues. What are the main elements in the statement?

```
    Censorship not only violates First Amendment rights

guaranteed by the Constitution but often popularizes the very

ideas it seeks to suppress.
```

The main elements might be "First Amendment rights," "Constitution," "popularizing ideas." Other elements that could be inferred from the statement include "democracy," "freedom of ideas," "tyranny," "public morals," "values," "power of the word." Any of these terms could be used as the starting point for the general statement opening your introductory paragraph.

```
    One of the unique features of democracy in this country

is the protection of free speech in all its various forms.


    History proves that the harder governments or groups try

to censor ideas in the name of the public good, the more popu-

lar those ideas become.


    One of the oldest justifications for censorship is the

claim by the censoring groups or officials that they are not

suppressing free thought but protecting public morality from

harmful ideas.
```

Any one of these opening statements will serve your purposes. From this point, you can move in a logical sequence to your thesis statement, gradually narrowing your focus from the broad statement to the thesis. Once your introduction is written you are ready to delve into the body of your paper.

Middle Paragraphs— Getting from One Point to Another

Middle or body paragraphs serve two purposes.

1. They develop each point in support of your thesis statement.
2. They build toward the strongest point before the concluding paragraph.

Although each paragraph in the middle section should be able to stand alone, it also is part of a larger whole. You can imagine each paragraph like a link in a chain. If the links are not connected, the chain falls apart. If your paragraphs are not connected, your paper is merely a collection of separate ideas. The reader will be unable to follow the development of your thoughts.

The connections between paragraphs are called *transitions*. Smooth transitions lead the reader from one point to another and clearly show the relationship between your main ideas. They unify your paper and give it a coherence and flow that make it a pleasure to read.

The function of transition words and phrases is easier to understand if you first look at how they unify ideas within a paragraph.

Transitions within Paragraphs

The major function of transitions is to link ideas that on the surface do not appear to be closely or logically related. Transitional words and phrases allow the reader to follow the writer's shifts in logic. For example:

```
Shakespeare is a brilliant writer. Some parts of his plays are

badly written.
```

These statements appear to contradict one another. However, add transitions, and the writer's intention becomes clear.

```
Although Shakespeare is a brilliant writer, some parts of his

plays are badly written.
```

Or

```
Admittedly, Shakespeare is a brilliant writer. Nevertheless,

some parts of his plays are badly written.
```

Transitions become even more important when you are developing an argument or analysis in a paragraph. Read over the sample paragraph below. How easy is it to follow the writer's thinking?

```
    The public feels the insanity defense is easily misused.

This belief is not entirely wrong. Courts sometimes apply the

insanity defense inconsistently. The major problem is that

newspapers do not print the clearcut verdicts but only those
```

```
that are ambiguous. People have the idea that the insanity
defense is unreliable and should be abolished. The courts get
confused over how to apply this defense. Lawyers tend to misuse
it for all types of cases. There is more confusion for the
courts. The key to telling when the insanity defense plea needs
revision is when the lawyers start to misuse it.
```

If you're like most readers, you are left wondering exactly what the author meant to say. Ideas come fast and furious; but without connecting links, it is hard to follow the author's reasoning. Once transitions are used to link ideas, the meaning becomes clear.

```
        The public feels the insanity defense is easily misused.
This belief is not entirely wrong, because courts sometimes
apply the insanity defense inconsistently. The major problem,
however, is that newspapers do not print the clearcut verdicts
but only those that are ambiguous. Because of what people read
in the press, they have the idea that the insanity defense is
unreliable and should be abolished. In addition, when the
courts get confused over how to apply this defense, lawyers
tend to use it for all types of cases. The result is more
confusion for the courts. Thus, the key to determining when the
insanity defense plea needs revision may be when the lawyers
start to misuse it.
```

Transitional words and phrases notify the reader that the next step in the argument or analysis is about to follow. They provide subtle cues that announce "and now I'm going to talk about . . ." without interrupting the flow of ideas. Some of the most common transitional words or phrases include the following.

admittedly	furthermore	obviously
although	however	of course
and	in addition	on the other hand
as a result	in conclusion	still
assuredly	indeed	therefore
because	in fact	thus
but	moreover	true
certainly	most important of all	undoubtedly
clearly	nevertheless	unquestionably
consequently	no doubt	while

These words and phrases, along with another device known as a paragraph hook, can be used to link paragraphs.

Transitions between Paragraphs

Although transitions are important within paragraphs, they become even more important when linking paragraphs. Particularly in an argumentative paper, you want to make sure the reader knows clearly where you are going as you develop your thesis. Transitional words and phrases are especially useful in presenting con and pro arguments, as shown below.

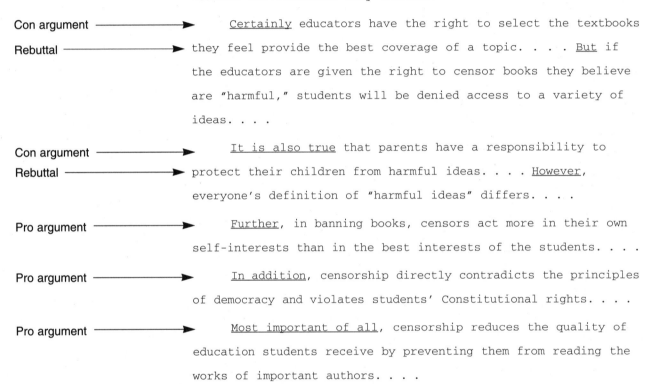

Censorship in education, far from protecting students from harmful influences, violates their Constitutional rights and weakens the education they receive.

Con argument ⟶ Certainly educators have the right to select the textbooks

Rebuttal ⟶ they feel provide the best coverage of a topic. . . . But if the educators are given the right to censor books they believe are "harmful," students will be denied access to a variety of ideas. . . .

Con argument ⟶ It is also true that parents have a responsibility to

Rebuttal ⟶ protect their children from harmful ideas. . . . However, everyone's definition of "harmful ideas" differs. . . .

Pro argument ⟶ Further, in banning books, censors act more in their own self-interests than in the best interests of the students. . . .

Pro argument ⟶ In addition, censorship directly contradicts the principles of democracy and violates students' Constitutional rights. . . .

Pro argument ⟶ Most important of all, censorship reduces the quality of education students receive by preventing them from reading the works of important authors. . . .

In conclusion. . . .

The transitions introduce each main point and lead the reader step by step to the strongest argument in the paper. They are particularly effective in short papers. For longer works, however, and in literary, position, or descriptive papers, such words and phrases can become repetitious and tiresomely obvious. You want the links to be a seamless part of your text, not stand out like flashing neon signs.

For a stronger, more subtle link, learn to use the *paragraph hook*. The paragraph hook picks up a phrase or concept in the last sentence of the preceding paragraph and uses it as a link to the next paragraph. Notice the difference in the examples below between a standard transition and a paragraph hook.

Transitional Phrase

The setting in many of Hemingway's novels and short stories reflects his love of nature. The tranquil streams of "Big

Two-Hearted River," the sweep of the veldt in <u>The Green Hills of Africa</u>, and the silent Michigan woods in the Nick Adams stories restore the main characters' sense of harmony and balance.

<u>In contrast</u>, cities, in Hemingway's view, are places where men and women lose what is essential to themselves. As a result, they betray confidences, entangle themselves in impossible relationships, and destroy each other's chances for happiness.

Paragraph Hook

The setting in many of Hemingway's novels and short stories reflects his love of nature. The tranquil streams of "Big Two-Hearted River," the sweep of the veldt in <u>The Green Hills of Africa</u>, and the silent Michigan woods in the Nick Adams stories restore the main characters' sense of harmony and balance.

<u>In stark contrast to this effect of nature</u>, cities, in Hemingway's view, are places where men and women lose what is essential to themselves. As a result, they betray confidences, entangle themselves in impossible relationships, and destroy each other's chances for happiness.

You can use the paragraph hook to repeat, summarize, or elaborate on a phrase or idea from the previous paragraph.

The tranquil streams . . . restore people's sense of harmony and balance.

Once people return to cities, in Hemingway's view, they lose this <u>harmony and balance</u>. . . . ◄——— Repeats one part of the previous sentence

Or

<u>Such a view of nature</u> contrasts sharply with Hemingway's view of cities. . . . ◄— Summarizes the content of the previous paragraph

Or

<u>Although Hemingway's view of nature is more benign than many authors'</u>, his view of cities is far less charitable. . . . ◄— Elaborates on the contrast and compares Hemingway to other authors

Experiment with your own writing—try creating paragraph hooks instead of using only transition words and phrases. By learning to use transition words and paragraph hooks, you can link your ideas and paragraphs into a well-connected chain. Readers may not notice how skillfully you are guiding the argument or description, but they will notice that the paper is well written and a pleasure to read.

Concluding Paragraphs— End with a Bang

Many beginning writers make it through the introduction and middle sections of their paper only to flounder at the end. They simply restate the thesis or present the reader with a list of all their main points without interpreting them. In T.S. Eliot's words, they end "not with a bang but a whimper."

Remember the function of the concluding paragraph is to begin with the thesis and end with a broad general statement about your subject. The conclusion resembles a pyramid—the opposite of the introduction with its funnel shape.

If you find yourself at a loss about how to begin the conclusion of your paper, go back to the introductory paragraphs and start with your thesis statement. Use transitional words or phrases to help begin the paragraph.

```
Thesis statement: Censorship in education, far from

protecting students from harmful influences, violates their

Constitutional rights and weakens the education they receive.


Concluding paragraph: In short, censorship in education,

far from protecting students from harmful influences, violates

their Constitutional rights and weakens the education they

receive.
```

If this straightforward restatement of the thesis sentence seems a bit stiff or awkward, you can rephrase the statement without changing its meaning.

```
     In short, censorship in education fails to protect

students from so-called harmful influences, violates their

Constitutional rights, and weakens the education they receive.
```

Or

```
     In short, censorship in education has little to recommend

it. The practice fails to protect students from so-called

harmful influences, violates their Constitutional rights, and

weakens the education they receive.
```

Now you are ready to tie in the middle section of your paper before your final broad statement. Avoid simply listing your main points—readers generally resent being told all over again what they just read. Instead, borrow the meaning of your main points and rephrase them. Compare the two concluding paragraphs below.

Avoid

        In short, censorship in education fails to protect
students from so-called harmful influences, violates their
Constitutional rights, and weakens the education they receive.
The preceding paragraphs have shown that censors act more
in their own interests than for the students, censorship
contradicts the principles of democracy and violates
constitutional guarantees of free speech, and it denies
students access to the works of important writers. Therefore,
censorship in education should not be allowed.

Better

        In short, censorship in education fails to protect
students from so-called harmful influences, violates their
Constitutional rights, and weakens the education they receive.
When educators try to censor the books students read, they
often act more from their own fears and prejudices than from
any real understanding of student needs. After all, who is to
say what is harmful to students; the criteria change from
generation to generation. Censors also contradict the very
principles of free speech and free access to the truth that
serve as the cornerstone of our democracy. Thus, students
educated under censorship not only receive a dangerously
incomplete picture of the truth, they may have trouble learning
the truth at all. The best protection for young people is not
censorship but an education system that teaches them to think
for themselves.

The second conclusion rephrases the thesis and extracts the meaning of the main points in the paper. The arguments are not repeated in a laundry list but interpreted in light of the entire paper. The reader is given a capsule summary of your arguments. The final broad statement not only maintains that censorship is wrong but offers a better alternative.

Use the techniques described in this section to end your paper with a bang. Look over your introductory paragraphs and middle paragraphs, then transform, interpret, and rephrase your main points. Leave the reader with a final, convincing statement that puts your topic in a broader perspective. The conclusion is your last chance to persuade or convince the reader of your point of view. Make the most of it.

A Final Word

You've made it through the revision process. Now read your paper over one last time before you type the final version. Ask yourself the following questions.

- Is my thesis statement clearly stated in the introductory and concluding paragraphs?
- Do my main points fully support the thesis?
- Have I organized the main points so they flow logically from the least important to the most important arguments?
- Have I supported my statements and opinions with evidence, examples, or illustrations?
- Are my transitions within and between paragraphs smooth?
- Does my conclusion rephrase, summarize, and interpret the thesis statement and main points in my paper?
- Have I cited all facts, other people's ideas or opinions, and direct quotes in the paper?
- Does my Works Cited list contain complete information for each reference?

If you spot any weaknesses in your paper, now is the time to correct them. In addition, Chapter 5 provides grammar and style tips, and Chapter 8 presents guidelines for typing your term paper or report in correct format. Look over these chapters before you prepare the final version. You have put a great deal of thought and effort into your paper so far, make sure it is the best representative of your ideas possible.

CHAPTER 5
Grammar and Style Tips

Compare these two passages.

Oppressed groups try peaceful change first, but history shows that peaceful attempts can lead to violence if there is too much repression over too long a time. People in power try to keep peaceful groups down. For example, American colonists resorted to war. Before that, they tried to change King George and Parliament without war. Even after several years.

History shows that oppressed groups generally go through a long period of peaceful attempts to win their rights from those in power before turning to violence. For example,

```
American colonists tried for years to change repressive English

laws by peacefully petitioning King George and Parliament. Only

after these nonviolent attempts failed did the colonists resort

to war.
```

In the first passage, a good idea lurks somewhere in all the verbiage and grammatical errors. Unfortunately, the reader is so distracted by what is wrong with the passage that the content is lost.

In the second passage, ideas are supported, not overwhelmed, by the language. The main concept is clear and subsequent arguments are concise and well expressed. The writer has corrected all grammatical mistakes.

These two examples illustrate the principal purpose of grammar and style—*to communicate your ideas clearly and effectively*. You may have a brilliant thesis, a clever argument, or a fascinating topic. But unless your writing communicates your ideas, the effect is lost on the reader. You owe it to yourself, and to all the research you've done, to put your best language forward.

This chapter provides easy guidelines for grammar and style questions regarding lively writing, subject-verb agreement, punctuation, capitalization, and numbers. Many students find such questions the most troublesome when they write.

Lively Writing

Beginning writers are often overwhelmed by advice on how to write well or how to improve their writing. Actually, if you learn how to use the active voice, eliminate *there* constructions, use parallel structure, and keep your language clear and fresh, you will possess the basics of writing with style.

Use Action Verbs and the Active Voice

Verbs are like the motor that drives a machine—they add power and energy to your writing. Weak verbs dilute your words. To improve your writing, keep these two guidelines in mind.

1. Use action verbs, not state-of-being verbs, whenever possible.
2. Use the active voice, not the passive voice.

Action Verbs. Action verbs—such as *run, talk, meet, explore, dictate, erupt*—show the reader that something is happening or that someone is taking action. These verbs bring your words to life and engage the reader.

On the other hand, state-of-being verbs—such as *can* or *should* and all forms of *to be (am, is, are, was, were, will be, been, being)*—simply sit in the middle of the sentence. These static verb forms are like a still photograph compared to a live-action film.

Whenever possible, change a state-of-being verb into an action verb in your writing.

AVOID:
```
Jack London's stories are exciting tales of how the

fittest survive in nature or in society.
```

BETTER: Jack London's stories <u>show</u> in vivid detail how the

fittest survive in nature or in society.

How can you spot the action verb in your sentences? Often the verb is buried in a noun that ends in *-tion* or *-ion*, such as *application, completion, realization, production.* These words can be changed into action verbs, rescuing your sentences from excessive "nounism."

Verbs Buried in Nouns

The <u>realization came</u> to him that all the foreign diplomats in Iran were closing down their embassies. His supervisor <u>gave</u> <u>authorization</u> to shred all secret documents.

Action Verbs

He suddenly <u>realized</u> that all the foreign diplomats in Iran were closing down their embassies. His supervisor <u>authorized</u> the shredding of all secret documents.

Other verbs, such as *to do, to seem, to make* lack power as well. See if you can choose other verbs that work harder for you. Compare the examples below.

AVOID: The author <u>seems</u> unwilling to give her characters any

power to change their lives.

BETTER: The author <u>gives</u> her characters little power to change

their lives.

Active versus Passive Voice.

The active voice describes who or what carried out an action. Like action verbs, active voice adds interest and liveliness to your writing. The passive voice is more static and describes who or what received the action.

Active	Passive
An aircraft <u>sank</u> the ship.	The ship <u>was sunk.</u>
Federal agents <u>arrested</u> Hodges.	Hodges <u>was arrested</u> by federal agents.

Besides adding unnecessary words to your sentences, the passive voice obscures the actors in your writing. Compare the two examples below.

When Charles Lindbergh returned to the United States, a huge parade <u>was given</u> in his honor in New York. Bells <u>were</u> <u>rung</u>, confetti <u>was thrown</u> from skyscraper offices, and shops <u>were closed</u>. Speeches <u>were given</u> by the mayor and several

```
dignitaries, and then Lindbergh was hurried away to meet the

governor of the state.
```

Who or what *gave, rang, threw, closed, hurried*? Besides Lindbergh and a few officials, no actors appear in this passage, yet a great deal is happening. By shifting to the active voice, you bring the actors back into the picture and give the writing more energy.

```
    When Charles Lindbergh returned to the United States, New

York City officials organized a huge parade in his honor.

Churches rang their bells, office workers threw confetti from

high above the street, and shopkeepers closed their businesses.

The mayor and several dignitaries spoke at length about

Lindbergh's achievement, then hurried him away to meet the

governor.
```

Now all the actors are present in the passage. In general, make your subjects *do* something in your sentences. Change the passive to the active voice whenever possible.

Occasional Use of Passive Voice. Should you always eliminate the passive voice? Not necessarily. It can be used when you wish to emphasize the subject's powerlessness or when you need a more neutral tone to avoid passing judgment on someone's actions.

Subject has no power to resist being fired. →
```
After Hill spoke out against another cut in wages, she was fired.
```

Passive voice emphasizes the child's helplessness. →
```
The child was struck by a train at the crossing.
```

Passive voice establishes a more objective tone in laying the background for subsequent arguments. →
```
    In the 1950s, atomic tests were conducted in the deserts

of Utah and Nevada. Soldiers were exposed to high levels of

radiation near the test sites, and many died of cancer over the

next twenty years. The question remains--did the government

know how many soldiers had received a dangerous dose of

radiation?
```

While these examples condone use of the passive voice, for the most part, be ruthless in changing the passive to the active voice in your writing.

Eliminate "There" Constructions

One of the most common errors beginning writers commit involves the seemingly innocent *there* and constructions like *there is, there was, there were.*

You can instantly improve your style if you work to eliminate "there" constructions from your writing.

If this sounds simple—don't be fooled. *There* crops up in sentences like the proverbial bad penny and is just as hard to eliminate. Although it is not grammatically incorrect, the word clutters sentences and encourages weak verbs and uninspired phrasing. In some instances, you can fix the problem by simply dropping *there* and its verb. Compare the two sentences below.

```
There was a storm raging last night.

A storm raged last night.
```

The second sentence—without *there was*—conveys more force than its weaker cousin.

In other cases, the problem may be more complex. You may need to reword the sentence and find a stronger verb. For example:

```
There was an argument between two men.
```

Eliminating *there was* leaves you with a sentence fragment *an argument between two men*. Look for an active verb to convey your meaning. Did the argument *erupt, break out, start*?

```
An argument erupted between two men.

An argument broke out between two men.

An argument started between two men.
```

Or even

```
The two men argued.
```

In other cases, the solution is buried in the sentence itself. In the example below, for instance, the subject comes after a preposition and the verb is hidden in the noun *disagreement*.

```
There is general disagreement among critics regarding which
poem is Christina Rosetti's finest.

Critics generally disagree on which poem is Christina Rosetti's
finest.
```

Don't be afraid to take your sentences apart, experiment with different verbs, or rephrase your thoughts. By eliminating *there* and its constructions, you develop your skill in using language.

Keep Your Structures Parallel

You can bring new clarity and force to your writing by mastering parallel structure. Briefly defined, parallelisms are words, phrases, or clauses in a sentence that possess the same grammatical structure. Once you learn the basics of parallelisms, you'll be able to spot errors quickly. The sentence below fails to maintain parallel structure.

```
He had authority to plan the campaign, to organize the

political workers, and after the campaign ended, he analyzed

all mistakes.
```

Once a parallel structure begins, the reader expects it to continue. Changing the structure confuses the reader and dilutes the impact of your ideas. Repetition can be an effective stylistic device. The sentence above should read as follows.

```
He had authority to plan the campaign, to organize the

political workers, and to analyze all mistakes after the

campaign ended.
```

Parallel structures can be simple or more complex. But they all share the same common element—repetition of a grammatical structure.

Articles and Prepositions. If you repeat an article or preposition once, repeat it with all the items in a series—or drop the article or preposition altogether.

INCORRECT: The ship carried a dinghy, an inflatable life raft, radio, and directional beacon.

CORRECT: The ship carried a dinghy, an inflatable life raft, a radio, and a directional beacon.

Or

```
The ship carried a dinghy, inflatable life raft, radio, and

directional beacon.
```

Nouns, Adjectives, Adverbs, Verbs. In some cases, you may need to condense several words into a single noun, adjective, adverb, or verb.

Nouns

INCORRECT: They traveled across deserts, valleys, mountains, and even went through swampland.

CORRECT: They traveled across deserts, valleys, mountains, and swampland.

Adjectives

INCORRECT: The first rocket design was clumsy, complicated, but didn't cost much.

CORRECT: The first rocket design was clumsy, complicated, but inexpensive.

Adverbs

INCORRECT: The jaguar strikes swiftly and <u>without a sound</u>.

CORRECT: The jaguar strikes swiftly and <u>silently</u>.

Verbs

INCORRECT: They have sold the tickets, tacked up the posters, and <u>the chairs were set up</u> for the concert.

CORRECT: They have sold the tickets, tacked up the posters, and <u>set up</u> the chairs for the concert.

Pairs and First/Second/Third. Pairs (*and, but, either/or, neither/nor, not only /but also*) and first/second/third constructions are often the hardest to control. Make sure that you maintain a balanced parallel structure on either side of the pairs, as in the examples below.

INCORRECT: They <u>not only</u> discovered the tomb <u>but also</u> a nearby burial site.

CORRECT: They discovered <u>not only</u> the tomb <u>but also</u> a nearby ◄— burial site.

> The verb *discovered* refers to both the tomb and the burial site. Thus, *not only* comes before the noun to set up a parallel structure. Compare this sentence with the one below.

INCORRECT: They discovered <u>not only</u> the tomb <u>but also</u> found a nearby burial site.

CORRECT: They <u>not only</u> discovered the tomb <u>but also</u> found a ◄— nearby burial site.

> The verb *discovered* refers only to *the tomb* while *found* refers to the *burial site*. Thus, *not only* comes before the first verb to set up a parallel structure.

INCORRECT: He turned down the offer <u>first because he felt unqualified and second that it paid too little money</u>.

CORRECT: He turned down the offer <u>first because he felt unqualified</u> and <u>second because it paid too little money</u>.

Be on the lookout for mistakes in parallel structure in your writing. Remember, mastering parallelisms can add considerable impact to your ideas.

Eliminate Clichés, Wordiness, Slang

Another quick way to improve your style is to eliminate clichés, wordiness, and slang from your writing. These expressions add nothing to your paper and reveal only a lazy mind too tired to think for itself.

Clichés. Clichés are trite, worn-out expressions that have been chewed and rechewed until they have no substance left. They come easily to mind because you have heard them all your life. Learn to spot these tired phrases in your writing and substitute your own language. Common clichés include the following.

dead as a doornail	keep your shirt on
stiff as a board	neat as a pin
getting in touch with	on the tip of my tongue
up to your ears	needle in a haystack
oldies but goodies	too good to be true
quiet as a churchmouse	on the warpath
white as a sheet (ghost)	a stitch in time

AVOID: Woolf's stories are a <u>gold mine</u> for the reader who wants to know more about <u>what makes people tick</u>. Her insights into human nature are <u>pearls of wisdom</u> and <u>put other writers to shame</u>.

BETTER: Woolf's stories are <u>deeply satisfying</u> to the reader who wants to know more about <u>the hidden aspects of human nature</u>. Her psychological insights <u>reveal her profound wisdom and far outstrip the abilities of most writers</u>.

Whenever you find a cliché in your writing, practice rephrasing the idea in your own language. You will find that the cliché has nothing of any significance to say.

Wordiness. Watch out for excess verbiage and redundant expressions that clutter your writing. Like clichés, wordy and redundant expressions spring easily to mind because they are so common in ordinary speech. Eliminate these offenders ruthlessly.

AVOID: The building was rectangular <u>in shape</u>.

Rectangular is already a shape.   **BETTER:**   The building was rectangular.

AVOID: <u>In the vast majority of cases</u>, writers do not show good financial sense.

BETTER: <u>In most cases</u>, writers do not show good financial sense.

A list of wordy phrases commonly used by writers is given below. Compare them with their more concise alternatives. Wherever you find the wordy phrases in your writing, change them to the shorter versions.

Wordy	Concise
at this point in time	at this time
blend together	blend
personal in manner	personal
meet together	meet
refer back to	refer to
blue in color	blue
consensus of opinion	consensus
during the course of	during
box that is heavy	heavy box
on a weekly basis	weekly
until such time as	until
person who is tall	tall person
storm that struck last night	last night's storm
due to the fact that	because
very necessary	necessary
the fact that she had come	her coming
engaged in the study of	studying
in spite of the fact that	although

Redundant words and expressions repeat or rephrase what has already been said. These errors are easy to spot once you know what to look for and where to find them.

AVOID: The detectives had to retrace the steps they had taken before.

BETTER: The detectives had to retrace their steps. ◄────────── *Retrace* means to go over steps taken before; the phrase *they had taken before* is unnecessary.

Slang. Slang words lower the tone of your writing and cause the reader to question your knowledge and credibility as a writer. Eliminate such words from your work.

AVOID: Some people might regard Fitzgerald as a real loser, like the guy couldn't make it in Hollywood, New York, or anywhere else he lived.

BETTER: Some people might regard Fitzgerald as a failure, unable to succeed in Hollywood, New York, or anywhere else.

As in the case of clichés and wordy expressions, slang takes up space without adding meaning or sense to your writing. Learn to spot these verbal freeloaders in your work and eliminate them or substitute your own words.

Subject-Verb Agreement

The standard rule for subject-verb agreement is simple: Verbs must agree with their subjects in person and number. A first-person, singular noun (I) takes the first-person verb form (am), while a third-person, plural noun (they) takes a third-person verb form (are).

FIRST PERSON: <u>I am</u> tired. <u>We are</u> thirsty.

SECOND PERSON: <u>You look</u> hot.

THIRD PERSON: <u>She swims</u> well. <u>He sings</u> off key. <u>It is</u> hard. <u>They sing</u> beautifully.

Singular	**Plural**
The <u>door is</u> open.	The <u>doors are</u> open.
<u>He arrives</u> tomorrow.	<u>They arrive</u> tomorrow.
<u>You teach</u> math.	<u>All of you teach</u> math.
The <u>car stalls</u> often.	The <u>cars stall</u> often.

Although the basic rule for subject-verb agreement is simple, at times it is not always easy to tell when a subject is singular or plural. The following guidelines will help you determine whether a singular or plural verb is the right choice for your sentences.

Compounds Joined by *and*— Singular and Plural Verbs

In most cases, compound subjects joined by *and* require a *plural* verb. You are speaking of two or more subjects.

<u>Two battleships and one destroyer were sunk</u> off the island.

<u>Beattie and Mason are</u> among our most talented young writers.

There are only two exceptions to this rule. Use a *singular* verb (1) when the subject is considered a unit (as in *research and development* or *secretary and treasurer*) or (2) when both parts of the subject are modified by *each* or *every*.

<u>Is the secretary and treasurer</u> going to attend the meeting?

<u>Each student</u> and <u>every teacher is</u> important to our school.

Compounds Joined by *or* or *nor*— Singular and Plural Verbs

Use the *plural* verb for subjects joined by *or* or *nor* when (1) the subject nearest the verb is plural or (2) both parts of the subject are plural.

Neither the television nor the two radios were damaged.

Are the toasters or the microwaves on sale?

Use the *singular* verb when (1) the subject nearest the verb is singular or (2) both parts of the subject are singular.

Neither the radios nor the television was damaged.

Is the toaster or the microwave on sale?

Collective Nouns—Singular or Plural Verb

When you are emphasizing the collective noun as a unit, use the *singular* verb. To refer to individuals that make up the unit, use the *plural* verb.

The school board has voted to fire the principal.

The school board have argued among themselves for hours.

No one understands how the city council works.

The council are divided on the bond issue.

Plural Nouns—Singular Verb

Plural nouns used as the titles of academic courses or subjects or as units of measurement (pounds, dollars, inches) take a *singular* verb.

Forty feet seems too long for a hobby craft.

Humanities is a difficult course!

Pronoun Usage

Pronouns take the place of one or more nouns or a group of words in a sentence. Like nouns, they can refer to a person, place, or thing.

Types of Pronouns

Pronouns have a variety of forms. Personal pronouns are shown below:

Person	Singular	Plural
First	I, me, my, mine, myself	We, us, our, ours, ourselves
Second	you, your, yours, yourself	you, your, yours, yourselves
Third	he, she, it; him, her, his, hers, its; herself, himself, itself	they, their, theirs, themselves

Other pronouns include *someone, no one, everybody, who, whom, which, that, those, this, these, nobody, each,* and *somebody.* These pronouns can be used to ask a question (*Which* car do you want to buy?); indicate nearness or distance (*this* book here, *that* book over there); and to avoid repeating a noun in the same sentence (The woman, *who* came early, left an hour ago).

Common Pronoun Errors

Students often have trouble using pronouns correctly. Some of the more common errors, and the correct usage, are given below.

Pronouns versus Contractions. Students confuse possessive pronouns with their look-alike or sound-alike contractions (*its/it's, his/he's, who's/whose*). To keep the possessive pronoun form straight, remember this simple rule: *Possessive pronouns never take an apostrophe.*

> **INCORRECT:** The ship destroyed <u>it's</u> enemy.

> **CORRECT:** The ship destroyed <u>its</u> enemy.

Pronoun-Antecedent Agreement. The antecedent of a pronoun refers to the word or words the pronoun replaces. For example:

Author is the ⟶ The <u>author</u> wrote the book in London. <u>She</u> completed the manu-
antecedent of *she.*   script in two months.

The antecedent to a pronoun should always be clear. Student writers often use vague pronouns such as *this* or *that* to refer to entire sentences or vague ideas. Keep your antecedents clear.

This refers to the ⟶ **Vague:** He wanted to raise the walls, put on the roof, and hang
sentence and not to any   the doors all in one day. <u>This</u> was unrealistic.
specific antecedent.

The pronoun now refers ⟶ **Clear:** His schedule was to raise the walls, put on the roof,
to the antecedent noun   and hang the doors all in one day. <u>This</u> was unrealistic.
schedule.

Double Antecedents. When *and* joins two antecedents, use a plural pronoun. If the antecedents are joined by *or* or *nor* use a singular pronoun.

> <u>An elm and a maple</u> cast <u>their</u> shadows on the street.

> Neither the <u>president nor</u> the <u>premier</u> has the full support of his country.

Who or Whom?

The confusion over when to use *who* or *whom* has plagued writers for many years. Yet the rules for their use are actually quite simple.

1. *Who* is always used as a subject.

    Who is the leader of the band?   ◄————————————   *Who* is the subject of the sentence.

    Can you tell who is coming tonight?   ◄————————   *Who* is the subject of the clause *is coming tonight*.

    The prize goes to whoever finds the formula first.   ◄————   *Whoever* is the subject of *finds the formula first*.

2. *Whom* is always used as an object.

    The letter was addressed "To Whom It May Concern."   ◄————   *Whom* is the object of the preposition *to*.

    Are there any friends whom you might like to invite?   ◄————   *Whom* is the object of the verb *invite*.

    The prize goes to whomever you choose.   ◄————   *Whomever* is the object of the verb *choose*. Compare this sentence to the one above using *who*.

Punctuation Guide

Punctuation has several purposes:

1. To show where one thought ends and another begins.

2. To indicate relationships among ideas.

3. To separate items in a series.

4. To express measures of time, quantity, weight, and so on.

The most common punctuation marks used in reports and term papers include periods, commas, semicolons, ellipses, apostrophes, parentheses, brackets, and quotation marks.

Period

The period marks a full stop at the end of a statement, indicating a complete thought. The period is also used in many abbreviations. When the abbreviation comes at the end of a sentence, only one period is used to mark both the abbreviation and sentence end.

    Joyce Carol Oates' stories dramatize our hidden fears.

    The Environmental Protection Agency (E.P.A.) is seeking to   ◄————   Abbreviation
    protect our national parks.

    One of the strongest protectors of our national parks is the

    E.P.A.   ◄————————————————————————————   Period ends abbreviation and sentence.

Comma

Commas are among the most overused and abused of all punctuation marks. Most beginning writers tend to insert commas wherever they feel a break in rhythm or phrasing occurs in their sentences. This tendency produces the infamous comma splice that afflicts many reports and term papers.

To avoid inserting commas where they don't belong, learn the basic rules for comma use.

1. *Two complete sentences.* Use commas before the coordinating conjunctions *and, but, or, yet, for* when they join two complete sentences. Do not insert a comma before these words when they join two verbs that share the same subject.

Two complete sentences ——➤ The issue of gun control is sensitive, and many people have
joined by *and*　　　　　　strong opinions on the matter.

Two complete sentences ——➤ The Constitution is over two hundred years old, but it still
joined by *but*　　　　　　serves our nation well today.

But

And joins the verbs *is* ——➤ The issue of gun control is sensitive and provokes many
and *provokes,* which
share the same subject　　strong opinions.
issue—no comma is used
before *and.*

2. *Introductory phrases, clauses.* Commas are used after introductory phrases and clauses, unless the phrases or clause is very short.

Introductory phrase ——➤ Although short on supplies, the American colonial troops
　　　　　　　　　　　managed to hold off the British attack for seven days.

Short phrase *in many* ——➤ In many ways World War II marked the beginning of the
ways requires no comma.　"American Century."

3. *Expressions such as "for example," "for instance," "however," "on the other hand."* Commas are always used to set off these expressions from the rest of the sentence whether they are placed at the beginning, middle, or end of the sentence.

For example, only a handful of Spanish soldiers conquered

the entire Inca empire.

Only a handful of Spanish soldiers, for example, conquered

the entire Inca empire.

Only a handful of Spanish soldiers conquered the entire Inca

empire, for example.

4. *Nonessential or descriptive material.* Commas separate nonessential or descriptive material from the rest of the sentence. Such expressions or descriptions can be dropped from the sentence without changing the meaning.

```
Prime Minister Thatcher, who arrived early, gave her speech
before an angry House of Commons.
```
← *Who arrived early* is not essential to the main idea of the sentence.

```
Japanese culture, long hidden from the West, stretches back
nearly 4,000 years.
```

5. *Items in a series.* Insert a comma between each item in a series and before the final *and, but, or* to avoid any confusion regarding the last two items in the series.

```
Senator Strom Thurmond has been called a great man, a
troublemaker, a bleeding-heart liberal, and an
old-fashioned conservative.
```

```
Sports native to America include basketball, football,
baseball, roller derby, and cockroach racing.
```

6. *Names, dates, and numbers.* Commas are used to separate the elements within names and dates and to provide proper punctuation within numbers 1,000 and over.

Georgia Harkness, PhD	Bernard Samuels, MD
Edward Youngman, Jr.	Theodore Hatfield, Sr.
May 27, 1945	27 May 1945 (note no comma)
13,000	245,000

Semicolon

A semicolon is a stronger break in a sentence than a comma but is not as complete a break as a period or colon. Semicolons have two functions.

1. *Two complete thoughts.* Semicolons link two closely related complete thoughts when the conjunctions *and, but, for, or, nor, yet* are not used.

```
The Cheyenne signed the treaty; their Sioux allies refused.
```

```
For years we ignored the warning signs; now we must reap the
consequences.
```

2. *Complete thoughts or items in a series that contain internal punctuation.* In some cases, one or both of two complete thoughts—or items in a series—already contain internal punctuation such as commas or parentheses. Semicolons are used to help the reader understand which part goes with which.

```
Student government, when well supervised, can be good
training for the future; many former student presidents have
found a career in public office.
```

```
The worst railroad accident in history (which took place
in upstate New York) killed 213 people; yet the railroad
officials responsible were never punished.
```

Colon

A colon represents a more complete stop than a semicolon but not as full a stop as a period. Colons are used before a series or list, between two complete thought, and in expressions of time.

1. *Series or list*. Colons, like periods, are used only after complete thoughts. They cannot be used following a fragment or phrase.

The first part of the sentence is a fragment. ⟶ **INCORRECT:**
```
Alexander's victory depended on: careful planning,
a full moon, and his famous luck.
```

Colon follows a complete thought. ⟶ **CORRECT:**
```
Alexander's victory depended on three elements:
careful planning, a full moon, and his famous luck.
```

INCORRECT:
```
On top of the ridge: a deserted cabin, two starving
horses, and an unmarked grave.
```

The phrase is now a complete thought. ⟶ **CORRECT:**
```
They came on a grim sight at the top of the ridge:
a deserted cabin, two starving horses, and an
unmarked grave.
```

2. *Two complete thoughts*. Like semicolons, colons separate two complete thoughts when such linking words as *and, but, or, nor, yet* are not used. The second complete thought may begin with either a small or capital letter.

```
By midnight Nimitz had only one choice: the fleet must sail
for Midway.
```

```
The discovery of Troy revealed one sure fact: Legends often
contain a solid core of truth.
```

3. *Expressions of time*. Colons are used when writing time in numerical form. Do not use *o'clock* with numbered time expressions. However, expressions such as *a.m., p.m., noon, in the morning,* and *midnight* can be used.

INCORRECT:
```
Galileo made his discovery at 12:00 o'clock.
```

CORRECT:
```
Galileo made his discovery at 12:00 noon.
```

```
The church offered high mass at 12:00 noon and
12:00 midnight.
```

```
         Trains leaving New York at 5:30 a.m. rolled into

         Chicago by 6:30 p.m. that same night.
```

Ellipses

Ellipses points (. . .) indicate that material has been omitted from a quotation or quoted material. When words are omitted at the end of a sentence, use a period plus the ellipses. If you are omitting lines of a poem, extend the ellipses for the length of the line omitted.

Prose

```
I cannot help but feel that our young, vigorous country must   ←—————  Original

lead the world in this most perilous and dark time. No one

nation, though it be given all of nature's virtues, can stand

aside indifferently while across the sea our sister nations

languish under tyranny--we must act.


Roosevelt wrote to Davis:
```

```
         I cannot help but feel that our . . . country must   ←—————  Quoted in paper;
                                                                       note final period after
         lead the world in this . . . dark time. No one nation          the ellipses.

         . . . can stand aside indifferently while . . . our

         sister nations languish under tyranny. . . . .
```

Poetry

```
Elizabeth Bishop's poem "Sandpiper" shows her use of vivid

imagery:
```

```
         The beach hisses like fat. On his left, a sheet

         of interrupting water comes and goes

         and glasses over his dark and brittle feet.

         . . . . . . . . . . . . . . . . . . . . . . . . .

         His beak is focussed; he is preoccupied.
```

Apostrophe

The apostrophe is used to show possession and to form the plural of many nouns and symbols. If you have trouble with this punctuation mark, look over the guidelines below.

1. *Possessive of singular and plural nouns.* The possessive of a singular noun is formed by adding *'s.*

    queen's   boy's   machine's

The possessive of a plural noun that ends in *s* is formed by adding only the apostrophe. All other plural nouns require *'s*.

horse**s'**   countrie**s'**   athlete**s'**

children**'s**   women**'s**   men**'s**

2. *Indefinite and personal pronouns.* Indefinite pronouns (*everyone, no one, anybody, everybody, someone, somebody*) require an apostrophe to form the possessive. However, personal possessive pronouns (*my/mine, our/ours, your/yours, his, hers, its, theirs*) do not require an apostrophe to form the possessive.

```
Everyone's car but hers has been stolen.

Our father brought home someone's umbrella.

In everyone's opinion, his story sounded false.
```

3. Individual and joint possession. When nouns are linked to show individual possession, both nouns require an *'s* to show possessive form. When nouns are linked to show joint possession, however, only the final noun takes an *'s*.

Individual Possession:

The king and queen have separate carriages. ⟶

```
The king's and queen's carriages were covered in gold
foil.
```

Joint Possession:

The carriage belongs to both the king and queen. ⟶

```
The king and queen's carriage was covered in gold foil.
```

One clue to whether possession is individual or joint is to look at the noun following the possessive. In general, if it is plural (*carriages*), possession is individual. If it is singular (*carriage*), possession is usually joint.

4. *Plural form of symbols and numbers.* The apostrophe or *'s* is used to form the plural of letters, numbers, symbols, signs, and words referred to as words.

```
It's easy to change all 3's to look like 8's.

The computer inserted %'s for #'s in the paper.

In the 1700s, s's were printed to look like f's.

How many to's can you find in the following sentence?
```

Hyphens

Hyphens have several important uses. They join two or more words in compound adjectives, indicate continuous numbers or compound numbers, connect some prefixes and suffixes to their root word, divide words at the end of a line, and clarify confusing or awkward spelling.

1. *Compound adjectives.* When compound adjectives are used before a noun, they are hyphenated. When they follow the noun, no hyphen is used. However, if one of the modifiers is an adverb ending in *-ly,* do not use a hyphen in the compound adjective.

Before Noun	**After Noun**
decision-making process	a process of decision making
long-range goal	a goal that is long range
high-flying idealist	an idealist who is high flying
a publicly owned park	a park publicly owned

2. *Prefixes and suffixes.* Prefixes *ex-, self-, all-* and the suffix *-elect* always take a hyphen whether they are used as modifiers or nouns. Hyphens are used with all prefixes before proper nouns and adjectives.

```
The ex-president spent the day resting comfortably.

Nothing is more important then self-esteem.

The environmental issue is all-encompassing.

Hughes, as governor-elect, made a rousing speech.

Are you pro-Republican or pro-Democrat this year?
```

3. *Continuous numbers and compound numbers.* Hyphens are used to link continuous numbers when they refer to dates of birth and death, pages of material, statistics, and other instances in which the relationship between the numbers needs to be shown.

```
Aldous Huxley (1894-1963) remains one of our most inventive
writers.

Only midway through the book does Emily Brontë describe
Heathcliff (pages 134-35).

The number of T-cells dropped 40-55% within 48 hours.

The oil embargo of 1976-77 dealt the U.S. a severe blow.
```

Hyphens are used with compound numbers from twenty-one to ninety-nine and with fractions used as adjectives. When fractions serve as nouns, however, no hyphen is used.

```
Pigafetti wrote in his journal: "We have spent twenty-nine

days at sea with no sight of land."
```

The fraction is an adjective modifying *majority*.

```
The bill must pass by a two-thirds majority.
```

The fraction is a noun, the subject of the sentence.

```
Two thirds of the legislators voted for the bill.
```

4. *Word division and avoiding awkward constructions.* Hyphens are used to divide words at the end of a line. Always check an updated dictionary to determine how a word should be hyphenated. Be sure you do not end more than three lines in a row with a hyphenated word.

```
Modern civilization had its earliest begin-

nings in the Middle East--at least scho-

lars have always believed so. Neverthe-

less, new evidence shows that North America

is the site of an even older culture.
```

Use hyphens to avoid awkward or confusing word constructions in sentences.

```
re-creation (avoids confusion with recreation)
```

Parentheses

Parentheses enclose material that interrupts the text to add information. In reports and term papers, parentheses are also used to enclose reference citations.

```
The huge waves of immigrants in the early 1900s (see Fig. 4)

nearly doubled New York's population.
```

```
Monroe believes that Hemingway's unhappiness stems from his

father's suicide (34-35).
```

If the enclosed material falls at the end of the sentence, the period or other end mark is placed *outside* the closing parenthesis. If the enclosed material is a complete sentence within itself, the end mark is placed *inside* the final parenthesis.

The enclosed material is part of the sentence— the period comes after the closing parenthesis.

```
The Treaty of Versailles sowed the bitter seeds of World War II

(see Appendix A for a complete copy of the Treaty).
```

The enclosed material is a complete sentence on its own—the period falls within the final parenthesis.

```
The Treaty of Versailles sowed the bitter seeds of World War

II. (See Appendix A for a complete copy of the Treaty.)
```

Brackets

Use brackets to enclose additions or corrections to quoted material or to material already enclosed in parentheses.

```
Part of Einstein's letter read, "We have discussed it [atom

bomb] at length and believe the Allies must develop it first."
```

```
Hemlines follow the ups and downs of the stock market (see

Figure 3 [Table 2] following page 18).
```

Quotation Marks

Quotations marks are used to enclose a direct quotation, that is, the repetition of someone's exact words. They are also used to enclose certain terms and expressions and the titles of poems, short stories, articles, chapters of books, and many other documents. Follow the guidelines below for correct use of quotation marks.

1. *Punctuation and quotation marks.* Commas and periods are always placed *inside* the closing quote marks, even if the quoted material is contained within the sentence.

```
Catherine the Great said, "Russia will become the center of ◄─── Direct quote

Europe."
```

```
Catherine the Great told her court that Russia would become ◄─── Quoted material is
                                                                  contained within the
"the center of Europe."                                           sentence.
```

Semicolons and colons are always placed *outside* the closing quotation marks.

```
The steamship became known as "Fulton's Folly"; actually,

Fulton had nothing to do with it.
```

```
Four states have been dubbed "new": New Mexico, New York,

New Hampshire, and New Jersey.
```

Question marks and exclamation points are placed inside the closing quote marks if they are part of the quoted material. Otherwise, they are placed outside the final quotation marks. Only one end mark is used at the end of a sentence.

```
When asked to surrender, John Paul Jones cried, "I have not ◄─── Exclamation mark
                                                                  is part of the quoted
yet begun to fight!"                                              material.
```

```
How many people know the truth behind "The Ballad of the Sad ◄─── Question mark
                                                                  punctuates the entire
Cafe"?                                                            sentence.
```

2. *Brief and long quotations.* Quoted material that is no more than one or two lines long is enclosed in quotation marks and included as a regular part of the text. However, longer passages of quoted material are set off from the rest of the text by being indented.

```
In Volume Two of her diary, Anaïs Nin says that poverty "is

the great reality. That is why the artist seeks it . . . It

has a spiritual significance."
```

```
In Volume Two of her diary, Anaïs Nin upholds the value of

poverty to the artist:

        Poverty is the great reality. That is why the artist

        seeks it. It was my only reality as a child. It gave

        me a closeness to human reality forever. . . . Poverty

        has a religious significance. It represents sacrifice,

        it is usually the outcome of a choice between artis-

        tic, spiritual values and the material ones. (Nin 201)
```

3. *Single quotation marks.* Single quotation marks are used to set off a quote, title, or document name within quoted material.

Notice the single quote comes after the period.

```
He said that his fondest memory was "at the age of sixteen

reading Yeats's 'Circus Animals' Dissertation.'"
```

```
The critic stated, "Katherine Ann Porter's 'Noon Wine' is

the finest short story written by an American."
```

4. *Titles, terms, and expressions.* Quotation marks are used to enclose the titles of several types of documents, including chapters of books, articles, poems, short stories, reports, many government pamphlets and short publications, and titles of proceedings or workshops.

"The Long Road Home" (chapter in a book)

"What's Wrong with American Management?" (article)

"Ode to Immortality" (short poem)

"Salad Dressing" (short story)

"How to Watch Your Cholesterol" (government pamphlet)

"Ultrasonics in the 1990s" (proceedings)

"Learn to Be Twice as Smart" (workshop)

When you first use terms or expressions considered unusual (such as slang in a formal report) or that may be unknown to the reader (technical or jargon terms) enclose them in quotation marks. Thereafter, do not use the quotations marks when repeating the terms or expressions.

```
Quarks, we are told, possess "charm." Such terms as charm
are merely ways to describe various physical properties.
```

Capitalization

The following guidelines offer basic rules for capitalizing names, titles of works, and nationalities and races. For more detailed guidelines, see the *MLA Handbook*.

Names of Persons

Capitalize all given and surnames in a person's name, including both names in a hyphenated surname, and all titles used with the name.

Charles R. Appleby   Helen Rodgers Lindon

Victoria Sackville-West   James John Elliot-Smythe

His Holiness Trang dan Djong   Rinpoche Mitzi Sishumi

Reverend Michael Norcome   Senator Clare Luce

Martin Luther King, Jr.   Charles Lindbergh, Sr.

Henry Ford III   Anne Quinlin, Esq.

In your reports and term papers, you can shorten the name after giving the full name for the first time. Use only the last name, without titles and without *Mr., Miss, Ms., Mlle.,* or any other formal designation.

```
Harriet Beecher Stowe's book created a storm of controversy
when it was first published. Southern slave holders claimed
Stowe had exaggerated the evils of slavery and misrepresented
Southern life.
```

The only exception to this rule is in the use of fictional characters' names. You may refer to them as the author does in the work (*Billy Budd, Little Nell*) and you may retain their titles (*Dr. Jekyll, Dr. Moreau*).

Titles of Works

When typing the title of a work, always use the title page as your reference, not the cover of a book or document nor the top of each page.

Capitalize the first word and all major words except for articles (*a, an, the*), the coordinating conjunctions (*and, but, or, for, nor, yet*), and prepositions under five letters (*over, under, to,* etc.). Unless the title has an end mark of its own, use a colon and a space to separate the main title from its subtitle. Include all punctuation that is part of the title.

Hallmark Cards: They Cared Enough to Sell the Very Best (book)

"When Lilacs Last in the Dooryard Bloomed" (poem)

Where did You Go? Out. What Did You Do? Nothing (book)

Sgt. Pepper's Lonely Hearts Club Band (album title)

"Don't Get Mad. Get Even with the Boss." (article)

Star Trek: Voyager (television show)

Jupiter Symphony (musical composition)

History of the English-Speaking People (both words in the hyphenated compound are capitalized)

Nationalities and Races

Capitalize the names of nationalities and ethnic groups. Recent usage permits the names of races to be either capitalized or lowercased, but *be consistent.* If you capitalize one race, capitalize them all.

Swedes	Mongolians
English	Masai
Chinese	Montagnards
Russians	white (White)
Kurds	black (Black)

CHAPTER 6

Works Cited and Works Consulted Lists

As discussed in Chapter 4, you prepare the Works Cited and Works Consulted lists before revising your final paper. These lists show what resources you used to write your term paper or report.

At this stage, your care in preparing your bibliography notecards will be invaluable. On each card, you should have all the information you need to complete your Works Cited or Works Consulted lists.

The Works Cited list contains the sources you actually quote or cite in your paper. The Works Consulted list itemizes additional materials that you have read to understand your topic but did not cite in the body of the paper.

This chapter reviews the basic styles for various publications, including books and reference works, magazines, newspapers, special collections, scholarly journals, and audiovisual materials. For more detailed explanations on styling references, see the latest edition of the *MLA Handbook*.

Arrangement of Entries

In most cases you will list entries alphabetically by the author's last name, using the letter-by-letter system. In this system, *MacGregor, Alice* comes before *McDermot, Andrew; Saint-Germain, Julia* before *St. Denis, Ruth.*

If the author is unknown, alphabetize the entries by the first word in the title other than *A, An,* or *The.* For example, *The Oxford Book of Verse* comes before *A Reader's Guide to American Novels.*

In some instances, your instructor may want your references broken down by specific categories: primary and secondary sources, books and magazines, subject matter (Renaissance and Marriage Laws, Renaissance and Military Laws), or by some other division. Entries within each division are still alphabetized according to the letter-by-letter system.

Books

Each entry in a list of works cited usually has three main sections—author, title, and publication information. Each section is followed by a period and two spaces.

```
Vann, Ted. Starflight Handbook. New York: Orion, 1988.
```

When other facts are required, a period and two spaces follows each additional item.

```
Vann, Ted. "Traveling in Hyperspace?" Starflight Handbook. Ed.
    Julia C. Harcourt. 2nd ed. New York: Orion, 1988. 44-56.
```

When citing books, information is usually arranged in the following order.

1. Author's or authors' name(s)

2. Title of a chapter, section, or appendix in the book

3. Title of the book

4. Name of the editor, translator, or compiler

5. Edition of the book used

6. Number(s) of the volume(s) used

7. Name of the series

8. Place of publication, name of the publisher, year of publication

9. Page numbers used

10. Any additional bibliographical information

The citation below illustrates this order. Notice where the periods are placed in this example.

```
Randolph, Edward. "Physics of the Curve Ball." Mechanics of

     Everyday Things. Ed. Greg R. Peterson. 5th ed. Vol. 3.

     How Things Work Series. New York: Putnam & Co., 1988. 67-

     78. 12 vols.
```

Guidelines for Citing Names

The following guidelines apply to the names of authors, editors, and translators of books used in your report.

1. Always reverse the author's name for alphabetizing, adding a comma after the last name and a period at the end of the name (Hemingway, Ernest.).

2. Always use the author's name as given on the title page. Never abbreviate a name given in full.

3. Omit titles, degrees, and affiliations that precede or follow names.

Not This	**But This**
Dr. Susan Blackwell	Blackwell, Susan
Saint Teresa de Jesus	Teresa de Jesus
Dame Edith Sitwell	Sitwell, Edith
Reverend Jean Carlyle	Carlyle, Jean
Sir Richard Burton	Burton, Richard
Stephen Hawkins, PhD	Hawkins, Stephen

4. Suffixes that are an essential part of a name appear after the given name.

Martin Luther King, Jr.	King, Martin Luther, Jr.
Henry Ford III	Ford, Henry, III

5. If the name of an editor or translator appears on the title page in addition to the author's name, it is usually included after the title of the work. The abbreviations *Ed.* and *Trans.* are used before the individual's name.

List the editor and translator in the order in which they appear on the title page. Likewise, if someone served as both editor and translator, state those roles as they are listed on the title page.

If only the editor and translator are listed, use the abbreviations after the editor's name, but list the translator after the book title.

In Addition to Author's Name

```
Ed. Laura C. Epstein. Trans. Stephen Mitchell

Trans. Stephen Mitchell. Ed. Laura C. Epstein

Ed. and trans. Laura C. Epstein

Trans. and ed. Laura C. Epstein
```

Editor and Translator the Only Names

```
Epstein, Laura C., ed. Modern French Poetry.
```

```
Epstein, Laura C., ed. and trans. Modern French Poetry.

Epstein, Laura C., ed. Modern French Poetry. Trans. Louis

     Valle.
```

Guidelines for Citing Titles

Follow these guidelines for citing the titles of books in your Works Cited list.

1. In general, state the full name of the book, including any subtitle. Separate the title and subtitle with a colon, unless the main title ends in a punctuation mark (for example, a question mark or exclamation point). Underline the entire title, including subtitle, but do not underline the period that follows the entire title.

```
A Bright Shining Lie: John Paul Vann and America in Vietnam.

Hurricane Alert: The Story of Hurricane Hugo.

Why Can't Johnny Read? Literacy in America.
```

2. If you are citing only part of a book—a chapter, preface, poem, article, or appendix—state the part's title or name after the author's name. Place a period after the title or name, skip two spaces, and begin the title of the entire book.

Chapter titles, article titles, poems, and short stories are in quotes.

```
Kingston, Maxine Hong. "Woman Warriors." China Men.
```

Preface, foreword, introduction are neither in quotes nor underlined.

```
Neil, Alfred S. Foreword. The Portable Joseph Conrad.
```

Titles of plays, novellas, and longer poems are underscored, like book titles.

```
Mamet, David. Speed the Plow. Playwrights of the 1980s.
```

Guidelines for Publication Information and Page Numbers

Publication information—city, publisher, and date—is obtained from both the title page and copyright page (back of the title page) in any book, as shown in Figure 6.1. Use the guidelines below for creating your bibliography cards and Works Cited lists.

City. Use only the first city listed. If the city is not well known or might be confused with another city with the same name, use the name of the state or country in abbreviated form.

```
Chicago: Academy Press, 1984.
```

No periods are used in the state abbreviation.

```
Athens, GA: OrangeTree, 1979.
```

Publisher. It's acceptable to use a shortened version of the publisher's name. Omit any articles and business titles. Use only the first name of the publisher. If the publisher's name is that of a person, use only the last name.

FIGURE 6.1   Publication Information

Title Page

Exploring the

Illinois
Countryside

Archie Satterfield

Printed on recyclable paper

PASSPORT BOOKS
a division of *NTC Publishing Group*
Lincolnwood, Illinois USA

Copyright Page

Library of Congress Cataloging-in-Publication Data

Satterfield, Archie.
    Exploring the Illinois countryside / Archie Satterfield.
        p.   cm.
    Includes bibliographical references and index.
    ISBN 0-8442-9459-4
    1. Illinois--Guidebooks. I. Title.
    F539.3.S28   1995
    917.7304'43--dc20   95-51252
                                                      CIP

Cover & Interior Design by Nick Panos
Cover & Interior Illustration by Julia Scharf

Published by NTC Publishing Group
4255 West Touhy Avenue
Lincolnwood (Chicago), Illinois 60646–1975, U.S.A.
© 1996 by NTC Publishing Group. All rights reserved.
No part of this book may be reproduced, stored in a retrieval
system, or transmitted in any form or by any means,
electronic, mechanical, photocopying, recording or otherwise,
without the prior permission of NTC Publishing Group.
Manufactured in the United States of America.

6 7 8 9 0 VP 9 8 7 6 5 4 3 2 1

Publisher   City   Author(s)   Copyright Date

Works Cited

Satterfield, Archie

    Exploring the Illinois Countryside.

    Lincolnwood, Illinois: Passport Books, 1996.

Publisher's Name	Short Form
Simon and Schuster, Inc.	Simon
Harcourt, Brace and Jovanovich, Inc.	Harcourt
HarperCollins San Francisco	HarperCollins
Wm. C. Brown Group	Brown
Bantam Books	Bantam

If a book is published by a university press, use only the letters *UP* instead of the words *University Press.*

Publisher's Name	Short Form
University of Chicago Press	U Chicago P
Berkeley Press	Berkeley P
Iowa State University Press	Iowa State UP
University of Georgia	U Georgia

Page Numbers. Do not include page numbers in the list of Works Cited unless you are using only a single chapter, article, poem, play, or story from a book.

```
Loudain, Barbara. "Crime in the Halls." School Daze: War on the

     Playground. Miami: U Miami P, 1988. 43-56.
```

The following guidelines show how to cite various types of books that you are likely to use as sources for your reports and term papers.

Single-Author Books, Anthologies, Multiple Listings

To list books by a single author, include the following: (1) author's name, (2) book title, including any subtitles, and (3) publication information (city, publisher, date).

```
Blume, Judy. Forever . . . Michael. New York: Random, 1983.

O'Keefe, Daniel Lawrence. Stolen Lightning: The Social Theory

     of Magic. New York: Vintage, 1982.
```

Anthologies and Collections. When a single author has put together an anthology or collection of works, list these roles after the author's name.

```
Pistorio, Janet S., ed. Battle for Your Mind: Advertising and

     the American Public. San Francisco; Ten-Speed Press, 1986.

Godolphin, Francis R., ed. and trans. The Latin Poets. New

     York: Modern Library, 1968.
```

Multiple Listings. In some instances, such as in a literary paper, for example, you will use several books written by one author. Rather than repeat the author's name for each book, type three hyphens (followed by a period) where the name would ordinarily appear. The works are alphabetized by title.

```
Hinton, S. E. The Outsiders. New York: Delacourte, 1967.

---. Rumblefish. New York: Delacourte, 1975.

---. Tex. New York: Delacourte, 1975.
```

Multiauthor Books, Anthologies, Multiple Listings

For books by two or three authors, list the names in the order in which they appear on the title page. Only the first author's name is reversed for alphabetizing. The other authors' names are given in normal order, even if the authors share the same last name.

Notice the use of commas and periods in creating a multiauthor citation.

```
Atwater, George, and Caroline Brewer. The Teen-Age Dilemma:
    Growing Up in an Affluent Society. 4th ed. Chicago:
    Contemporary, 1987.

McLuhan, Marshall, Kathy Hutchon, and Eric McLuhan. Media
    Messages and Language. Lincolnwood, IL: National Textbook,
    1980.
```

If there are more than three authors, list only the first name followed by a comma and the abbreviation *et al.* (which means "and others").

```
Meichenbaum, Michael, et al. Exploring Choices: The Psychology
    of Adjustment. Glenview, IL: Scott, 1988.
```

Anthologies and Collections.
If the names listed on the title page are editors, translators, or both, add the appropriate abbreviation after the final name.

```
Rosenberg, Alan, and Gerald E. Myers, eds. Echoes from the
    Holocaust: Philosophical Reflections on a Dark Time.
    Philadelphia: Temple UP, 1988.

Brell, Jacques, and Anthony DuValle, eds. and trans. Modern
    French Poetry: New Voices of the Twentieth Century. New
    York: Knopf, 1982.
```

Multiauthor Listings.
In some instances, one author may write a book on his or her own as well as collaborate with other authors on different books. The style for listing these works alphabetically is as follows.

```
Yeats, William Butler. The Celtic Twilight. London: Smythe,
    1981.

---, and Lionel Johnson. Poetry and Ireland. Dublin: Cuala,
    1970.
```

```
---, and Thomas Kinsella. Davis, Mangan, Fergueson. In Anglo-
        Irish Studies Series. Dublin: Dufour, 1971.
```

When two or three people coauthor various books, use three hyphens after the first citation in place of the authors' names.

```
Denitte, Benjamin, Susan Davis, and Robert Howard. Critical
        Studies in South American Fiction. Boston: Little, 1978.

---. Octovio Paz: From Writer to Revolutionary. Tempe: U
        Arizona P, 1981.
```

Books by Corporate Authors

In your research, you may need to cite references in which no individual authors are listed. Instead, the corporate author may be a company, a commission, or even a government agency. List the corporate name first, followed by a period.

```
Boston Computer Society. Things the Manual Never Told You. Ed.
        Jack McGrath. New York: Addison-Wesley, 1985.

National Geographic Society. Splendors of the Past: Lost Cities
        of the Ancient World. New York: National Geographic
        Society, 1981.

U.S. Department of Health and Human Services. The Graying of
        America: Our Aging Population. Washington, DC: U.S.
        Government Printing Office, 1986.
```

Translation of a Work

In citing a translated work, list the original author first, then the title, then the translator's and editor's names in the order in which they appear on the title page.

```
Rimbaud, Arthur. Season in Hell. Ed. Carol Fischer. Trans.
        Louis Valle. New York: Random, 1972.
```

Work in an Anthology

The order of information for citing work in an anthology is as follows.

1. Author of the piece

2. Title of the work (enclosed in quotes if it is an article, short story, or poem, but underlined if the work is a play, novella, long poem, or novel)

3. Title of the anthology

4. Name of the editor or translator of the work

5. Publication information

6. Page numbers of the piece

```
Forché, Caroline. "Ourselves or Nothing." New American Voices.
     Ed. David Smith. San Francisco: New Directions, 1984. 44-
     43.
```

```
Graham, Harold. The Suburban Crawl: Plays for Modern Times. Ed.
     Carlton Trish. New York: Macmillan, 1976. 127-43.
```

Preface, Introduction, Foreword, or Afterword

To cite these parts of a book in a bibliographic list, follow these guidelines.

1. Author of the book, *unless* a different person wrote the preface, introduction, foreword, or afterword. In that case list that person instead of the book's author.

2. Name of the part cited (do not use quote marks or underlining)

3. Title of the work

4. Author of the work—if different from the person who wrote the preface, introduction, foreword, afterword. The author's name is preceded by the word *By* (note capital *B*).

5. Publication data

6. Page numbers

```
Berke, Joseph H. Introduction. The Tyranny of Malice: Exploring
     the Dark Side of Character and Culture. New York: Summit,
     1988. 11-15.
```

```
Kumin, Maxine. Foreword. The Complete Poems. By Anne Sexton.
     Boston: Houghton, 1981. xix-xxxiv.
```

Work in a Multivolume Series or Collection

Citing works in multivolume series or collections can be confusing. Look over the following guidelines carefully to determine which category applies to your references.

Each Chapter by Separate Author. When each chapter in a multivolume series is written by a separate author, use the following style.

```
Volaine, Sarah. "Constance Urdang." Encyclopaedia of Women

     Writers. Eds. Trudy Silverman and Irene Young. Vol. 8.

     Toronto: Summit, 1983. 56-64.
```

Each Volume with Its Own Title. When each volume in a series has its own title, the volume title is treated like a book title. The volume number and name of the series should follow the volume publication data, as shown below (listing the total number of volumes is optional).

```
Durant, Will, and Ariel Durant. The Age of Napoleon. New York:

     Simon, 1975. Vol. 11 of The Story of Civilization. 11

     vols.
```

Multivolume Work with No Editor; Article with No Author. When a multivolume work has no editor, use the following style.

```
Putnam, George G. "Manhattan Project Revisited." Dictionary of

     American Science. Vol. 3. New York: Pantheon, 1979. 345-

     78. 10 vols.
```

In some instances, articles in a multivolume work will be written anonymously.

```
"Laser Surgery." Dictionary of American Science. Vol. 2. New

     York: Pantheon, 1979. 546-82. 10 vols.
```

Cross-References

If you are using more than one article or work from a collection in a single volume, you can avoid repeating the entire citation every time you list another article. Cite the collection as a separate entry. All references to works within the collection can be listed with the following information.

1. Author of the article

2. Title of the article (in quotation marks)

3. Editor or compiler of the collection work (if more than one editor or compiler is listed, use only the last name of the first editor listed)

4. Page numbers of the article you are citing

```
Randolph, Julie, and Sergio Ramon, eds. Things That Go Bump in

     the Night: A Psychological Study of Horror Stories. 2nd

     ed. Atlanta: Hanover, 1983.

Underhill, Evelyn. "Origins of the Ghost Story." Randolph 213-

     45.
```

Reference Works

In most instances, your instructor will not allow you to use information from general encyclopedias in your Works Cited list. However, you may be able to list them in the Works Consulted. The following styles are used for articles with or without an author. Notice that *ed.* (for "edition") follows the year of publication. This tells the reader which updated version of the encyclopedia you are using.

For general encyclopedias, you need to give only a shortened form of the publication information.

```
Driver, Harold E. "Indians, American." Encyclopedia Americana.

    Danbury, CT: Grolier, 1987 ed.


"Strategic Weapons System." Encyclopaedia Britannica:

    Micropaedia. 1985 ed.
```

For less familiar references, more complete publication information is generally given.

```
Beacham, Walton. "Short Fiction: Toward a Definition." Critical

    Survey of Short Fiction. Ed. Frank N. MacGill. Vol. 1.

    Englewood Cliffs, NJ: Prentice, 1981. 1-17. 7 vols.
```

Pamphlets

Pamphlets are cited in the same manner as books, with the order of information arranged in the same sequence. If the pamphlet lists no authors, begin with the title. Where a pamphlet number is indicated, type it after the date of publication.

```
Strauss, Harold, ed. On the Delights of Japanese Novels. New

    York: Knopf, 1957.


Food Additives and Hypersensitivity. Summit, NJ: American

    Council on Science and Health, 1982. No. 23.
```

Newspapers and Periodicals

Citations for periodicals and newspapers generally give the information in the following order.

1. Author's name
2. Title of the article in quotation marks, with the period *inside* the closing quote mark ("And the Wall Came Tumbling Down—Berlin, 1989.")
3. Name of the periodical, underlined but *not* followed by any punctuation. Drop *A, An,* and *The* from the periodical title (*The New York Times* becomes *New York Times*)

4. Volume number—use this only when day and month are not listed
5. Date of publication—day and abbreviated month, followed by year (for example, 3 Feb. 1987)
6. Page numbers, separated from the year by a colon

Article from Newspaper

Different editions of the same day's newspaper contain different material. As a result, specify the edition you used, preceded by a comma and a space, after the date. The name of the edition (*national, western, late, early*) is generally listed along with the name of the paper on the front page.

```
Rickover, Paul. "Mysterious Lights Baffle Air Force Experts."

     Phoenix Daily News 5 May 1986, late ed.: 17.
```

Although finding the edition is fairly easy, citing which section of the paper you used can be a little more complicated. Some sections are designated by letters (*A, B, C, D*), others by numbers (*section 1, section 2*). In general, page numbers may be followed by the appropriate section letter or preceded by *sec. 1, sec. 2,* and so on.

```
Andrick, Vivian. "Debate Over Greenhouse Effect Heats Up."

     Detroit Free Press 13 Apr. 1988, natl. ed., sec. 2:4.

Lui, Anita. "Japanese Women Don Business Suits." Miami Herald

     24 Oct. 1987: 24A-25A.
```

Article from Weekly/Biweekly Periodical

Articles from these periodicals may or may not list an author's name (known as a "byline"). Notice in these citations that no period follows the magazine name, no comma follows the month, and the letter *p* is not used with page numbers.

```
Perle, Richard. "Bush's Summit Favors Gorbachev." U.S. News and

     World Report 18 Dec. 1989: 27.

"Learning How to Bottle the Immune System." Science 13 Dec.

     1989: 1250-51.
```

Article from Monthly/Bimonthly Periodical

The style for these references follows that of weekly periodicals with one change. You use only the month and year of the publication. Do not list the volume and issue number. If the page numbers are not in order (interrupted by advertisements, for example), use the first page number and a plus sign (for example, *98+*).

```
Gackenbach, Jayne, and Jane Boswald. "Taking Control of Your

        Dreams." Psychology Today Oct. 1989: 27+.
```

Article from a Scholarly Journal

Scholarly journals publish original research intended for other specialists and students in a particular field of study. Unlike weekly/biweekly or monthly/bimonthly periodicals, scholarly journal citations list the volume and issue number along with year of publication and page numbers.

For journals that number pages continuously throughout the entire volume, use the following style.

```
Dearing, James W. "Setting the Polling Agenda for the Issue of

        AIDS." Public Opinion Quarterly 53 (1989): 309-29.
```

For journals that begin each issue with page 1, you must include the issue number after the volume number. The two numbers are separated by a period.

```
Sterling, Wade. "Leadership in the '90s: Who Do We Follow?"

        Statesman. 10.4 (1989): 92-115.
```

For journals that use only issue numbers, treat the issue number as you would a volume number.

```
Ellington, Kyle. "Decaying Protons--A Clue to the Universe's

        Demise." Astrophysics Quarterly 4 (1985): 24-28.
```

Social Issues Resource Series (S.I.R.S.)

When you use articles located in the S.I.R.S., style them according to the type of source—newspaper or periodical—then add the information about the S.I.R.S. volume.

```
Terwillinger, Ray. "No One Hits the Long Ball Anymore." Cleveland

        Plain Dealer 18 July 1978, sec. 2: 24. SIRS: Sports vol. 2,

        art. 17.
```

Guidelines for Other Sources

In addition to books, periodicals, and newspapers, your research may also include computer software and computer services, literary or artistic reviews, audiovisual materials, interviews, and radio and television programs. Each of these references has its own style.

Reviews

Reviews of books are cited listing the reviewer's name first, then the title of the book reviewed and its author, followed by the periodical in which the review appeared.

```
McClintock, Anne. Rev. of Lives of Courage: Women for a New South
        Africa, by Diana E. H. Russell. New York Times Book Review
        17 Dec. 1989: 11.
```

Interviews

When you are quoting from an interview of a notable person published in a book or magazine, list the interviewee's name first, followed by the word *Interview,* then the title and publication information of the source.

```
Capote, Truman. Interview. Southern Writers in Exile. Ed. George
        Johnson. New York: Dodd, 1983. 117-32.
```

If you have conducted the interview yourself, either in person, over the phone, or via correspondence, use the following style.

```
Capote, Truman. Personal correspondence. 13 May 1985.
```

At times, you may conduct an interview or receive correspondence through your electronic mail (or e-mail) connections on your computer. Use the following formats to cite these works in your reference list.

```
Hamper, Robert. "Strategic Marketing Update." E-mail to the
        author. 12 Jan 1996.

Christopher, Karolyn. "Preparing the House for Home Care of
        Relatives." E-mail to Dr. Lynn Souyez. Rush Community Health
        Care Center. Seaview, CA. 24 June 1995.
```

Computer Software and Computer or Information Services

Entries for computer software should list the writer of the program (if known), the title, underlined, along with the version of the program; the words *computer software;* the software company producing the program; and the year of publication.

```
WordPerfect. vers. 5.1. Computer software. ISS, 1989.

Saunders, Alex. Paywrite. vers. 2.3. Computer software.
        Accounting Ware, 1990.
```

Material retrieved from a computer or information service is treated like any other printed material with a reference to the service added at the end. List the following information for your Works Cited page.

1. Author's name (if given)

2. Title, publisher, and date of the reference

3. Title of the database (underlined)

4. Publication medium (CD-ROM)

5. Name of the vendor (if relevant)

6. Electronic publication date

```
Benares, Ashok. "India and China: An Uneasy Peace." International
     Policy Oct-Dec 1976: 22-45. Dialog file 67. On-line data-
     base. Item 332917 115638.

Arthur, Thomas E. "Discovering Antimatter in the Laboratory."
     Science Nov. 1995: 23-27. INFOTRAC: Magazine Index Plus.
     CD-ROM. Information Access. Dec. 1995.
```

If you use material on a diskette as a reference, cite the diskette as you would a book, adding the medium of publication.

1. Author's name (if given)

2. Title of the work (in quotation marks)

3. Title of the product (underlined)

4. Edition, release, or version (if relevant)

5. Publication medium (CD-ROM)

6. City of publication

7. Name of the publisher

8. Year of publication

```
Gutierrez, Martha. "Latin Poetry: 1940-1990." South American
     Cultural Series. 3rd ed. Diskette. Houston: Gila Press,
     1994.
```

Sources taken from an electronic journal, electronic network, electronic newsletter, or electronic conference document should consist of the following.

1. Author's name (if given)

2. Title of the article or document (in quotation marks)

3. Title of the journal, newsletter, or conference (underlined)

4. Volume number, issue number, or other identifying number

5. Year or date of publication (in parentheses)

6. Number of pages or paragraphs (if given) or *n. pag.* if no page numbers

7. Publication (On-line, CD-ROM)

8. Name of the computer network (Internet, BITNET, World Wide Web)

9. Date of access

```
Stuart, Brenda. "New Shakespeare Manuscript Discovered--So They
        Say." Shaksper 3.205 (5 May 1994): n. pag. On-line. BITNET.
        8 Aug 1994.

Chin, Ling-Jie. "Growth in Personal Communication Devices: Star
        Trek Is Only a Phonecall Away." Wired Communicator 8.0143
        (10 Apr 1995): 12 pp. On-line. Internet. 13 May 1995.
```

Radio and Television Programs

Information for radio or television entries usually appears in the following order.

1. Title of the episode, if known (in quotation marks)
2. Title of the program (underlined)
3. Writer, producer, director (if known)
4. Title of the series, if known (underlined)
5. The network on which the program appeared
6. The local station broadcasting it and city (for example, WFMT, Chicago)
7. Broadcast date

```
"Mind over Matter." Narr. Ernest Faulkner. Writ. and prod. Joan
        Washington. An Owner's Guide to the Brain. National Public
        Radio. WBEZ, Chicago. 26 Mar. 1985.

Magellan's World-Shaking Voyage. Narr. Sir Hugo Richards. Dir.
        Oliver Stanowski. Prod. Ruth Eddington. NBC special. KORC,
        St. Louis. 15 May 1968.
```

If you are citing the radio or television program as part of a report or term paper on one individual, list that person's name first before the title.

```
Welles, Orson, dir. War of the Worlds. Writ. Howard Koch. Based
        on H. G. Wells's War of the Worlds. Mercury Theatre of the
        Air. CBS Radio. WCBS, New York. 30 Oct. 1938.
```

Films, Filmstrips, Slide Programs, Video Materials

Entries for films usually begin with the title, underlined, and include the director's name, the distributor, the year, and the size and length of the film. You may also include other information, such as the writer or producer, the actors, and musical score composer.

As in the case of radio and television programs, if you are featuring the work of any particular individual in your paper, list the person's name first, before the title.

```
Lean, David, dir. Lawrence of Arabia. Prod. Sam Spiegel.

     RCA/Columbia Pictures. 1963. 180 min.
```

When listing an entry for a filmstrip, slide program, or videotape, include the medium after the title, followed by the same information as that given for films.

```
Reverse Your Roles. Sound filmstrip. Argus Communications, 1981.

     82 fr., 15 min.
```

```
Super Bowl XX. Videocassette. VHS. MCA/Turner Television, 1986.

     192 min.
```

Typing Works Cited and Works Consulted Lists

These pages follow the last page of your term paper or report and are numbered as part of the paper. For example, if the last page of your text is 10, the Works Cited list would be numbered as page 11.

The formats for Works Cited and Works Consulted pages are exactly the same. Type your last name and the page number in the upper right-hand corner, half an inch from the top of the page. Center the title one inch from the top of the page. Double-space to the first entry. The first line of all entries begins flush with the left margin. Second and third lines of each entry are indented five spaces. Double-space throughout the list, both within entries and between entries. See samples in Figure 6.2.

In some cases, you may want to arrange your Works Consulted list by some other method than alphabetically. For example, you may list your resources chronologically by publication date; or group them into books, articles, or references; or arrange them according to whether they are primary or secondary sources. Whatever system you use, the format for margins, spacing, and page numbering remains the same.

FIGURE 6.2 Sample Works Cited and Works Consulted

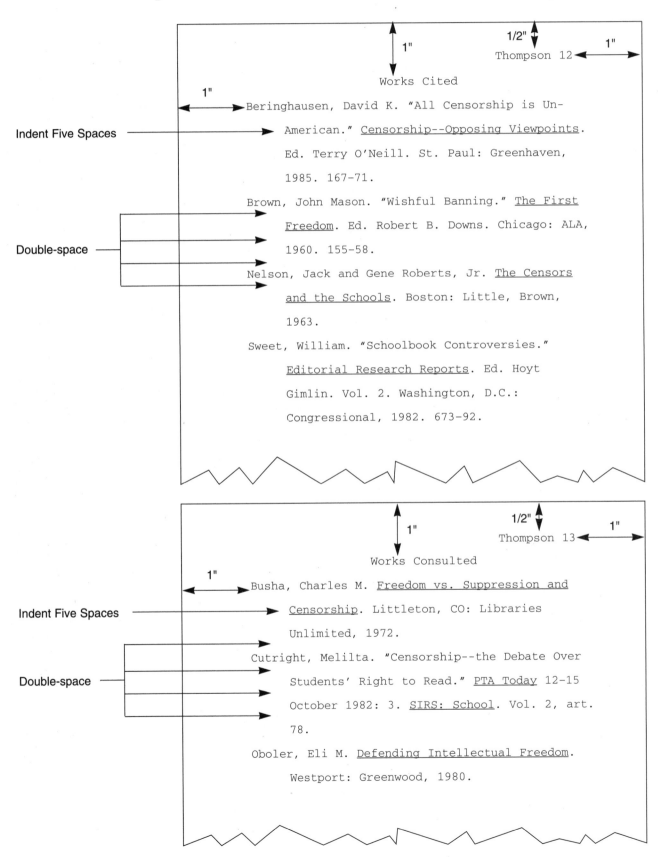

PART 3
Final Touches

CHAPTER 7
Illustrating Your Paper

The right illustration—chart, map, table, photograph—in the right place adds interest and clarity to your term paper or report. This is particularly true if you are discussing a complex or controversial topic. The combination of words and pictures or symbols can bring your subject alive for the reader.

This chapter presents a few key guidelines to help you choose and design the right illustration for your paper.

Words or Graphics— When Do You Need Illustrations?

Writers have been combining words and pictures for thousands of years—but how do you know when to use words and when to use illustrations in your paper? Keep the following criteria in mind when you are writing your first draft.

Tables, charts, and graphics are better than words when:

1. *You are describing complex technical or physical processes.* How does cocaine affect the human body? In this case, one picture may be truly worth several thousand words. You can include a diagram that traces the effects of this drug from the time it is ingested until the remaining amount is eliminated from the body. You can number or letter various stages and refer to them throughout your description.

2. *You have complex numerical or statistical data to convey.* You are summarizing two decades of public opinion surveys on the subject of prayer in schools. One table or chart can save you a page or two of text.

3. *You are describing a particular event or subject such as a battle, city plan, or interior of a building.* A map, blueprint, or other illustration can orient your readers and give them a visual reference as your text continues.

4. *You want to present information the reader will need to remember.* In general, most people remember visual images better than they do words. If you want your readers to remember information you give early in your paper, find a way to present it visually. Suppose, for example, you want the reader to remember six dimensions of religion that you will be discussing. You could present the information visually, as shown in Figure 7.1.

FIGURE 7.1   Representing Text Visually

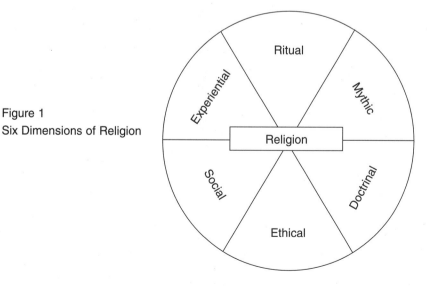

Figure 1
Six Dimensions of Religion

This figure will make it easier for the reader to remember the six dimensions of religion discussed in the text.

As you outline your paper and write your first draft, note in the margins where you think tables, charts, or other graphics will be needed. Use the next section to determine how many and what type of illustrations to select for your final draft.

How to Use Illustrations

The art of using charts, tables, or other graphic material effectively is based on two principles.

1. *Illustrations should be essential to your report and not used to conceal a lack of content.* Some writers use photographs, charts, and diagrams when they run out of things to say about their topic. Illustrations must provide important information and not be used simply to fill out the page number requirements or to impress the instructor.

2. *Illustrations must support and clarify the text, not stand in place of it.* The right illustration can convey information in a fraction of the time it takes to describe the same features in words. Imagine trying to describe the structure of a DNA molecule, for example. One picture can show the structure in beautiful detail.

   But the best illustration is useless if it is not properly labeled, is not inserted in the right place, or is not explained in the text. You must interpret the information you present in graphic form; don't assume the reader will understand what the information means.

A term paper is likely to contain more charts, tables, and graphics than an ordinary report, but the two principles above apply equally to both types of papers.

Types of Illustrations

You have five basic forms available to you to illustrate your paper: tables, circle graphs (pie charts), bar charts, line charts, and pictures or symbols (which include flow charts). Figures 7.2 through 7.6 provide examples of all five types of illustrations. Which one you choose depends on the information you have to display and the point you are trying to make.

For example, suppose you are writing a paper on the "graying" of the U.S. population, that is, the increasing number of people in the 35 and above age brackets that make up the total population. The paragraph of text in your rough draft runs as follows.

```
Over the next ten years, the population over age 65 will

increase from 32 million to 55 million, representing 15 percent

of the population, compared to only 10 percent today. The

number of 35- to 55-year-olds will also rise significantly,

from 114 million to 125 million, accounting for 42 percent of

the population. In ten years, this group will be at or near
```

retirement age. In contrast, the number of people age 18 to 25
will decrease from 95 million to 70 million and make up only 18
percent of the population, compared to 22 percent today.

A lot of numbers for the reader to absorb! You can arrange the information
in a table to help the reader see the figures at a glance (see Figure 7.2). This
method presents the information in a convenient form but offers little visual
interpretation of the data.

Suppose you wanted to present the information more graphically to underscore a point you are making in your paper. For instance, your point may
emphasize that older groups are the fastest-growing segments in our population—a fact which will have an impact on advertising, health care, entertainment, and other commercial enterprises. A bar chart would show the population figures in relation to each other and enable the reader to spot easily
which groups are increasing at the fastest rate (see Figure 7.3).

FIGURE 7.2 Sample Table

Age Group	1990		2000	
	Millions	% of Total	Millions	% of Total
18–25	95	22%	70	18%
35–55	114	39	125	42
65+	32	10	55	15

Source: U.S. Census Bureau

FIGURE 7.3 Sample Bar Chart

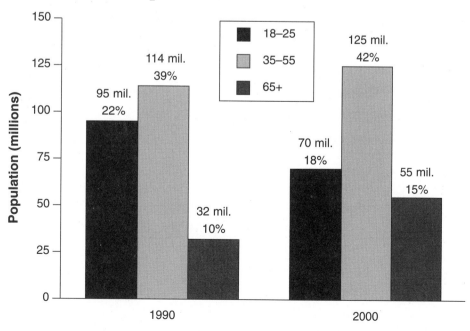

On the other hand, suppose you wanted to show that the older groups account for an increasingly greater percentage of the total population figure. A circle graph would be the best choice to illustrate your point (see Figure 7.4). Each group is represented by a certain sized wedge of the circle. The combination of figures and symbols enables the reader to grasp more easily the amount of "space" each group occupies in the whole. You can then explain in the text how the oldest group, which will take up an increasingly larger segment of the circle, may actually receive less of the available resources.

Now suppose instead that you want to depict population trends over time to alert your readers to potential problems—increasing burdens on Social Security, health care, younger workers, and so on. A line graph would enable you to make this point, illustrating in a steady progression how some groups will rise in population, while others fall (see Figure 7.5). You can explain in your text what these coming trends mean in terms of resources needed to meet the health care, housing, and employment needs of these groups. Line graphs can be used to act as an early warning system, saying in effect, "Here is where we are now—here is where we will be in the future."

Finally, suppose you simply want to show the reader that the population groups are changing—as in the table format. You can use symbols for the different groups and enlarge or shrink the symbols to depict an increase or decrease in population size (see Figure 7.6). Your major purpose here is to present the data in an easy-to-read format and to add interest and liveliness to your paper by depicting it in pictorial form.

Your text may emphasize a point based indirectly on the data—for example, how the themes of movies are likely to change to accommodate the shifts in population. If the older group is increasing at such a rapid rate, will studios make fewer action films and more movies that stress relationships, memories, and dreams lost or attained?

Guidelines for Using Illustrations

The guidelines below can help you to avoid the most common mistakes students make when they use illustrations in their papers. In most cases, students

FIGURE 7.4 Sample Circle Graphs

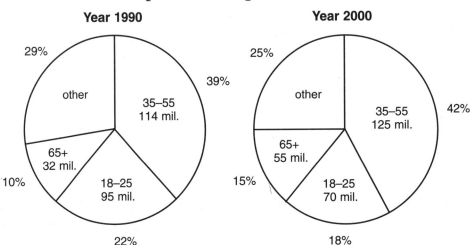

FIGURE 7.5   Sample Line Chart

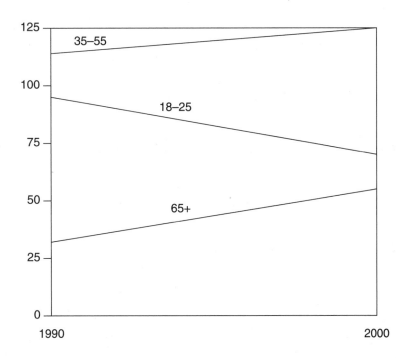

FIGURE 7.6   Sample Symbol Chart

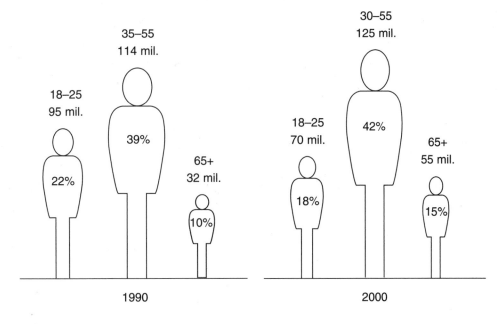

try to use too many graphics, do not explain them well, and do not indicate where in the text the graphics belong. Follow these guidelines to use illustrations effectively in your papers.

- *Use a minimum number of graphics.* Most students believe that if a few graphics are good, more are better. They clutter their papers with charts, tables, and pictures that overwhelm the reader and bury the text.

Select only those graphics that emphasize a point, explain key facts in the text, or help the reader to remember essential information.

- *Use the smallest-sized graphic that conveys the information clearly.* Another common mistake is using oversized graphics. It is better to use one or two smaller-sized illustrations than one over-sized one. Illustrations should complement the text, not overwhelm it.

- *Make sure all your graphics are designed so that words, lines, scales, and other elements are the same size.* Avoid broad discrepancies in size between one graphic and another—for example, a line graph that takes up a quarter page and a circle graph that takes up a full page. Use the same scale for your line, bar, and circle graphs.

- *Make sure the terms you use in the graphic are the same terms used in the text.* If you talk about pounds in the text, use pounds in your graphics. Don't change terms or symbols in your illustrations or you will confuse and aggravate the reader. If you are copying a graphic from another source, adapt the terms so they are consistent with your text (for example, changing tons to pounds).

- *Cite the graphic in the text as close to the relevant information as possible.* Let the reader know the graphic exists early in the relevant paragraph. Don't wait until the next page to mention it.

```
As recent surveys show, more Americans are rating quality

of the environment as one of their top priorities (see

Figure 3).
```

- *Type the table and figure titles flush with the left margin, and capitalize only the first letter of each word over five letters long.* For tables, type the number and title above the table as follows.

```
Table 1
```

Table begins here ⟶ `Worldwide Expenditures on Elementary Education--1990`

For figures, abbreviate the word *figure* followed by the figure number and a period (Fig. 1.); leave two spaces and begin the title. Type the figure number and title at the bottom of the figure, above the source line.

Bottom of figure ⟶ `Fig. 1. Sites of Toxic Dumps in the United States`

`Source: Environmental Protection Agency`

- *Number all graphics consecutively throughout your paper.* Number tables and figures consecutively and refer to the illustrations by number. Tables and figures are separate types of illustrations, so number them as Table 1, Figure 1; Table 2, Figure 2, and so on. Do not number them Table 1, Figure 2 as if the figure were the second illustration after the table.

Do not refer to illustrations as *the table below* or *the figure on the next page.* By the time your paper has gone through a few revisions, the table or figure may not be below or on the next page. Instead, use such phrases as *see Table 1* or *as shown in Figure 3, page 12.*

- *Comment on the major points of the graphic.* Help the reader interpret the information given in the graphic. If you are presenting a bar chart on the increasing level of pesticides in our food supply, for instance, tell the reader what the increase means.

```
As shown in Figure 3, the level of Trichloride-D has risen

200 percent in the past three years, an increase that

presents a clear health threat, according to USDA standards.
```

- *Cite your source for the information in your graphic.* What was your source for your figures, statistics, or other data? In most cases, cite the source in a note at the bottom of the illustration.

Interpreting Illustrations

Always tell your readers what the illustrations mean in terms of your paper. Why are you showing the information? What does it mean that hospitals are closing in record numbers in most major U.S. cities? What is the importance of the diminishing rain forest in Latin America?

Don't merely repeat the data already shown in the illustration. As the writer, you are the reader's guide, pointing out what is significant or important about the information the reader is seeing. See Figure 7.7 and compare the two examples that follow in which the writer is making a point about the need for peer counseling in high schools to help prevent teen suicides.

FIGURE 7.7   Sample Line Chart

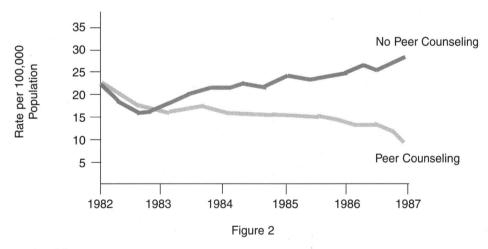

Figure 2

Avoid

```
    As shown in Figure 2, suicide rates among teens in

schools without peer counselors rose from 22 per 100,000

population to 30 per 100,000 population over five years, 1982

to 1987. In schools with peer counselors, the suicide rate fell

from 23 per 100,000 population to 12 per 100,000 population

over the same period.
```

The paragraph simply repeats information presented in the line chart.

Better

The paragraph interprets the data in the line chart, telling the reader what the trends indicate.

>   Peer counseling can have an important effect in reducing the rate of suicide among teenagers. As shown in Figure 2, over a period of five years the suicide rate in schools with peer counselors declined over 50 percent, from 23 per 100,000 population to 12 per 100,000 population. In schools that did not provide peer counseling, the suicide rate continued to rise steadily. These statistics strongly suggest that peer counseling could help save hundreds of lives a year.

Whenever you use illustrations in your papers, ask yourself if you have interpreted the data or simply inserted it into your paper.

Once you know what illustrations you would like to include in your paper and how to use them to your best advantage, you are ready to create your graphics. The next section reviews the main purpose of each type of graphic and offers brief tips on how to create them.

Designing Tables, Charts, and Graphics

While each graphic has its own requirements, there are a few general guidelines for designing effective illustrations.

- The word *Table* and the number of the table are typed flush with the left margin and above the title of the table. The title is also typed flush left. The table number and title appear *above* the table.

- The word *Figure* (sometimes abbreviated *Fig.*) and the number of the figure are typed flush with the left margin, followed by a period, and the title of the figure. The figure number and title appear below the illustration (but above the source line).

- If the graphic contains more than one part, label each part with a letter (A, B, C, . . .).

- Make sure all elements of the graphic are properly labeled. In a line chart, for example, label all lines clearly so the reader can easily distinguish then.

- Place keys, or "legends," to the graphic and any notes containing explanations or source citations below the graphic.

- In designing charts, use black ink for the final version, preferably not ballpoint, which tends to blot and smudge. Sketch out your charts in pencil first, then draw the final version in ink.

- If you are creating graphics with a computer, be sure your printer can produce clear, readable copies.

Tables—Showing Numbers

Tables are particularly useful for displaying numbers in columns. They have the added advantage of being easy to produce on a typewriter or computer—no special artists' equipment is needed.

A table has at least two columns, with headings on the sides and tops of the columns to indicate what the figures represent. The headings on the top are called *boxheads*; the far left column is known as the *stub*. For clarity, lines may be drawn between groups of columns.

When preparing tables, follow these guidelines.

1. Stub, column, and boxhead labels are typed with initial capitals only.

2. All figures are aligned on the right. Commas, decimal points, dollar or percent signs, and other symbols are aligned vertically. In most cases, numbers should contain only two decimal points.

3. Abbreviations are used without periods. Unusual symbols or notations should be explained in a note below the table.

4. Single-space rows of numbers within tables, but double-space between groups of data and between the headings and the first row of figures.

The examples in Figure 7.8 (a–c) show how tables can be prepared.

FIGURE 7.8(a)   Sample Table

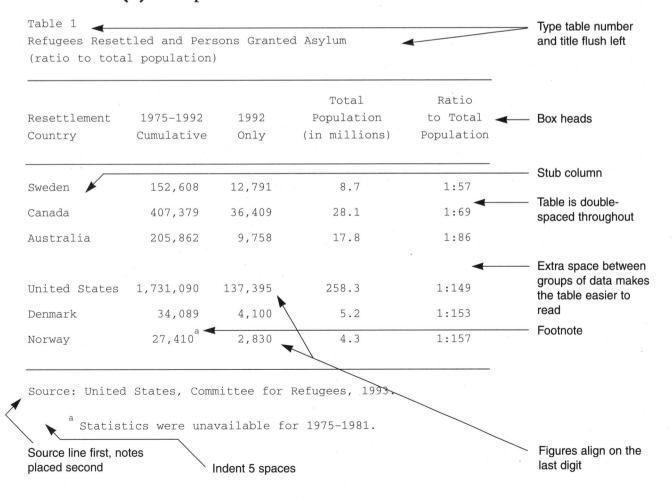

Table 1
Refugees Resettled and Persons Granted Asylum
(ratio to total population)

Resettlement Country	1975–1992 Cumulative	1992 Only	Total Population (in millions)	Ratio to Total Population
Sweden	152,608	12,791	8.7	1:57
Canada	407,379	36,409	28.1	1:69
Australia	205,862	9,758	17.8	1:86
United States	1,731,090	137,395	258.3	1:149
Denmark	34,089	4,100	5.2	1:153
Norway	27,410[a]	2,830	4.3	1:157

Source: United States, Committee for Refugees, 1993.

   [a] Statistics were unavailable for 1975–1981.

Type table number and title flush left

Box heads

Stub column

Table is double-spaced throughout

Extra space between groups of data makes the table easier to read

Footnote

Source line first, notes placed second

Indent 5 spaces

Figures align on the last digit

FIGURE 7.8(b)   Sample Table

Table 5
Student Participation in Athletic Extracurricular Activities: 1990
(in thousands)

Vertical rules help group data

Extracurricular Activities	Sex		Race		
	Male	Female	White	Black	Asian
Baseball/softball	19.2	12.1	16.0	13.7	13.9
Basketball	24.3	15.4	18.2	30.9	22.8
Cheerleading	1.7	10.0	5.3	9.9	2.8
Football	28.9	2.9	14.7	22.6	16.2
Soccer	9.1	6.1	7.9	4.0	10.2
Swimming	3.9	3.9	4.1	2.8	5.2

Source: United States, Dept. of Education. Office of Educational
Research and Improvement. National Center for Education
Statistics. Digest of Education Statistics, 1992. (Washington:
GPO), 1992, p. 136.

Source lines are indented 2 spaces

Figures align on decimal points

FIGURE 7.8(c)   Sample Table

Table 2
World's Five Biggest Chocolate Eaters

Country	Annual Consumption (pounds per person)
Switzerland[a]	18.9
Britain	17.6
Norway	17.1
Austria	17.0
Belgium[b]	13.2

Source: Milton Moskowitz. The Global Marketplace.
(New York: Macmillan), 1987, p. 405.

[a]Leading nation for three years in a row.

[b]Figures are estimated through December.

Note: Does not include Germany, as figures were
not available at the time of publication.

Bar Charts—Showing Relationships among Groups

Bar or column charts depict relationships among groups of information, such as the number of compact discs produced in different countries in any one year. Bars can be arranged vertically or horizontally. Use these guidelines when creating bar charts.

1. Draw the chart as a rectangle.

2. Label the horizontal and vertical scales clearly and mark any appropriate divisions (miles, amounts of money, etc.) to show the scale you are using.

3. Label each bar clearly. If you use more than one bar, provide a label or key for the reader's convenience.

Notice that the sample bar charts in Figure 7.9 (a–b) can be constructed either vertically or horizontally.

FIGURE 7.9(a) Sample Horizontal Bar Chart

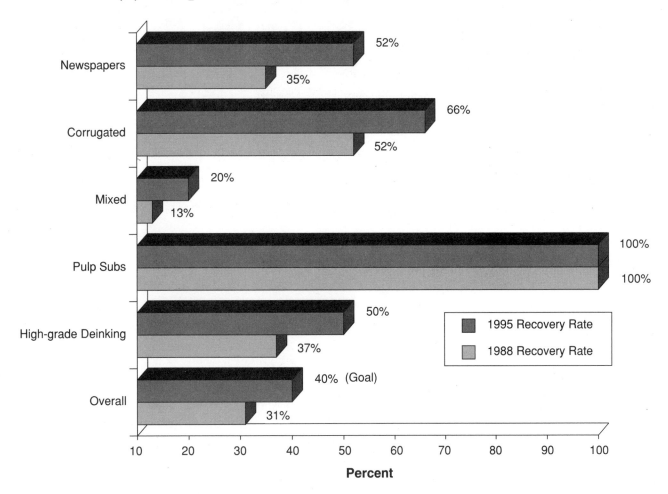

Figure 5   Potential Waste Paper Recovery Rates

Source: American Paper Institute and Franklin Associates, Ltd.

FIGURE 7.9(b) Sample Vertical Bar Chart

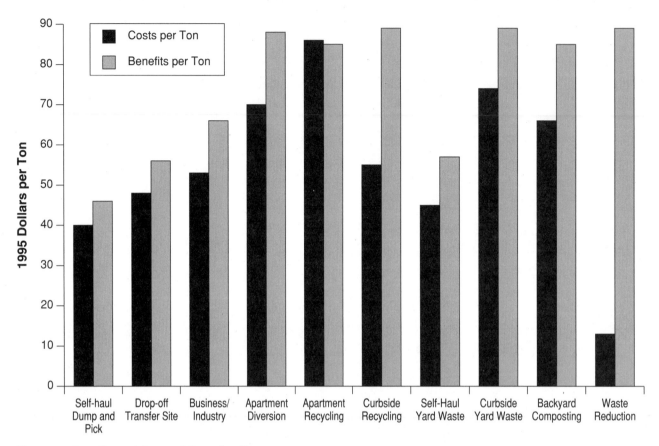

Figure 3   Benefits and Costs of Recycling Programs

Source: Seattle Solid Waste Utility.

Circle Graphs—Showing Relationship to the Whole

Circle graphs, or pie charts, are particularly useful when you want to show the relative sizes of groups of information compared to the whole. However, the segments are not placed at random. Follow these steps in preparing your circle graphs.

1. Sectors are arranged clockwise according to size, beginning at "twelve noon" with the largest sector.

2. Whenever you are using a segment labeled "other," it is always placed last.

3. Label each segment clearly, using percentages carried only to one decimal point.

4. To construct a circle graph, convert percentages to degrees using the following formula:

   $360° \times$ percent converted to decimals = degrees°

   arc on the circle: $360° \times .12 = 43.2°$ (round to nearest whole degree = $43°$)

Some common percentage values of a circle are as follows:

$$100\% = 1.00 \times 360° = 360°$$
$$50\% = .50 \times 360° = 180°$$
$$25\% = .25 \times 360° = 90°$$
$$10\% = .10 \times 360° = 36°$$
$$5\% = .05 \times 360° = 18°$$

The examples in Figure 7.10 (a–c) show various uses of circle graphs.

FIGURE 7.10(a)   Sample Circle Graph Showing Proportion of Each Group to the Whole

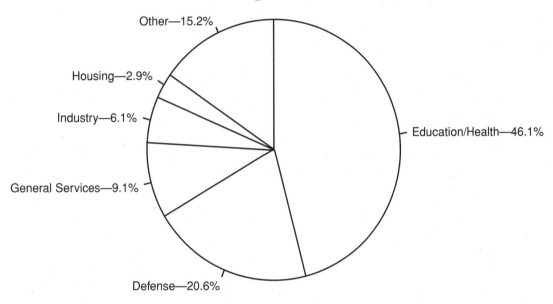

Figure 2   United States Government Expenditures, 1992

Source: Statistical Abstract of the World, 1994.

FIGURE 7.10(b)   Sample Circle Graphs Showing Two Separate Groups of Data

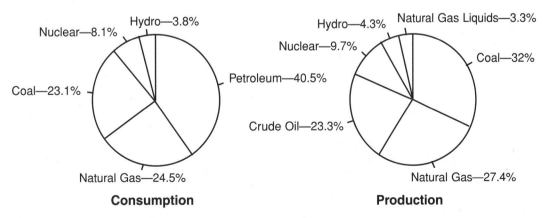

Figure 6   Commercial Energy Consumption and Production

Source: United States Department of Commerce, 1993.

FIGURE 7.10(c) Sample Circle Graphs Showing Progressive Changes

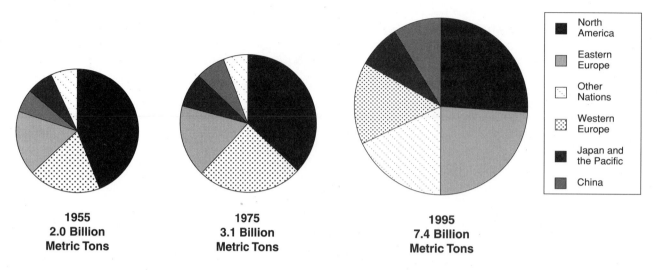

Figure 1 Carbon Dioxide Emissions by World Area

Source: World Resources Institute, 1995.

Line Charts—Showing Trends

Line charts allow readers to see trends in data over time. The continuous line makes the rise or fall of your information easier to follow. When designing line charts, keep these guidelines in mind.

1. Use the same rectangle form as in bar charts. Line charts are generally constructed horizontally.

2. Use no more than three or four lines in your charts—too many will confuse the reader.

3. Use different types of lines—solid, dashed, broken, lighter, or heavier—to depict different groups of data. Label all lines carefully.

4. Label the horizontal and vertical scales and all divisions along the scales.

Figure 7.11(a–c) shows a variety of line charts.

Pictorial or Symbol Graphics

Some of the more common pictorial or symbol graphics include maps, photographs, diagrams, and flow charts. Flow charts are particularly useful in showing steps in a process and in depicting organizational structures in businesses and institutions. In preparing these graphics, follow these guidelines.

1. Make sure all symbols are clear. If you are using a symbol to represent food groups or population groups, for example, make sure the symbols are easy to identify.

2. Make sure the symbols accurately represent differences in size or percentages. Because you are using a graphic representation, not numbers,

FIGURE 7.11(a)   Sample Line Chart

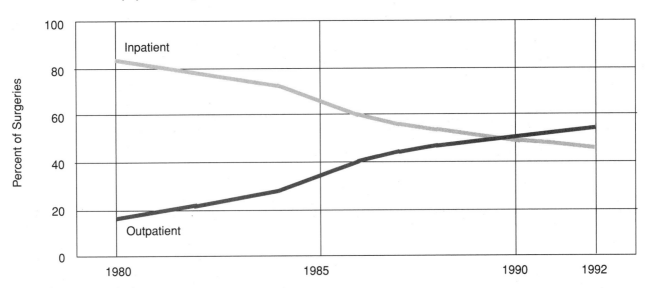

Figure 2   Inpatient and Outpatient Surgeries in Short-stay United States Hospitals.

Source: American Hospital Association: Hospital Statistics, 1992.

FIGURE 7.11(b)   Sample Line Chart

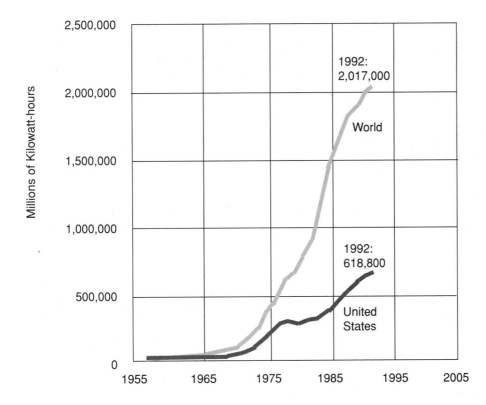

Figure 4   Growth of Nuclear Energy Production

Source: United States Energy Information Administration.

FIGURE 7.11(c) Sample Line Chart

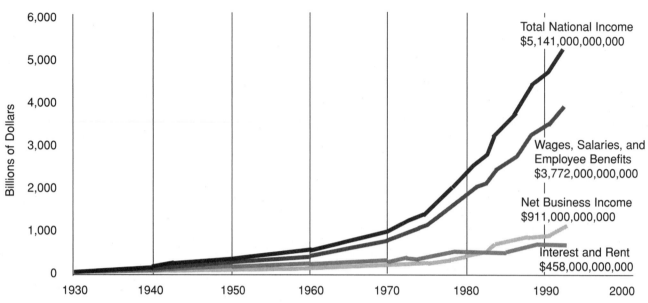

Figure 3   United States National Income, 1930–1993

Source: Bureau of Economic Analysis, United States, Department of Commerce, 1993.

bars, lines, or sectors, be sure that the sizes of your symbols are in direct proportion to the amounts they are supposed to represent.

3. Label all important elements on a map, photograph, diagram, or flow chart. For some maps you will need to include a scale in miles or kilometers and indicate direction of north, south, east, and west.

4. Type any explanations or source citations in a note below the graphic.

The examples in Figures 7.12, 7.13, and 7.14 show correctly drawn and labeled pictorial and symbol illustrations.

List of Illustrations Page

Once you have finished your graphics, you will need to create a List of Illustrations for your paper. This list follows the same format as your Works Cited page (see Chapter 8). You can list tables separately from figures or simply arrange all illustrations in the order in which they appear in your paper. The List of Illustrations is placed either immediately after the title page or at the end of the paper before the Works Cited page. If you place the list before Works Cited, number the page (see Figure 7.15).

The guidelines and tips in this chapter can help you produce effective graphics that will enhance your paper.

FIGURE 7.12(a)   Sample Organizational Flow Chart

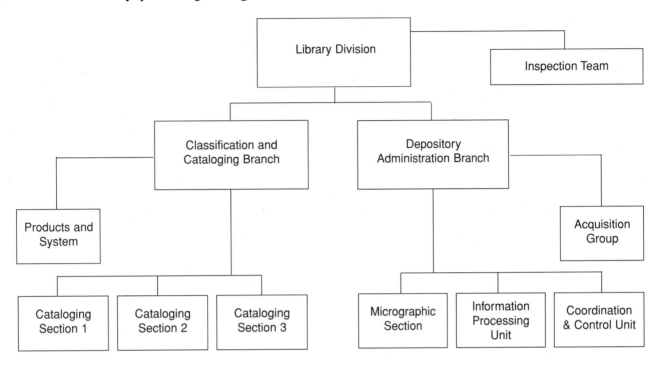

Figure 6   Organization Chart of USGPO's Library Division

Source: United States Government Printing Office.

FIGURE 7.12(b)   Sample Process Flow Chart

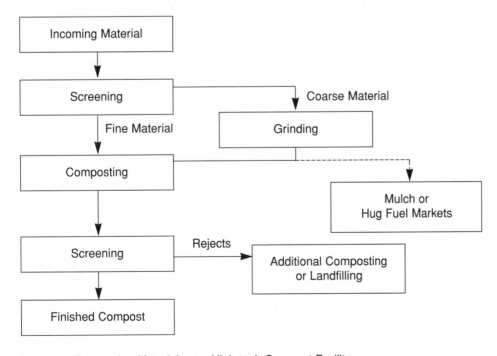

Figure 2   Processing Materials at a High-tech Compost Facility

Source: United States Environmental Protection Agency.

FIGURE 7.13   Sample Pictorial

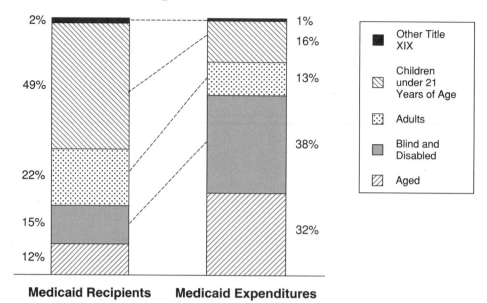

Medicaid Recipients · Medicaid Expenditures

Legend:
- Other Title XIX
- Children under 21 Years of Age
- Adults
- Blind and Disabled
- Aged

Note: Other Title XIX includes some participants in the Supplemental Security Insurance Program.

Figure 3   Medicaid Recipients and Expenditures by Eligibility, 1993

Source: Health Care Financing Administration.

FIGURE 7.14   Sample Map

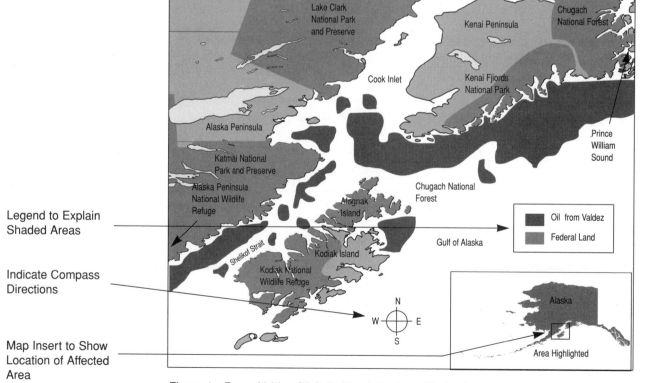

Legend to Explain Shaded Areas

Indicate Compass Directions

Map Insert to Show Location of Affected Area

Figure 4   Exxon Valdez Oil Spill, March 24–May 18, 1989

Source: United States Environmental Protection Agency, 1991.

FIGURE 7.15 Sample List of Illustrations Pages

After Title Page

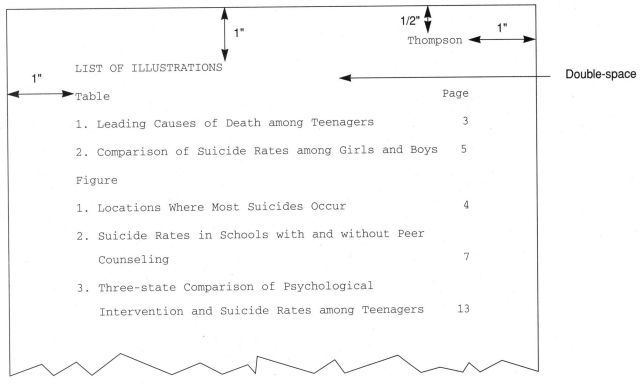

Before Works Cited

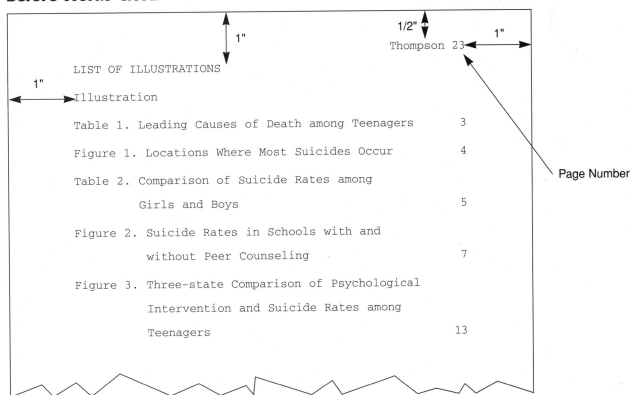

CHAPTER **8**
Typing and Word-Processing Guidelines

Once you have written your paper, you are ready for the final stage: preparing the report or term paper to hand in to the instructor. After all your research and painstaking care, you want to make the final product the best representation of your efforts possible. This is no time to get careless.

This chapter is divided into four sections: preparation for typing, typing the paper, word-processing tips, and proofreading your paper.

A Word about Handwritten Papers

Although handwritten papers are rapidly becoming a thing of the past, some instructors do allow students to turn in handwritten papers. If you must do so, make sure you use black or dark-blue ink, use lined paper, leave space between each line, and write on only one side of the paper. Observe the guidelines below for margins and paragraph indentions.

Preparing for Typing

Before you start typing, you need to consider the type of equipment you will use, the kind of paper you need, any requirements for margins and spacing your instructor may have, and methods for making corrections.

Type of Equipment

Modern technology has made a bewildering array of equipment available to the writer. It ranges from the old standby, the manual typewriter, to the newer electronic, computerized typewriters, to word-processing personal computers, or PCs. If you use a manual or electric typewriter, follow these guidelines.

- *Make sure your typewriter is in good working order.* Check to see that your margin-setting keys, platen roll, single- and double-space settings, tab keys, spacing bar, and all letter, number, and symbol keys function properly. You may want to have your typewriter cleaned by a professional before you start or clean it yourself if you know how.

  If your typewriter has special features, such as boldface type, italics, automatic recall of sentences or pages, automatic page numbering, or repeating characters, test those features before you start typing your paper. You don't want a special feature to quit in the middle of a paper when you have no substitute available.

- *Clean your typewriter.* In particular, check the *o, e, a, d, s, p, q,* and *g* keys, which tend to become clogged with lint or dirt. Cleaning kits are available at most office supply stores, or you can make your own kit with a bottle of cleaning fluid, cotton, and toothpicks.

  Also, make sure the platen roll and other surfaces of the typewriter are clean. Otherwise, you may put smudge marks on your paper as you handle it.

- *Use a new, black ribbon in the typewriter.* Don't use colored ribbons—brown, green, red, or blue. Also, make sure your ribbon is new. Few things are as irritating to the reader as a report typed with an old, faded ribbon. Instructors have been known to hand reports back to students or give them an "F" on the basis of a paper's appearance alone. The harder you make it for the instructor to read your paper, the more your work—and your grade—is likely to suffer.

- *Use pica, not elite type whenever possible.* Pica type is larger and more legible than elite type. The example below shows the difference between the two.

```
This is elite type, 12 characters per inch.
```
```
This is pica type, 10 characters per inch.
```

However, many typewriters have only elite keys. Before you start typing, check with your instructor to determine if elite type is acceptable.

- *Do not use all script, italic, or other special type styles.* Script and italic type styles are difficult to read when they make up the entire report. Stick to the basic type styles—Courier, Prestige, or Gothic—found on most typewriters and on the default setting in most word-processing software. Script or italic can be used to emphasize words but only within a sentence or paragraph.

If you are using a personal computer to prepare your report or term paper, use the following guidelines.

- *Make sure you have enough memory in your machine to complete the paper.* Some smaller word-processing PCs have limited memory. Make sure your machine can handle the size file you will create in preparing your report.

- *Make sure your computer and software are in good working order.* Few things match the terror that strikes a writer's heart when a computer error locks up a file, inserts garbage in the middle of a report, or refuses to carry out routine commands. Make sure your disks are formatted properly and are error-free. You can use your DOS program or any one of several utilities programs to check the disks for bad sectors or file errors.

  Also, make a quick check of your word-processing master disk to ensure it is in good order. Clean your disk driver heads using any one of several kits available and insert a new ribbon or cartridge in your printer when printing out the final copy.

- *Use standard type styles and a high-quality printer.* As with typewriters, avoid fancy scripts and type styles. Also, check with your instructor about the quality of printout that is acceptable. In many cases, dot-matrix printers are of marginal quality and will not be accepted. Figure 8.1 shows the difference between dot-matrix, near letter-quality, and letter-quality printing. Generally, near letter quality is acceptable for most term papers and reports.

More tips for word processing can be found later in this chapter.

Paper Size and Selection

Whether you use a manual or electric typewriter, or a word processor, prepare your report on 8 ½ by 11-inch white bond paper. The paper should be at least 20 weight, which gives it a heavier texture. *Do not use a coated or erasable bond paper, as the coating on the surface smudges ink and type.*

For word-processing printers that use fanfold paper, be sure to purchase what is known as "micro-perf" paper. That is, the sides of the paper have been laser-cut so that the fanfold holes tear off without leaving a jagged border.

For any type of printer—fanfold or single sheet—make sure that you use 20-weight paper in your printer. Thinner, 16-weight paper tears easily and is difficult to handle.

FIGURE 8.1   Dot-Matrix, Near Letter-Quality, and Letter-Quality Printing

This is an example of dot-matrix printing. Notice that the letters are made up of a series of dots. Thus, they are not as clearly formed, making the entire text more difficult to read. This type is generally not acceptable for term papers and reports.   ← Dot-Matrix Printing

This is an example of near letter quality printing. It resembles the type of print found in typewriters and letter-quality printers. In most cases, this type is acceptable for term papers and reports.   ← Near Letter-Quality Printing

This is an example of letter quality printing. It is the type available on typewriters and high-quality printers. Letter quality is the easiest to read because the characters are sharp and clear. This type is the preferred form for term papers and reports.   ← Letter-Quality Printing

General Margins and Spacing

Check with your instructor for any special guidelines regarding margins and spacing. If there are none, then follow these guidelines.

General Margins. Set a 1-inch margin on the left side of the paper and at the top, right side, and bottom of the page. However, if your paper is to be inserted into a three-hole binder, leave a $1\frac{1}{2}$-inch margin on the left. This will allow enough space for the binder rings.

Most instructors, however, do not want papers bound, stapled, or otherwise fastened together. Binding only makes it harder to read the paper and write comments in the margins.

Ragged Right or Justified Right Margins. If you are using a word processor, ask your instructor if he or she prefers a ragged right or justified right margin. *Ragged right* means that each line ends close to the right margin, but the edge itself is uneven. *Justified* means that the computer automatically adjusts line spacing to make all lines end at the right margin. Thus, both left and right margins are aligned down each side of the page. The only problem with a justified margin is that sometimes words are stretched apart to accommodate the differences in line length, creating a distracting appearance on the page.

Ragged right and justified right margins are illustrated in Figure 8.2.

FIGURE 8.2   Ragged Right and Justified Margins

Ragged Right Margin ⟶

This is an example of a ragged right paragraph in which the lines are not aligned at the right margin. Most instructors prefer ragged right margin because it maintains proper spacing between letters and words.

Justified Right Margin ⟶

This is a good example of a justified right margin in which all lines are aligned at the right side of the paper or report. This gives an even appearance to both right and left margins but may result in disproportionate spacing between letters and words.

Line Spacing. If you are using a word processor, set the spacing to double-spacing. Since you have already set the margins at 1-inch, the word processor will automatically skip to the next page when you have reached the bottom margin. If you are using a typewriter, set the line spacer so there are six vertical lines to the inch. Thus, a paper 11 inches long will hold 66 typed lines.

Double Spacing. Make sure you have set your typewriter or word processor on double spacing. All reports and term papers should be double-spaced, including quoted material, notes, and works cited.

Margin and Spacing Guide. If you are using a typewriter, you can create a margin and spacing guide like the one shown in Figure 8.3. Insert this paper behind each sheet to act as a guide for right and left margins and page number location, and to let you know when you are approaching the 1-inch margin at the bottom of the page.

Paragraph and Tab Indentions. Standard indentions for paragraphs and tab settings are 5 spaces or half an inch. For example, if your left margin is set at 10 spaces, your tab indentions would be set at 15, 20, 25, 30, and 35 spaces. Generally, you will not need any more than four or five tab settings.

Page Numbering. The title page, outline and table of contents (if included), generally are not numbered. All other pages are numbered in the upper right-hand corner one-half inch from the top of the page and one inch from the right edge (see Figure 8.3 for proper location). Type your last name before the number. If the pages become jumbled, it will be easy to tell whose paper the pages belong to.

Do not use the abbreviation *p* before the page number or insert hyphens, stars, or any other symbol before or after the number. Use only the number itself.

If you are using a word processor, go to the beginning of the file and create a header consisting of your name. Most word-processing programs will then automatically print your name and insert the proper page number.

If your instructor requires that the outline and table of contents pages be numbered, use small roman numerals at the bottom of each page, centered one inch above the bottom edge at line 60 (see Figure 8.3).

FIGURE 8.3 Margin and Spacing Guide

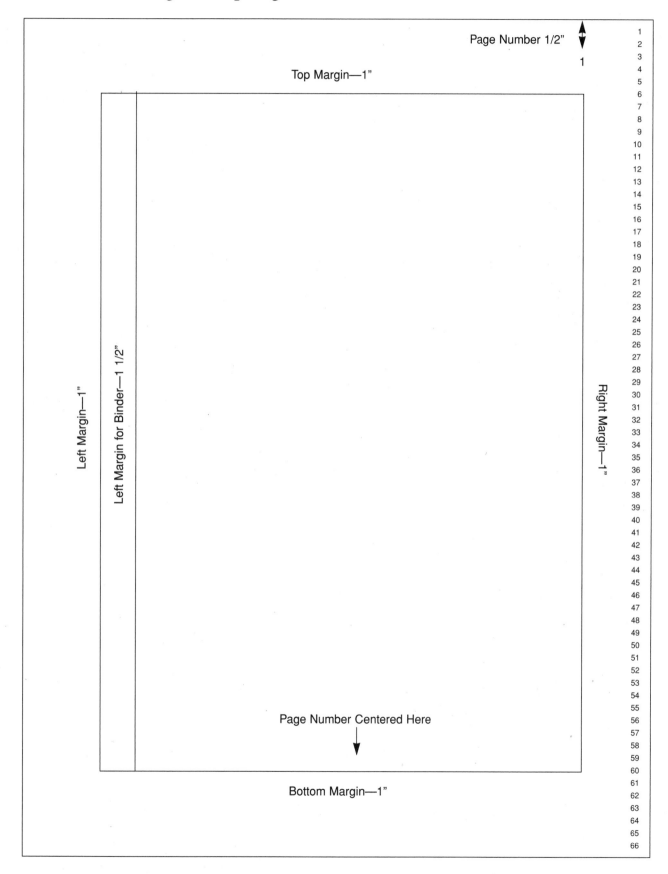

Making Corrections

Guidelines for making corrections in reports and term papers vary considerably from one instructor to another. Some insist on no more than two corrections per page; others are more lenient. Ask your instructor about the rules for corrections before you start typing your paper.

In general, the following guidelines apply.

- *Strikeovers, misspelled words, omitted words or letters or punctuation, and other obvious mistakes are never permitted.* If you cannot make neat corrections, retype the page.

- *To correct errors as you type, use correction fluid or correcting paper to cover up the mistake. Then retype the correction.* These two methods are preferable to trying to erase the error, which can tear the paper or smear the words above and below the correction. Correction fluid or correcting paper are available at any office supply or stationery store.

- *To correct errors after you have finished a page, learn how to adjust the soft carriage return and proportional spacing key to reposition the typewriter keys exactly within a word or line to make the correction.* Use correction fluid or correcting paper and retype the correct word or words.

- *If permitted, insert missing words or corrected words, numbers, symbols, or punctuation marks by using a caret (^) and writing in the correction above the line in ink.* Figure 8.4 shows examples of acceptable and unacceptable corrections.

FIGURE 8.4 **Acceptable and Unacceptable Corrections**

Acceptable Correction

during the

The Soviet Union invaded Afghanistan summer of 1979.

Unacceptable Corrections

during the

The Soviet Union invaded Afghanistan summer of 1979.

(Correction pulled out to margin is not acceptable.)

We fönd few examples in history to support the liberal stand.

(Strikeover is not acceptable.)

Air bagsshave proven their worth in preventing serious injuries.

(Smeared erasure is not acceptable.)

The American Revolution marked the first pop^{ular} uprising in

North America.

(Correction is not aligned.)

- *Corrections on a word processor can be made without any special correcting fluids or papers.* In addition, you can use a spell checker and grammar program to go through the paper for any errors, correct them on screen, and print out the corrected page. With such convenience, there is no excuse for handmade corrections on a paper prepared on a word processor.

Typing the Paper

This section explains how to type various parts of a paper and presents brief tips on typing special inserts, punctuation marks, and other common symbols.

Parts of a Paper

For most term papers, you will have a title page, outline, table of contents, body of the report, Works Cited, and Works Consulted. Shorter reports will generally have only the body of the paper and Works Cited.

Separate footnotes at the bottom of the page or at the end of the report are no longer used, according to the Modern Language Association style guidelines. In addition, "Bibliography" is now called "Works Cited." Some instructors also require a listing of "Works Consulted." These are books, articles, or other resources that served as background material in the course of your research but were not cited in the main body of the report. The style for these two lists is presented in Chapter 6.

Title Page. In general, only longer reports and term papers have title pages. Type the title, capitalizing only the first letter of each important word. Do not capitalize prepositions and articles unless one is the first word of the title. Center the title on line 23 of the page. Space down to line 44 and type your name, the name and number of the course, the instructor's name, and the date you submit the paper. Double-space between each line. Figure 8.5 shows a sample title page.

Outline. If you must submit an outline with your paper, it comes directly after the title page. Begin 1 inch from the top of the page, type the word *outline* in all capitals and center it on the page. Double-space to the first roman numeral and begin your outline flush with the left margin. Subsequent headings are indented five spaces each, as shown in the example below.

```
                        OUTLINE

     I. Gun control

         A. Arguments against

             1. right to bear arms guaranteed

             2. right to protect self and home

         B. Arguments for

             1. automatic weapons far too lethal

             2. guns used more often against family members
```

FIGURE 8.5   Sample Title Page

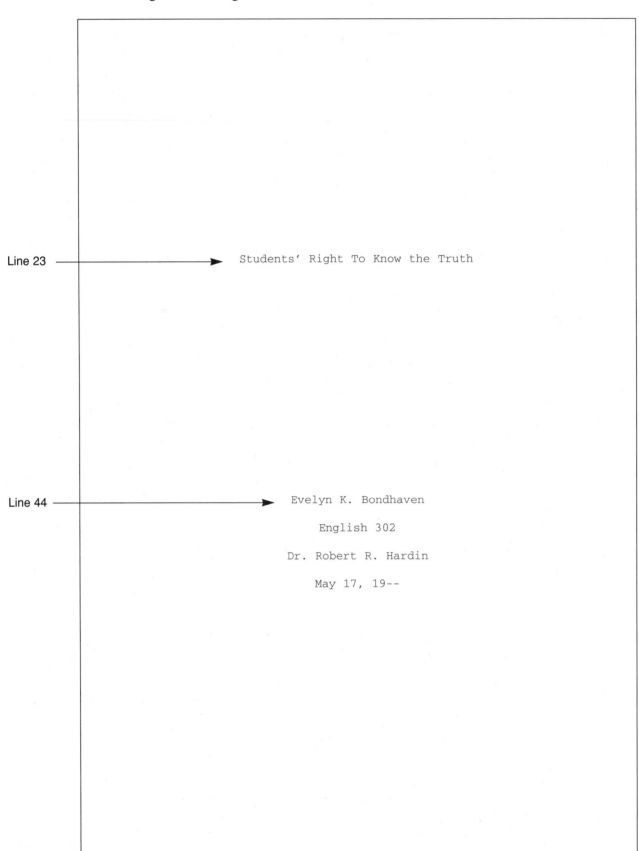

First Page of the Paper. If you have a title page, the title will also appear on page 1. Put your last name and the page number in the upper right-hand corner one-half inch from the top and one inch from the right edge of the paper. Leave a top margin of 3 inches and center the title on the page. Do not underline the title, put it in quotation marks, or type it in all capitals. Space down two lines, indent five spaces, and begin typing the first line of your paper.

If you do not have a title page, put your last name and the page number in the upper right-hand corner. Then begin 1 inch from the top of the page and flush with the left margin. Type your name, the instructor's name, the course name and number, and the date on separate lines, double-spacing between each line. Double-space after the date and type the title of your paper, centering it on the page. Double-space after the title and begin the first line of your paper, indenting it five spaces.

Compare the two formats for first pages in Figure 8.6.

FIGURE 8.6 Formats for First Pages

First Page Following a Title Page

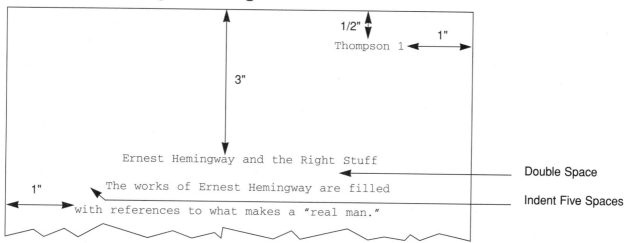

First Page of a Paper without Title Page

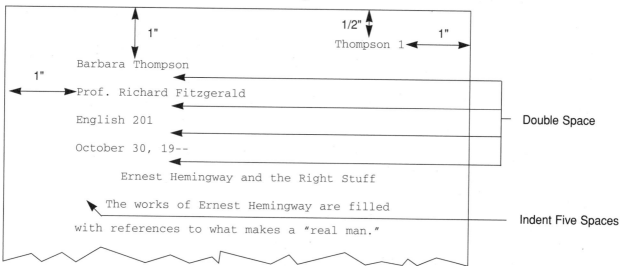

Body of the Paper. The body of the paper is double-spaced throughout, including all notes, quotations, and works cited. It is best to avoid hyphenating words at the ends of lines. If a hyphenated word is unavoidable, however, follow these guidelines for dividing words and paragraphs.

- *Dividing words.* Avoid dividing words at the ends of more than three succeeding lines. For example:

```
We must remember that most work-

ing men did not enjoy the bene-

fits of paid vacations or pensions

before World War II.
```

Avoid dividing a word at the end of the last line on a page, as this would mean carrying only part of a word to the first line of the next page. Consult the latest dictionary for the proper division of all words.

- *Dividing paragraphs.* As much as possible, avoid carrying only one or two words at the end of a paragraph over to the next page. Likewise, avoid typing only one line of a paragraph at the bottom of a page. It is better to begin the entire paragraph on the next page.

Last Page. The last page should not have *The End*, *Finis*, or any other concluding line. The last line of your report is all the ending you need.

Works Cited and Works Consulted Lists. These lists appear at the end of the report and are arranged in alphabetical order, using the letter-by-letter system. The format for various books, articles, and other resources is given in Chapter 6. These pages are numbered as part of the report. An example of the format for typing a Works Cited list is given in Figure 8.7. The format for a Works Consulted list is exactly the same.

FIGURE 8.7 Format for Works Cited

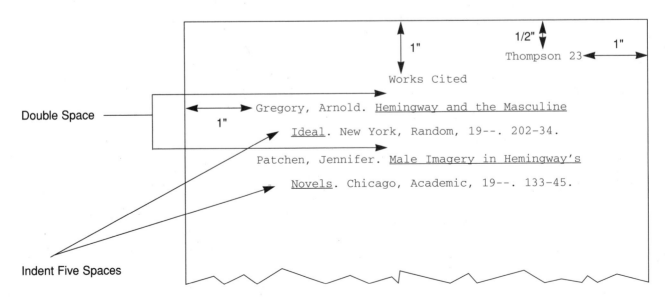

Other Typing Guidelines

In your report, you will probably use block quotes of prose or poetry, some scholarly abbreviations, and various punctuation and typographical marks. The following is a brief review of how to type such elements.

Quotations. Block quotations of prose are indented one inch or ten spaces from the left margin and double-spaced.

```
Call me Ishmael. Some years ago--never mind how long

precisely--having little or no money in my purse,

and nothing particular to interest me on shore, I

thought I would sail about a little and see the

watery part of the world.
```

Quotations from poetry are indented ten spaces or one inch from the left margin and end where the line of poetry ends.

```
The sky puts on a darkening blue coat

held for it by a row of ancient trees;

you watch; and the lands grow distant in your sight,

one journeying to heaven, one that falls;
```

Scholarly Abbreviations. In your report, you may have occasion to use some scholarly abbreviations such as *sic, Ibid., i.e., e.g.,* and the like. In general, these abbreviations are no longer italicized (or underscored), but may be set off by commas, brackets, or parentheses, or in some other way distinguished from the general text. Follow the guidelines established in the *MLA Handbook* for these abbreviations.

Punctuation Marks. The following guidelines should be used for punctuation marks in your paper.

- *Periods, exclamation points, question marks, and colons.* These marks are always followed by two spaces when they punctuate a sentence. However, colons used to separate time and ratios—and periods used internally in abbreviations—are not followed by a space.

```
Did any single event cause World War I? Most historians

would say no. However, they point to one fact: the

assassination of the Archduke at 4:30 p.m. on June 28, 1914,

provided the excuse for nations to go to war. It was perhaps

one of the most costly bullets ever fired! Following the

Archduke's death, millions of people would die over the next

five years.
```

- *Commas and semicolons.* These marks are always followed by only one space.

```
Medieval Europe, along with China and Japan, had some form of
moveable type by the fifteenth century. Both Western and
Eastern nations could print documents; however, only Western
nations developed printing on a massive scale.
```

- *Ellipses.* These punctuation marks are used to indicate words or text omitted from quoted material. Ellipses are typed using the period key with one space inserted between each dot. If the ellipses come at the end of a sentence, a fourth dot is added to serve as the period for the sentence quoted.

  If you are omitting an entire line or paragraph from quoted material, type a line of spaced dots from the left to right margin. In poetry, the dotted line is only as long as the line or paragraph of poetry omitted.

```
Lincoln stood on the podium, his tall, spare figure outlined
against the sky . . . The speech he gave that day lasted
exactly two minutes and forty-five seconds.
```

```
Those for and against nuclear energy both have deep
convictions about their respective points of view. . . .
```

```
Under the sloped snow
pinned all winter with Christmas
lights, we wait for your father
to whittle his soap cakes

. . . . . . . . . . . . . . . . . . . . . . . . . . . . .
Holding each other's coat sleeves we slide down the roads.
"As Children Together," Carolyn Forché
```

- *Brackets and Parentheses.* Square brackets [ ] can either by typed or, if your typewriter does not have a bracket key, drawn in by hand with ink. Only one space precedes the first bracket and only one space follows the closing bracket. The same rule of space applies to parentheses.

```
In 1941 Churchill said, "This island [England] stands alone
against the gathering darkness of tyranny."
```

```
Studies have shown that as the speed limit drops to 55 miles
per hour, yearly traffic fatalities also drop (see Table 2).
```

- *Dashes and hyphens.* Dashes are made by typing two hyphens together with no spaces before, between, or after the marks. Hyphens are also used to join compound words or inclusive numbers and to mark word divisions. There are no spaces before or after hyphens.

```
The military is not a democracy--only the leaders can have
decision-making authority. If everyone was permitted to vote
on a military decision, nothing would ever be decided (see
Military Strategy, pages 44-52).
```

- *Italics and underlining.* Italics are used to mark book, magazine, movie, and play titles and to emphasize words. Some typewriters and word processors can insert italic type styles. In other cases, use the underscore key to indicate words that would appear italicized in type or to emphasize words or phrases. In general, underscore only the words, not the spaces between words. Punctuation immediately following, such as a comma, is also underscored.

  If you are emphasizing words in quoted material that are not stressed in the original, type the phrase *italics mine* or *emphasis mine* in parentheses at the end of the quotation.

```
     William Butler Yeats's autobiography, A Vision, tells
of his family's peculiar psychic abilities. He recalls one
instance in which he was imagining vividly what it would be
like to have a broken arm in a sling. Later that day, his
sister asked their mother, "When did William hurt his arm?"
(emphasis mine) Although Yeats had only imagined the event,
his sister had mentally "seen" it.
```

Word-Processing Tips

As the cost of word-processing equipment continues to come down, more students are preparing their papers on personal computers. If you are thinking about this step, or if you have a word processor already, here are a few tips to keep in mind.

Learn It Before You Need It

Do not try to learn a word-processing system a few days before your paper is due. To become competent on a computer takes time and some expert instruction or help. You will be under enough pressure to finish your research and writing without the added anguish of trying to master the basics of a word-processing software and hardware system.

If you know you want to learn word processing for your schoolwork, invest your time in courses that teach some of the more popular word-processing programs: WordPerfect, Microsoft Word, MacWrite, and others. Become familiar with your computer, printer, and software before you need it for your reports and term papers. This step can save you a good deal of gnashing of teeth and pulling of hair when it comes time to prepare your final paper.

Establish Good Computing Habits

Computers are complex, sensitive machines that require careful handling. Establish good working habits to save yourself from disastrous mistakes. The following are among the most important guidelines.

- *Make sure your equipment is properly wired and protected.* Check to see if you have a grounded electrical socket in the wall and make sure you have installed a surge protector.

- *Keep your computer working area clear of clutter, food, or magnetized items.* Food or dirt getting into your system can damage the equipment. Magnetized scissors, toys, or other items can damage your computer's memory core and erase data on the diskettes.

- *Date all files.* When you first log onto your computer, insert the current date and time if you do not have an automatic calendar and clock. This will be extremely helpful to you in determining which version of your paper is the latest one.

- *Label all diskettes.* Nothing is more frustrating than knowing you have a completed paper somewhere on one of your disks—but which one? Put the name of your paper on the disk label along with any other information—such as *version 1* or *draft 1*.

- *Have a special storage box for your diskettes to protect them and keep them free of dust.*

- *SAVE, SAVE, SAVE!* This point cannot be stressed strongly enough. Save your work as you go, create backup files in case something happens to your original, and don't exit the word-processing program without making sure you have saved your work. In some word-processing programs, if you do not save before you exit, you not only lose all the work you have done, you also lose the automatic backup file.

A few moments observing these basic guidelines can save you hours of frustration and anguish retyping lost work. Computers are very unforgiving. If you lose your data and have no backup and no printout—your work is gone.

Learn the Special Functions

Most software word-processing programs have special functions that can streamline your work.

- *Page format.* This feature allows you to set margins, page numbering, line spacing, hyphenation, and headers automatically for the entire document.

- *Hard indentions.* In most word-processing programs, special function keys will set temporary margins for indented material. This can save you the bother of tabbing over from the left margin for each line of indented text you need to write.

- *Macros.* Macros are special codes that can be created easily when you have the same material to insert over and over. For example, a long title or complex name may crop up frequently in your work. You can create a macro by assigning a special code to that title or name. When you type the code, the computer will automatically insert the title or name for you.

- *Search and replace.* Suppose you finish your paper and then notice you have misspelled an important name throughout the text. Or perhaps you notice that in one instance you hyphenated a word and in another place you made it one word. The search and replace function will search for the incorrect word so that you can replace it with the correct term. With this feature, you can be sure you have not missed any incorrect names or words.

- *Editing features.* These special functions are the heart of most word-processing programs. They include the block and move, cut and paste, delete, center, copying, and overwriting functions. With them you can move sentences or blocks of text, delete them, write over them, copy them, and center them. Learn to use these features—they will make the task of preparing your report a great deal easier.

- *Split screen or window.* Many word-processing programs allow you to split the screen so that you can work on two "spaces" at once. This feature is especially helpful when it comes time to create the Works Cited list. You can split the screen and scroll through your report until you come to a reference. You then move to the window, type in the full reference, and continue scrolling through the text. This will ensure that you have accounted for all your references. All that remains is to alphabetize your Works Cited list.

- *Graphics.* Some word-processing software includes a simplified graphics program. You can use this program to create bar charts, graphs, flow diagrams, or other basic illustrations. More complex graphics usually require special software and extensive computer memory.

- *Thesaurus and spell checker.* Word-processing programs provide thesaurus and spell-checking features to help you choose the right word and proofread your text.

Advantages and Disadvantages of Word Processors

Like any other type of equipment, computers have their advantages and disadvantages.

The advantages include the automatic features that help you to set page format, edit material, create graphics, proof your spelling, and print out final copies. Changes and corrections can be made easily and new copies simply printed out. It is like having a magic slate to help you prepare your work.

The disadvantages of computers include their cost and the time it takes to master the word-processing programs. Also, if your system or disks are damaged, you can lose your entire paper before you have a chance to print out a copy. It is possible to delete a page or an entire file accidentally—particularly if you are working late and are tired or become careless. You are completely dependent on the computer's technology.

Proofreading

The final step before handing in your paper is to proofread it carefully. The best way to proofread your paper is to go through it systematically, looking for only one or two things at a time. If you try to proof for page numbers, spelling, grammar, and sense all at the same time, one or more of those elements will suffer. Follow this system for proofreading your paper.

1. *Check your format.* Make sure you have numbered your pages consecutively, maintained correct margins throughout, indented paragraphs and other material the correct number of spaces, and set up your title page, outline, table of contents, first page, and Works Cited pages correctly. Don't read the paper, simply check the format.

2. *Read through the paper for grammatical and spelling errors.* Don't read for content, just look at spelling and grammar elements. Do not rely on spell-checking programs to catch all spelling errors. If a word is spelled right but used incorrectly (*to* for *too* or *there* for *their*) the spell checker will not notice.

3. *Read through the paper for content.* Have you left out any words? Are your facts accurate? Have you referenced all your illustrations? Does your argument build logically?

By going through your paper systematically, you will catch far more errors than by trying to look for everything at once. If you have time, give your paper to someone else to proofread as added insurance against errors. You've put a lot of hard work into your paper—it deserves to be as error-free as you can possibly make it.

CHAPTER 9
Giving an Oral Presentation

On occasion, you will have to give an oral presentation based on your report or term paper. For many people, the prospect of giving a speech is even more intimidating than writing the report in the first place. Opinion surveys have found that speaking in front of a group ranks high on people's list of things they fear the most. The only items ahead of it are fear of dying a lingering, painful death and fear of losing members of one's family. As you can see, speaking in front of a group is equated with life-threatening situations!

The Four Rs of Public Speaking

If you fear public speaking, you're in good company. Winston Churchill, renowned for his ability to memorize, found that when he stood up in Parliament to give his first speech, he had forgotten everything he intended to say. Humiliated, he sat down without uttering a word.

Mahatma Gandhi had an even more unpromising beginning as a public speaker. When he rose to give his first speech before the Indian Congress in South Africa, he fainted from fright. He fainted the next three times he tried to give a speech. Eventually, he managed to reduce his fear and became a powerful public speaker. Even John F. Kennedy, whose public-speaking skills helped him win the U.S. presidency, often had to clamp his hands on the podium to keep them from shaking.

Each of these three people, like thousands of others, learned ways to manage their fear and speak comfortably in public. You can give successful oral presentations by learning the four Rs of public speaking: *Respond, Restructure, Rehearse, Relax.* When you put these four principles into practice, you can manage your fear and even enjoy speaking in front of a group.

Respond

The first R, *Respond*, involves two steps: responding to your material and responding to your audience. These key concepts can get you involved in your subject and help you tailor your oral report to your audience.

What Is Interesting about Your Subject?

Take a good look at your written report and ask yourself the following questions.

- *What do I find interesting about this subject?*
- *What made me want to write about it in the first place?*
- *What do I want to tell other people about this subject—what do I think they would like to know?*

You might have some surprising facts about a subject people think they know well. For example, the battle of Gettysburg started when a group of Confederate soldiers were out scavenging for boots and stumbled onto an advance unit of Yankee cavalry. This chance encounter touched off a chain of events that marked one of the major turning points of the Civil War.

Or you might address an issue that your audience is also concerned about—how to say "no" to drugs, whether abortion on demand should be legal in every state, how to handle the pressure to conform when you don't like what the group is doing.

It's important for you to get excited about communicating your topic to other people. If you're not interested in what you have to say, your audience will sense it and lose interest as well. Why should they pay attention if it's obvious you don't really want to be there?

On the other hand, by finding something about your topic you want to communicate, you are taking a big step toward mastering your fear.

Enthusiasm is infectious. Even if not everyone in the audience is interested in your topic, *your* interest in it can capture their attention.

Find the idea or facts that you believe can serve as the basis for a good report. Write them down, either free-writing, listing, or mapping them. These ideas are the structure on which you will build your oral presentation. For example, suppose you have written a report on modern superstitions. Your main idea may be that human beings in our highly technological, modern world are nearly as superstitious as our less sophisticated ancestors.

You might then list the types of superstitions we have and how we adjust our lives to accommodate these beliefs. Do people have lucky colors, numbers, days? What do superstitions do for us, and why do we seem to need them? What famous people are highly superstitious? These ideas are likely to capture your audience's attention.

Do You Know Your Audience?

The second step is to tailor your presentation to your audience. If you get excited about theories of time or of parallel universes, will you be able to talk about them at a level your audience will understand? How do these theories relate to their lives? Why should people care about them?

You need to know something about your listeners before developing your presentation. One way to accomplish this step is to draw up an "audience profile," like the one shown in Figure 9.1. After each category, jot down what you know about your audience. How many people will there be? What is their level of knowledge about the subject? What are they likely to be interested in? Does the composition of the group—gender, ethnic background, or age—make a difference?

FIGURE 9.1 Audience Profile

Number of people in the audience

_____

Their interest in topic

_____

Their level of knowledge about topic

_____

Composition or special considerations (gender, ethnic background, age, etc.)

_____

Other considerations

Once you feel more familiar with your audience, you can start tailoring your presentation. For example, instead of simply describing different theories of time, you might start out with questions to pique their interest. What would it be like to slow down time, speed it up, stop it? Is time travel really possible? What if you could reverse time? Imagine being able to live a day over again, this time getting everything right. You might relate your talk to various movies that have dealt with the subject of time travel—how realistic or probable are these movies according to current theories of time?

At this point, it is helpful to talk over our ideas with someone who may be in the audience (a member of your class) or who fits your audience profile. Find out if they think the ideas you have selected are appropriate for your audience and if your approach will communicate your ideas successfully.

Once you have completed the two steps of responding to your material and to your audience, you are ready to begin preparing your oral report.

Restructure

Most people feel they could get through an oral presentation if only they could read their report word-for-word. Not many instructors permit this approach. They consider—and rightly so—that a written report and an oral presentation require different formats.

As a result, you will give your talk either from an outline or note cards. This means you will need to use the second R, *Restructure,* and rework your report from its written form to an oral format.

In nearly all instances, you can use an inverted pyramid format for your presentation. As shown in Figure 9.2, the inverted pyramid begins with the most important facts, questions, summaries, or issues first. Information following supports or explains the most important elements of your talk. The final points reemphasize or restate your conclusions, argument, or main points.

FIGURE 9.2 Inverted Pyramid Order for Oral Presentations

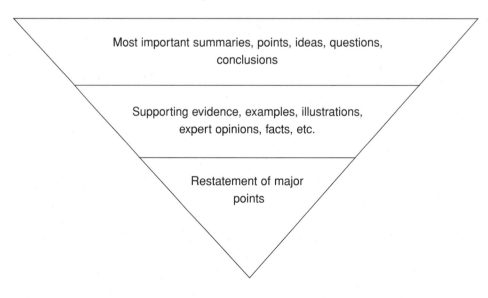

In a literary paper, for example, if your audience is unfamiliar with the book you are analyzing, your opening statements would be a brief summary of the story. Once everyone understands the basic conflicts and characters involved, you can continue with your analysis. If everyone already knows the story, you can begin with your major conclusions, opinions, or criticisms about the work and support them with examples, comparisons with other books by the author, and expert opinions.

The Outline Approach

In some cases your instructor may want you to work from an outline to make your presentation. Or you may find it easier to use an outline yourself. The main principle in using an outline is to construct one that is the most helpful to you in giving your talk. In some instances, key words or phrases may be all you need, as in the outline below.

```
    I. Modern people superstitious

       A. Lucky colors, numbers, days

       B. Sports, entertainment figures' superstitions

       C. Effects of superstitions on behavior

   II. Need for superstitions

       A. Why need them

       B. How they change

       C. What experts say

  III. Always need them?

       A. Always have uncertainty, unknown

       B. Need feelings of control

       C. Superstitions likely to change, but persist
```

This type of outline is good for a subject you are comfortable with and know well. You bring enough background and knowledge to the subject that you need only key words or phrases to trigger your thinking and the flow of your talk.

For less familiar topics, an outline that combines complete sentences and key words or phrases may be a better choice. This type of outline, presented below, gives more information on paper. If you find yourself suddenly at a loss for words, the sentences will help you orient your thoughts and pick up the thread of your talk.

```
    I. Although we live in a technologically sophisticated

       culture, we still believe in superstitions. Many of us

       avoid walking under open ladders, cringe when a black cat

       crosses our path, and declare that breaking a mirror means

       seven years' bad luck.
```

A. Nearly every one has lucky colors, numbers, or days.

B. Many sports and entertainment figures highly superstitious. Give examples.

C. Often go to ridiculous lengths to avoid or prevent "unlucky" situations. Give examples.

II. Apparently there is something in the human psyche that needs to believe in superstitions.

A. Feel superstitions can influence the outcome of events.

B. The type of superstitions has changed through history.

C. Experts say help us feel in control, safe.

III. As we continue to learn more about ourselves and the world, will we continue to need superstitions?

A. The unknown will always be with us.

B. Superstitions help control our fears.

C. As in the past, superstitions likely to change, but need for them persists.

The Note Card Approach

Some instructors require note cards for an oral presentation. Unlike an outline, which enables you to see the entire structure of your talk at a glance, note cards present one main idea at a time. While this approach has its drawbacks, you may be able to say more about each main point on a note card than you can on an outline. This can provide your memory with better cues.

It's a good idea to create an outline for your talk first, then transfer the main points to notecards. The outline format provides a check and balance against one main point receiving too much attention while another gets too little.

As in the outline format, you can use key words and phrases or sentences on your note cards (see Figure 9.3). Put only one or two main points on each card. Number the cards in the upper right-hand corner to prevent them from getting shuffled out of order.

Audiovisual Aids

Finally, whether you use note cards or outlines, write down where in your talk you might use audiovisual aids—slides, graphs, photographs, charts, samples, or other illustrative material to enhance your listeners' understanding. If you are reporting on the destructive power of volcanic explosions, for example, you might display photographs of Mount St. Helen's eruption—before and after. The blast flattened trees for several miles around the volcano and tore 1200 feet off the height of the mountain.

FIGURE 9.3   Note Cards for Oral Presentations

**Key Word
Format**

```
                                              ( 1 )

    I.   Modern people superstitious
         (Give examples from daily life that
         show how we are superstitious)
```

**Sentence
Format**

```
                                              ( 1 )

    I.   Despite our highly sophisticated,
         technological achievements, we
         are still superstitious people.
         —Lucky days and numbers
         —No thirteenth floor in many buildings
         —Black cat, broken mirror beliefs
```

While you can describe the destruction, a few photographs will *show* it. You can then use the time to talk about what the destruction means. The appropriate illustration or exhibit can add considerable impact to your talk.

Rehearse

Now that you have restructured your topic, you are ready for the third R, *Rehearse*. This step is perhaps the most important secret in giving an oral presentation. Think of it as similar to rehearsing lines in a drama, or practicing movements for a dance or gymnastics exhibition, or going over and over key plays in sports. You are preparing yourself to the best of your ability for your presentation.

Rehearsal involves five important steps.

1. Fit your talk to the time allowed.

2. Include any audiovisual aids you want to use.

3. Practice your talk in front of a mirror or before a "preview" audience of friends or family.

4. Adjust and correct your talk as you rehearse.

5. Arrange with your instructor ahead of time if you need audiovisual equipment or displays for your talk.

Fit Your Talk to the Time Allowed

Few things irritate an audience—or instructor—more than when a speaker runs over the time allowed. Some instructors have been known to use timers, alarms, or bells to cut off long-winded students. At the very least, they take a few points off the offender's grade.

Most oral presentations in class run from five to fifteen minutes. When you know your time limit, run through your presentation using a clock or watch to determine how long it takes. If you run over, study your outline to see what items you might eliminate or condense. If you are short of the limit, go back to your original paper and see what you might add to fill out the time.

Keep going over the talk until you have it as close to the allotted time as possible. You will make the final adjustments after you have included any audiovisual aids and given the talk before your practice audience.

Include Audiovisual Aids

Select only those slides, graphs, photographs, or illustrations that support your main points. Don't rely on the aids to tell your story for you, only to support your talk.

For example, if you are describing the sinking of the *Titanic*, do you need photographs of the *Titanic*'s sister ships, the dock where the ship was launched, and all the notable passengers? Or would it be better to summarize these facts briefly and instead show pictures of the ship as it was recently found at the bottom of the Atlantic? Such pictures would depict how the ship settled and show various artifacts still intact after some seventy years. The more recent photos could make the subject vivid and immediate to your listeners.

Practice Your Talk before an Audience

Once you have trimmed down your talk to the allotted time and selected any audiovisual aids, you are ready for your first dress rehearsal. Ask your friends, roommates, or family members to act as a live audience. Ask them to critique the following elements.

- Is the content informative and interesting?
- Is the talk well organized, do ideas flow in a logical manner?
- Do the illustrations, if any, seem appropriate?
- Do you present a good appearance and deliver your speech well? Do you talk too softly, slowly, quickly, loudly?
- Do you have any distracting mannerisms such as twirling your pencil, tugging at your ear, clearing your throat too often, or jiggling keys or change in your pockets while you talk?

If you don't have an audience to critique your talk, record your presentation on audio- or videotape, or give the talk in front of a full-length mirror. As you listen to or watch yourself, ask the questions listed above. You may be amazed at what you hear or see—personal quirks that are so automatic you are unaware of them.

One student, for example had no idea that after nearly every sentence she interjected an annoying "uuuhh." Only when she played back her recorded presentation did she hear this distracting mannerism. It made her sound unsure and timid. She was able to correct the problem and deliver a better talk.

Adjust and Correct Your Talk

Feedback on your practice talk is likely to focus on content and your delivery. You might find that your illustrations are not clear or that they come in the wrong place. Perhaps your main point is mentioned only at the end of your talk. Maybe you speak too softly or gradually increase the pace until you are speed-speaking by the end of your talk.

If you need to remember to speak more slowly or to pause in certain places, write a note to yourself on your outline or notecards. It is a well-known phenomenon that people's sense of time undergoes strange distortions when they are under stress. Most people tend to speed up when they talk in front of others, as if trying to hurry through what seems like an endless experience.

Be aware that this is likely to happen to you, and make a note on your cards to speak slowly. Don't rely on memory. Strong emotions can wipe out the mental notes you make to yourself. Even if you feel you are speaking too slowly, chances are you sound normal to your audience. Remember, their sense of time passing during your talk is likely to be quite different from yours.

Whatever the criticism, listen to it carefully, make adjustments and run through the talk again. Don't expect to get it right the first time . . . or even the second or third. The main point is to rehearse enough so that when it comes time for you to give your talk, you feel confident and prepared.

Make Arrangements for Your Presentation

Part of good preparation is making sure you have all the equipment and aids you need for your talk. Check with your instructor beforehand if you will require an overhead projector, slide projector, standup easels, display board, or other equipment. Are there sufficient electrical outlets handy? Will you need an extension cord or extra light for the projectors? Are there other students who need the same equipment? It may be that you can share projectors or display boards.

If it is appropriate, you might recruit one of your friends to handle the equipment or visual aids for you while you give your talk. In that way, you are free to concentrate on what you have to say while someone else is responsible for changing slides or display boards.

Relax

You've responded, restructured, and rehearsed. You're fully prepared—and still terrified. Now comes the last and least understood of the four Rs: *Relax.* There are two parts to this step: understanding the physiology of fear, and learning strategies to manage it.

Notice that the word is *manage* fear, not *eliminate* or *master* it. Being afraid in a new or unfamiliar situation is normal. It is not possible or desirable to eliminate your fear. Rather, your goal is to keep it within limits so that it does not paralyze or disable you.

Understanding the Physiology of Fear

When you face a threatening situation, your sympathetic nervous system moves into action. Hormones from your adrenal glands pour into your bloodstream, increasing heart rate and breathing rate, constricting blood supply to your organs and increasing it to your muscles, and galvanizing your entire body to fight or flee. Normally, when the threat is over, your parasympathetic nervous system shuts off the fight-or-flight reaction and restores your body to its normal state.

But in a case of prolonged threat, as the prospect of an oral presentation is likely to be, the parasympathetic system does not have a chance to shut off your red alert. You continue to pump adrenaline into your system and stay in a hyperactive state. After a time, your muscles tense, resulting in headaches, nervous tics, and backaches. Your hands and feet may feel cold or you may find yourself perspiring a great deal. You may become nauseated or develop diarrhea or both.

Because your breathing tends to be rapid and shallow, you may not be sending enough oxygen to your brain. This phenomenon is one of the factors behind the experience frightened people have of their minds "going blank." They cannot remember even the most basic facts, let alone what they have to say in a formal talk.

How do you get yourself calmed down enough to be simply nervous, and not terrified?

Strategies to Manage Your Fear

The secret to managing fear lies in a simple principle: *It is impossible to be physically relaxed and emotionally terrified at the same time.*

The art is in learning how to relax yourself when you are in a state of fight or flight. The key words in this process are breathing, moving, and supporting yourself.

The first step is to *breathe*. You breathe more rapidly when you are afraid. Deliberately take slower, deeper breaths.

The change in breathing pattern has a dramatic physiological effect. It signals the body that the emergency is not life-threatening. No one is going to shoot you if your talk doesn't go exactly as planned. Deeper breathing also can relieve the nausea you may experience and calm down your intestinal tract. As your body relaxes, your emotional anxiety also declines.

The second step is to *move*. Walk around, do aerobics, exercise. This burns up some of the adrenaline in your body, and signals your brain that the emergency is not so severe.

When you are in class waiting for your turn, deliberately tense and relax your legs, hands, and arms as you sit in your chair. Focus on slowing down your breathing. Give your body something to do that reduces the fight or flight response.

The third step is to *support* yourself emotionally. Does it help to have a podium in front of you? Arrange beforehand to make eye contact with a friend in the audience so you feel supported when you give your talk.

If you don't know anyone in the audience well enough, pick out a spot in the back of the room and imagine a friendly face there. Emotional support helps you to feel less isolated and exposed during your talk and reduces your fear.

Also, make sure that you arrange the podium, microphone, or other aids to be comfortable for you. If you have to bend over or stand on your tiptoes to speak into the mike, you are not going to be very relaxed. You have the right to adjust equipment or props to meet your needs.

Remember, the idea is not to eliminate your fear but simply to reduce it to manageable levels. A certain amount of adrenaline is good—it makes your perceptions sharper, your reactions quicker, and your thinking clearer. But too much adrenaline overwhelms your body and has the opposite effect. You tend to develop tunnel vision, over- or underreact, and have difficulty thinking.

By changing your breathing patterns, engaging in some type of physical movement, and getting emotional support, you can relax enough to actually enjoy being in front of people. You may want to write on your outline or note cards the three key words: *breathe, move, support.*

Oral Presentation Checklist

Here is a checklist of the main points covered in this chapter. Each time you are required to give an oral report, review the checklist to make sure you are fully prepared.

1. *Respond*
   - *To your subject:* Have you picked out the ideas or facts that interest you and that can serve as the basis for your presentation?
   - *To your audience:* do you know the composition of the group and their level of knowledge and interest in your subject?

2. *Restructure*
   - Have you used the inverted pyramid format to put the most important facts, conclusions, summaries, or arguments first?
   - If you use the outline approach to create your talk, will key words suffice, or do you need to use complete sentences?
   - If you use the note card approach, have you placed only one or two key points on each card? Have you numbered your cards?
   - Have you marked in your talk where and what type of audiovisual aids you might use?

3. *Rehearse*
   - Does the length of your talk fit the time allowed?
   - Have you rehearsed in front of a practice audience, recorded yourself, or given the talk before a mirror?
   - Have you incorporated any criticisms into your revised presentation?

- Have you made notes on your outline or cards of things you need to remember during your talk (such as *speak more slowly, loudly—look up at the audience*)?

- Do you present a good appearance and is your talk free of distracting mannerisms?

- Have you made prior arrangements with your instructor for any equipment you may need?

- Have you prepared all your materials the day or night before your presentation so you won't forget anything?

4. *Relax*

- Do you understand how you can breathe, move, and gain emotional support to manage your fear?

- Have you written on your outline or note cards to *breathe, move,* and *support* yourself before and during your talk?

- Can you arrange with friends to make eye contact with you during your talk or to help you with audiovisual equipment or displays?

APPENDIX A
Writing and Research

Many books on research and writing are published each year, but the ones listed below have proved to be among the most valuable for beginning writers. Nearly all of these books are available in paperback editions at local bookstores. They can help you to improve your writing not only during your academic career but on the job as well.

Topics for Research

Lamm, Kathryn. *10,000 Ideas for Term Papers, Projects, and Reports.* 3rd ed. New York: Arco, 1991. An indispensable book that groups topics according to 130 general subjects ranging from architecture to zoology. The author also provides key questions on the topics and lists major reference materials as a starting point for your research.

Miller, Walter James. *Sourcebook for English Papers: 1001 Ideas for Term Papers, Projects, Reports, and Speeches.* New York: Arco, 1987. The author suggests hundreds of literary topics and breaks them down according to theme, level of difficulty, and availability of information. The author also provides questions for research.

Research Guides

Beasley, David. *How to Use a Research Library.* New York: Oxford UP, 1988. An authoritative guide on locating and using materials from research libraries, including an excellent section describing computer-assisted research.

Croteau, Maureen and Wayne Worchester. *The Essential Researcher.* New York: Harper Perennial, 1993. A practical guide to resources in many research fields. Includes print, online, and CD-ROM sources.

Felknor, Bruce L. *How to Look Things Up and Find Things Out.* New York: Quill, 1988. An excellent book to help you locate key references for any discipline in the school curriculum. This book makes your research time count.

Metter, Ellen. *The Writer's Ultimate Research Guide.* Cincinnati: Writer's Digest Books, 1995. Complete information on how to find and use the latest research available. Gives addresses and phone numbers of many institutions, agencies, and private organizations.

Writing with Style

Gibaldi, Joseph. *MLA Handbook for Writers of Research Papers.* 4th ed. New York: Modern Language Association, 1995. Style guide used by most high schools, colleges, and universities for term papers and reports. Make sure you have the latest edition.

Howard, V. A., and J. H. Barton. *Thinking on Paper.* New York: Quill/Morrow, 1986. Learning by writing—how to generate, express, and refine ideas by understanding the processes of the mind when applied to writing.

Kane, Thomas S. *The New Oxford Guide to Writing.* New York: Oxford UP, 1988. Covers every aspect of the writing process and shows the reader how to write with more color, clarity, and force.

Kaye, Sanford. *Writing under Pressure: The Quick Writing Process.* New York: Oxford UP, 1987. Knowledgeable tips for overcoming writer's block, breaking any topic into manageable bits, getting started, and revising your work.

Miller, Casey, and Kate Swift. *The Handbook of Nonsexist Writing*. 2nd ed. New York: HarperCollins, 1988. Practical guidelines for using inclusive language in your writing.

Payne, Lucille Vaughan. *The Lively Art of Writing*. New York: NAL/Dutton, 1989. An excellent guide to mastery of writing reports and term papers. Written in an appealing, wonderfully readable style.

Strunk, William, Jr., and E. B. White. *The Elements of Style*. New York: Macmillan. Still one of the best books available on how to write well. Highly recommended—again, make sure you have the latest edition.

APPENDIX B

Sample Term Papers and Reports

The sample term papers and reports in this appendix show how the principles and elements discussed in the text are applied. *Some of the references in the Works Cited or Works Consulted lists have been inserted solely for the purposes of illustration. These references are not authentic and should not be cited or used in your own papers.*

This appendix contains examples of the four types of papers—argumentative, position, descriptive, and literary. Key elements and concepts pertinent to each paper are noted in the margins to highlight their use by the writers.

Descriptive Paper

Ainsle 1

Darryl Ainsle
Mrs. Aracebo
English 205
March 15, 19--

Taking Out the Radioactive Trash

What do you do with something that is harmful to plant and animal life; cannot be burned, sent into outer space, or dumped in a landfill; and can remain deadly for up to 10,000 years? That is the problem facing today's waste engineers and nuclear scientists who have to "take out the radioactive trash," waste materials generated by the use of nuclear energy and nuclear products. These engineers and scientists must find ways to store the world's growing stockpile of nuclear byproducts without harming the environment. They realize that solutions for disposing and storing radioactive waste must solve the problem not just for one generation but for many generations to come.

Radioactive waste is produced by a wide range of processes used in industry, science, and medicine. Waste materials include clothing, equipment, chemicals, contaminated soil and water, and nuclear fuel rods. The health risk of radioactive materials is related not only to the high-energy alpha, beta, and gamma rays they emit but also to their half-life or how long they remain radioactive (Altman 8-9). The "half-life" of radioactive materials refers to the time it takes for half the atoms to break down into a stable, harmless form. The half-life of some isotopes, especially those artificially made, can last less than a billionth of a second (Altman 8-9). On the other hand, the half-life of plutonium is about 5,000 years (Altman 9).

Question as opening to catch reader's attention

Thesis statement

Background information

Ainsle 2

The uses of radioactive compounds are widespread in industry. For example, food manufacturers use radioactive isotopes to irradiate food and kill harmful bacteria and other microorganisms (Joseph and Wells 23-24). Manufacturing companies also produce radioactive waste when they mine uranium, build nuclear weapons, and conduct nuclear research (Altman 11-12). In science and medicine, radioactive compounds and isotopes are used to diagnose diseases, treat cancer and other disorders, and aid in research (Sheldrake and Bouton 28-31). In medicine, for example, radioactive isotopes are used to trace the action of certain drugs through the body and to determine how well specific organs are functioning (Sheldrake and Bouton 32-33). These isotopes can also be used in chemotherapy to target cancer cells and destroy tumors.

Radioactive waste is divided into three categories: low-level, moderate-level, and high-level radioactive materials (Joseph and Wells 17-18; Zuefle 3). Each type of waste poses different health risks and requires different kinds of containment for safe disposal.

Low-level radioactive waste consists of clothing, such as gloves, overalls, and footwear, and protective equipment used by people who work with radioactive materials (Zuefle 3-4). This type of waste emits primarily alpha rays, which can be stopped easily by even thin barriers such as skin, clothing, paper, wood, or glass. The materials pose little health hazard to humans unless radioactive particles are inhaled or swallowed. Once in the lungs or digestive tract, they can cause cellular mutations and increase the risk for cancer of the lungs, colon, stomach, bladder, and rectum (Zuelfe 4-6).

Background information →

Setting up the topics to be discussed as the main points —

Describes what the materials are, their health risks, and disposal methods →

Ainsle 3

Low-level radioactive materials will decay to harmless
inert compounds within a few hours, weeks, or months.
These radioactive materials can be disposed of in sealed
metal containers and buried in only a few feet of earth
(Altman 25-26). Once the materials become nonradioactive,
they can be recovered and recycled (Altman 26;
Zuefle 6).

Moderate-level radioactive materials pose a more
difficult problem. They consist of nuclear byproducts,
such as radioactive isotopes (Sheldrake and Bouton 40-42).
In addition to alpha rays, these materials also emit beta
rays, which are higher energy particles than alpha rays.
Beta rays also present a graver risk to human health and
to other life forms. Exposure to these rays can result in
skin burns, illness, tumors, and significantly increased
risk for cancer (Altman 31). Beta rays travel nearly twice
as far as alpha rays and are stopped by one to three
inches of wood, glass, steel, or concrete (Joseph and
Wells 22).

Moderate-level radioactive waste is usually stored in
sealed steel canisters and buried deep underground or
deposited in designated ocean sites (Zuefle 7). However,
in some storage areas, seawater has corroded these
canisters and radioactive materials have leaked into the
surrounding waters (Zuefle 7-8). Canisters buried
underground in some sites have also leaked, contaminating
ground water which feeds into municipal water supplies.
Waste management companies and government scientists are
working on new types of containers and new sealing methods
to eliminate the problem of the accidental release of
radioactive waste into the environment.

Shows
increasing
levels of
danger to
human health

Describes
storage
problems

Ainsle 4

Establishes
this category
as the
greatest risk

High-level radioactive materials are those that emit dangerous, high-energy gamma rays. These rays can travel several miles and are stopped only by heavy shielding-- either several inches of lead or several feet of solid concrete (Lin 42; Zuefle 9). Direct exposure to gamma rays for even a few minutes can cause severe burns, radiation sickness, and death (Altman 33-34). The most hazardous of the high-level radioactive materials is plutonium, a byproduct of nuclear power plants and nuclear weapons

Details given
to show
magnitude of
the problem

manufacture (Joseph and Wells 26). Not only are these materials highly toxic, they will remain deadly for several thousand years. They must be heavily shielded from all contact with the environment; and their containment area must be earthquake proof, flood proof, fire proof, and tamper proof for several thousand years (Zuefle 9-10). As one scientist put it, "If the ancient Egyptians had used nuclear energy, we would still have to deal with their waste products--4,000 years later" (Zuefle 9).

Scientists and government officials are trying to design safe, secure containment and storage for high-level radioactive waste. One proposal under consideration would place an underground storage vault deep in the mountains in western Nevada (Lin, 48; Zuefle 12-13). According to

Discusses
one proposed
solution

geologists, this area appears to be among the most geologically stable in the country. However, no one can predict whether the earth will cooperate with government plans. There is no guarantee that a selected site will remain geologically stable for several thousand years. Should an earthquake break open a high-level radioactive waste site, the release of deadly radiation could contaminate an area covering several thousand square miles (Zuefle 14).

Ainsle 5

Plans for one type of storage vault, shown in the figure on page 6, include constructing an underground chamber, lined with concrete, some 2,000 feet below the surface (Altman 48; Lin 49-50). High-level radioactive material would be sealed in lead containers and lowered through air shafts into the vault below (Lin 49). The containers would be packed by automated equipment into the concrete flooring--like eggs in a carton. The advantage of this method is that it would isolate the material from the environment and provide permanent storage away from human settlements (Altman 50). The disadvantage is the cost and the risk of possible earthquake damage to the vault.

Clearly, disposing of nuclear waste is a lot more complicated than simply "taking out the trash." Because of the long life of some of these materials, any containment must protect not only today's generation but hundreds of generations to come. In particular, no secure, long-term method of storing and containing high-level radioactive waste materials currently exists. Perhaps the solution lies in permanent, underground vaults. In a sense, this approach would bring the nuclear industry full circle. People have taken uranium out of the earth to use in industry, science, and medicine; they would be putting the radioactive waste materials back into the earth for permanent safekeeping.

Describes the solution in more detail

Conclusion restates thesis statement and underscores nature of the dilemma

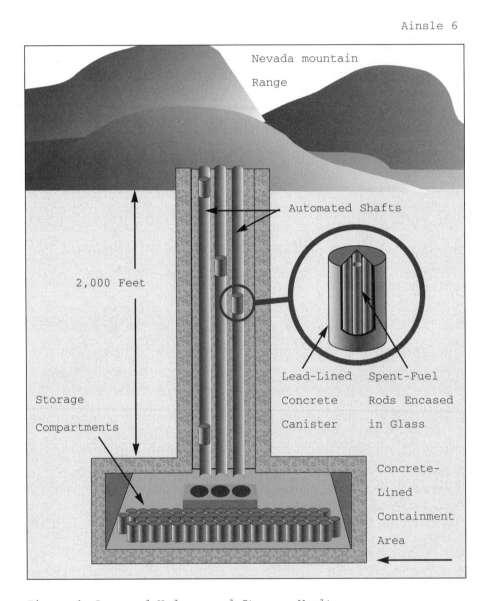

Figure 1 Proposed Underground Storage Vault

Source: Altman, Helen. Radioactive Waste: The 10,000 Year
        Dilemma. New York: Morrow, 1992. p. 150.

Ainsle 7

Works Cited

Altman, Helen. <u>Radioactive Waste: The 10,000 Year Dilemma</u>.
    New York: Morrow, 1992.

Joseph, Bernard, and Theodore Wells. <u>Nuclear Waste</u>. San
    Francisco: HarperCollins, 1993.

Lin, Chou-San. "Why Can't We Send It into Outer Space?"
    <u>Nuclear News</u> 8 July 1993: 42-50+.

Sheldrake, Carla and Edward Bouton. "Nuclear Waste in the
    Medical Industry." <u>Guidance Information Systems</u>. 18th
    ed. Diskette. Cambridge: Riverside, Houghton, 1993.

Zuefle, Norman. "Long-Term Storage Problems in Nuclear
    Waste Disposal." <u>Nuclear Technology</u> 3.401 (5 May
    1993): 15 pages. Online. BITNET. 4 Jul 1993.

Position Paper

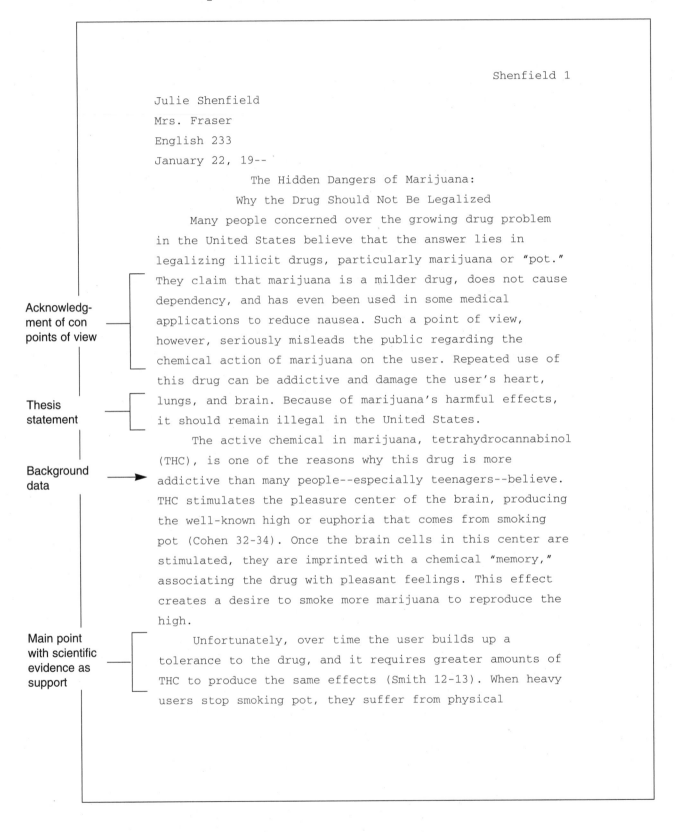

Shenfield 1

Julie Shenfield
Mrs. Fraser
English 233
January 22, 19--

The Hidden Dangers of Marijuana:
Why the Drug Should Not Be Legalized

Many people concerned over the growing drug problem in the United States believe that the answer lies in legalizing illicit drugs, particularly marijuana or "pot." They claim that marijuana is a milder drug, does not cause dependency, and has even been used in some medical applications to reduce nausea. Such a point of view, however, seriously misleads the public regarding the chemical action of marijuana on the user. Repeated use of this drug can be addictive and damage the user's heart, lungs, and brain. Because of marijuana's harmful effects, it should remain illegal in the United States.

The active chemical in marijuana, tetrahydrocannabinol (THC), is one of the reasons why this drug is more addictive than many people--especially teenagers--believe. THC stimulates the pleasure center of the brain, producing the well-known high or euphoria that comes from smoking pot (Cohen 32-34). Once the brain cells in this center are stimulated, they are imprinted with a chemical "memory," associating the drug with pleasant feelings. This effect creates a desire to smoke more marijuana to reproduce the high.

Unfortunately, over time the user builds up a tolerance to the drug, and it requires greater amounts of THC to produce the same effects (Smith 12-13). When heavy users stop smoking pot, they suffer from physical

Acknowledgment of con points of view

Thesis statement

Background data

Main point with scientific evidence as support

Shenfield 2

withdrawal symptoms, including irritability, sleep
disorders, digestive problems, and loss of appetite. These
reactions show that marijuana is physically, as well as
psychologically, addictive. In addition, people who develop
high tolerances to marijuana must turn to other, more
potent drugs such as heroin, crack, cocaine, barbiturates,
and even LSD to get the same high they used to achieve
with pot. These more potent drugs are far more addicting
and can lead to sudden death.

Marijuana is not only addictive but it damages the
user's health as well (see figure on page 3). As indicated
in the figure, continued use of the drug can harm the
immune defenses of the lungs (Cohen 63). Alveola
macrophages, the cells designed to attack and destroy
foreign material and bacteria entering the lungs, are
far less effective when they come into repeated contact
with THC and other chemicals in pot. Regular marijuana
smokers suffer from chronic bronchitis, chest pain,
sinusitis, and other respiratory ailments. Pot also changes
the heart function, increasing the heart rate by as much
as 50 percent. In addition, marijuana smoke contains at
least as much carbon monoxide as tobacco and adversely
affects the circulatory system. Carbon monoxide molecules
bind with red blood cells and reduce the amount of oxygen
in the blood.

Along with the lungs and heart, the brain is also
affected by continued use of marijuana, as shown in the
figure. Studies of brain wave activity in adolescent pot
smokers revealed that each adolescent's brain suffered from
an inability to produce fast beta wave activity (Heath
70). Inhibited beta waves mean inhibited powers of problem

Main point
detailing
further harm
of drug and
strengthening
writer's
position

Main point
showing most
critical harmful
effect on
user's lifestyle

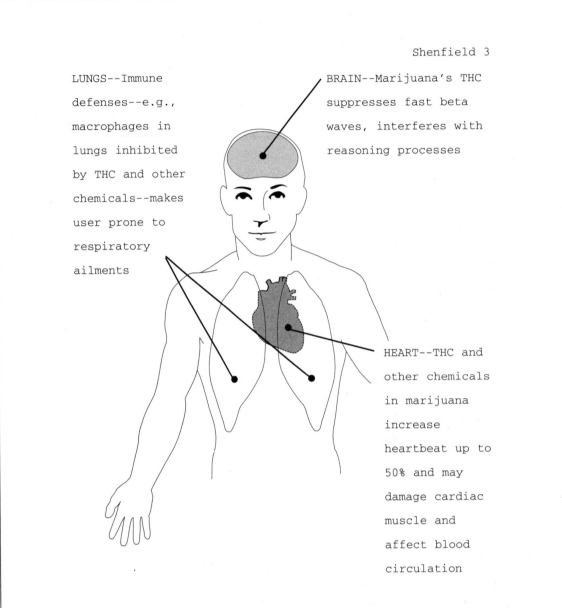

Shenfield 3

LUNGS--Immune defenses--e.g., macrophages in lungs inhibited by THC and other chemicals--makes user prone to respiratory ailments

BRAIN--Marijuana's THC suppresses fast beta waves, interferes with reasoning processes

HEART--THC and other chemicals in marijuana increase heartbeat up to 50% and may damage cardiac muscle and affect blood circulation

Figure 1 Effects of Marijuana on Heart, Lungs, Brain of Users

Source: Snyder, S. H. <u>Effects of Marijuana on Mind and Body</u>. New York: Wiley, 1988. p. 42

Shenfield 4

solving, discrimination, and analysis. Thus, marijuana can affect a user's ability to learn, assimilate, and remember information. Users become less able to handle schoolwork or deal effectively with personal problems and stresses.

Legalizing pot would do nothing to eliminate the harmful effects of marijuana. Because marijuana is a highly sensitive plant, the government could not control the quantity of THC in the plants it would grow. Climate, soil conditions, altitude, and processing all affect the THC levels in the plant (Wellington 25). If THC levels are too low, users would not get the chemical reaction they want. Instead, they would turn to black market suppliers who could provide more potent forms of the drug. An active black market would negate the very goal of legalizing pot--to regulate its use and cut down on the number of those addicted to the drug.

Because marijuana produces numerous harmful effects, it should remain illegal in the United States. Clearly, those who feel that marijuana should be legalized have not examined the facts carefully and overestimate the government's ability to regulate this drug. The damage marijuana produces in the heart, lungs, and brain is significant and may be irreversible. At the very least it impairs the quality of life for heavy users. Admittedly, the United States has a serious drug problem. The answer, however, lies not in legalizing illicit drugs but in educating young people about the damage even so-called mild drugs like marijuana can inflict on users.

Major point to which all other points have built

Restatement of thesis and discussion of supporting rationale based on evidence presented

Shenfield 5

Works Cited

Cohen, Miriam. "Marijuana: Its Effects on Mind & Body."
     <u>Encyclopedia of Psychoactive Drugs</u>. Ed. Solomon H.
     Snyder. New York: Chelsea, 1985.

Heath, Robert G. <u>Marijuana and the Brain</u>. Rockville, MD:
     American Council on Marijuana, 1981.

Smith, Teresa R. "Tolerance to THC in marijuana and dosage
     levels in heavy users." <u>Psychopharmacology</u> 14 (1988):
     12-15.

Snyder, S. H. <u>Effects of Marijuana on Mind and Body</u>. New
     York: Wiley, 1988.

Argumentative Paper

Paula Juralski
Prof. Peter Russell
English 256
May 24, 19--

Outline

Introduction--Because censorship not only reduces the quality of education students receive but directly violates their basic constitutional rights, censorship of books in the educational system should not be allowed in the United States.

I.   Con--It is true that educators and parents have the right to choose the textbooks and reading matter they feel provide the best education for students.

   Pro--But educators and parents should not be given the right to censor books, or students will be denied the right to investigate the truth and examine ideas.

II. Con--It is also true that parents and educators have a responsibility to protect children from "harmful ideas."

   Pro--Criteria for "harmful" changes must be defined in a broader context than simply ideas or beliefs that contradict a parent's or educator's.

III. Obscenity is often used as a criteria for censorship, but the notion of what is obscene changes with generations.

   A. What is obscene one generation, harmless the next
      1. Clothing example
      2. Hawthorne's <u>The Scarlet Letter</u>
   B. Obscenity refers to an emotional state, therefore must censor all activities that cause sexual arousal

        1. Survey of boys aged 12 to 16

        2. Censorship of books inconsistent

Conclusion--Censorship in education reduces the quality of education students receive and contradicts the very principles of democracy that schools should be teaching.

IV. Most censors act in their own interests rather than in the best interests of the students

    A. Avoid facts of adolescents' lives

    B. Create false picture of reality

    C. Try to bury the past (<u>Uncle Tom's Cabin</u>).

V. By limiting information students can receive, censorship seriously reduces the quality of education students are given.

    A. Forced to see world through someone else's eyes

        1. Poem about rape censored

        2. Message--don't talk about experiences

    B. Adolescents need to develop own ideas and views

VI. More importantly, censorship strikes at the heart of a democratic society and its institutions.

    A. Critical review should expand range of ideas

    B. Purpose of democratic education to teach students to form own opinions (<u>Pico</u> case)

VII. Finally, censorship is a direct violation of Constitutional rights guaranteeing freedom of speech, press, and expression.

    A. First Amendment protects freedom of press

    B. Fourteenth Amendment applies First to individual states

    C. Provision for freedom of speech stated explicitly

    D. Democracy works only when individuals determine value of ideas

Juralski 3

Against Censorship of Books in Education

The Constitution of the United States guarantees people certain rights, including freedom of speech, freedom of press, and freedom of expression. These rights are essential not only to a democratic form of government but to the educational system that underlies it. At the present time, some individuals are challenging the right to the free expression of ideas by advocating the censoring of certain books in education. These censors believe that students should be protected from harmful ideas as expressed in certain works. Yet for the most part censors act only in their own interests, interfere with the educational process, and violate the very democratic principles they claim to uphold. Because censorship not only reduces the quality of education students receive but directly violates their basic Constitutional rights, censorship of books in the educational system should not be allowed in the United States.

It is true that educators and parents have the right to choose the textbooks and reading matter they feel provide the best education for students. Indeed, education consists of a selective presentation and explanation of ideas. Justice Rehnquist of the U.S. Supreme Court defends this position by saying, "The effective acquisition of knowledge depends upon an orderly exposure to relevant information" (Sweet 685). But if educators are given the right not merely to choose books but to censor them, then students will be denied the fundamental right to investigate the truth and examine ideas wherever and however they wish (Cutright 14).

It is also true that parents and educators have a responsibility to protect children from "harmful ideas"

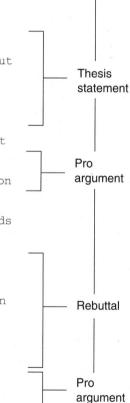

Thesis statement

Pro argument

Rebuttal

Pro argument

Juralski 4

Rebuttal

(Pincus 146). But the criteria for what is deemed "harmful" or "offensive" change with each generation. The table on page 5 provides a list of books banned at one time and the reasons censors gave for banning them. As the table shows, many books once considered harmful for students to read are among the classic works of literature whose insights into human nature cut across generational and cultural lines. As a result, harmful ideas need to be defined in a broader context than simply ideas or beliefs that contradict a parent's or educator's views (Rogers 105). As Donald Rogers states in his book on censorship in the schools:

Supporting data from experts

> . . . as human beings, we will seldom find a perfect balance between the need to protect and the right to honor. The golden mean will often exceed our grasp. But, whether we emphasize protection or knowledge, let us all strive for the wisdom to respect points of view that differ from our own. (106)

Censors have the burden of providing a clear connection between a harmful idea and actual damage to a child or a community--a connection that so far has never been proved satisfactorily (Rogers 105).

Specific examples supporting main point

The most common criteria used to define harmful ideas, particularly regarding materials for young people, is the charge of obscenity. However, as in the case of political or social ideas, the concept of what constitutes "obscene" material is highly dependent on cultural and social context. For example, some people now in their 80s may still remember when it was considered immoral for a woman to wear a skirt that showed her ankles. A hundred

Juralski 5

Table

Works Banned by Various Groups

Book	Reason for banning the book
Baum, THE WIZARD OF OZ	inappropriate for children, not literary
Carroll, ALICE'S ADVENTURES IN WONDERLAND	culturally, ethically unsuitable, not literature
Childress, A HERO AIN'T NOTHING BUT A SANDWICH	Too ethnic, inappropriate for young readers, obscene, antireligious, portrays unethical behavior
Dante, THE DIVINE COMEDY	obscene, too political, pornographic
Frank, ANNE FRANK: THE DIARY OF A YOUNG GIRL	inappropriate for young readers, obscene
Hawthorne, THE SCARLET LETTER	inappropriate for young readers, obscene, and portrays unethical behavior
Hughes, THE BEST SHORT STORIES OF NEGRO WRITERS	too ethnic, inappropriate for young readers, obscene, unethical, not literature
Salinger, CATCHER IN THE RYE	inappropriate for young readers, objectionable language, obscene, too political, antireligious, unethical
Sendak, WHERE THE WILD THINGS ARE	inappropriate for young readers, not literature
Steinbeck, GRAPES OF WRATH	inappropriate for young readers, objectionable language, too political, antireligious
Twain, THE ADVENTURES OF HUCKLEBERRY FINN	antiblack, inappropriate for young readers, objectionable language, unethical behavior, not literature
White, CHARLOTTE'S WEB	inappropriate for young readers

Source: American Library Association, 1987

Juralski 6

Specific examples supporting main point

years ago, Nathaniel Hawthorne's <u>The Scarlet Letter</u>, dealing with the subject of adultery, was found unfit for modest maidens to read (Gelhorn 23). It is now considered a classic and is required reading in many high school and college English classes. Thus, what is regarded as obscene in one era is considered harmless in another.

The word obscenity itself refers to an emotional state of arousal rather than an object (Gelhorn 22). In a survey of boys aged 12 to 16, the years of adolescence which censors are so worried about, 85 percent of them reported "genital commotions" from carnival rides, playing a musical solo, driving a car fast, and watching parades (Wittenberg 246). Obviously censors would not consider banning these as obscene activities. Yet they believe that reading books which talk about sexuality will in some way irreparably damage young minds and souls. If censors want to ban books judged obscene because they arouse normal sexual behavior, they must also ban perfume, music, and warm spring nights that produce the same result.

Main points showing motives of censors, supported by examples

Thus, in banning books, most censors act more in their own self-interest than in the best interests of students. When they ban books that portray accurate pictures of adolescent life, such as Judy Blume's novels, they are essentially avoiding facts that may force them to look at the reality of their own children's lives (Broderick 44). For example, in Blume's novels, teenagers talk frankly about sex and discuss their fears and expectations. To pretend that teenagers are not interested in the subject or do not need to talk about it is turning a blind eye to the facts. More importantly, by eliminating what censors feel is harmful to society, they participate

Juralski 7

in creating a false picture of reality, attempting to mold future generations in their own image (Thomas 158).

In addition, some censors use book banning in an attempt to bury their own past. For example, some protesting black groups tried to ban Uncle Tom's Cabin because it depicted blacks in what they felt were unflattering terms (Brown 151). However, they ignored the fact that Mrs. Stowe made the slave owner the antagonist and the slave the protagonist of the story. The book not only advanced the abolitionist cause in the 1850s but today depicts how far relations between whites and blacks have come in this country. All in all, censors are serving their own private interests far more than the so-called public good.

By limiting the information adolescents receive about themselves and their world, censorship seriously limits the quality of education students receive. When books for adolescents that deal with such issues as puberty, sexuality, and the like are banned, censors are forcing adolescents to see the world through someone else's adult views. Such actions prevent them from developing their own creative concepts of the world (Broderick 48). In one particular case, a book of poems was censored because it contained a poem about rape written by a fifteen-year-old who had gone through the experience. The schoolboard, in defending their decision, said it was not a poem because it did not rhyme (Broderick 51).

The unstated message to the adolescents in the community was they could not talk about such experiences but had to hide them from adults. Adolescents should be encouraged to explore their thoughts and feelings without

Transition to main point highlighting harm of censorship

having to conform to censors' views about what is proper to explore and what is not. Thus, censorship limits adolescents' opportunities to develop the ability to discern right from wrong, truth from falsehood, appropriate versus inappropriate modes of behavior (Cutright 15).

Moving into major points

More importantly, censorship strikes at the heart of a democratic society and its institutions. Critical review of reading material should expand the range of books offered in education not limit it (Sweet 678). The purpose of education in a democracy is to allow children to form their own opinions, not to restrict their views to only those considered "acceptable" and "correct" (Rogers 105). The U.S. Supreme Court agreed with this view and ruled in the <u>Island Trees Board of Education v. Pico</u> case that:

> School officials may not remove books for the purpose of restricting access to the political ideas or social perspective discussed in them, when that action is motivated simply by the officials' disapproval of the ideas involved. (Sweet 684)

The principles of democracy promote the idea that through intellectual discussion and free debate lies the best chance of preserving a democratic way of life.

Final major point leading to close of argument

Finally, censorship is a direct violation of Constitutional rights guaranteeing free speech, press, and expression. The First Amendment forbids Congress to pass any laws that go against freedom of the press. The Fourteenth Amendment went so far as to make the First Amendment apply also to individual states, further prohibiting any restriction on the people's right to freedom of expression. Thus, these amendments assure the rights of people to express their views and judgments

Juralski 9

freely (Busha 66). Provisions in the Constitution for
freedom of speech state explicitly:

> Every citizen has the right to express his
> opinions freely in word, writing, or picture; to
> circulate them; and to obtain information without
> restrictions from generally accessible sources.
> (Busha 67)

Freedom of expression, as guaranteed in the
Constitution, expressly prohibits censorship of material.
The authors of the Constitution understood that democracy
can work only when individuals--not the government or one
supreme person acting for all--decide on the value of
ideas (Sheinfeld 205).

Unquestionably, books should not be censored in the
educational system in the United States. No one person or
group has the right or wisdom to decide what is proper and
appropriate for all people, whether adults or adolescents.
Censors not only serve their own self-interests more than
the best interests of students, but they contradict the
very principles of democracy the schools should be teaching
and reduce the quality of education students receive. Far
from protecting students from harmful ideas, censorship
makes it hard for students to investigate and discover the
truth for themselves. Indeed, the best protection against
harmful or negative ideas is not to ban books but to teach
students how to think in order to make wise choices. The
framers of the Constitution appear to have had this
concept in mind when they guaranteed to citizens in the
United States the inalienable rights of freedom of speech,
freedom of the press, and freedom of expression.

Conclusion and summary, leading reader from minor to major points

Juralski 10

Works Cited

Broderick, Dorothy M. "Adolescent Development and
    Censorship." <u>School Library Media Annual</u>. Eds. Shirley
    L. Aaron and Par R. Scules. Vol. 1. Colorado:
    Libraries, 1983. 43-53. 6 vols.

Brown, John Mason. "Wishing Banning." Downs 155-158.

Busha, Charles H. <u>Freedom vs. Suppression and Censorship</u>.
    Littleton: Libraries, 1972.

Cutright, Melilta. "Censorship--the debate over students'
    right to read." <u>PTA Today</u> 12-15 October 1982: 3.
    <u>SIRS: School</u>. vol. 2, art. 78.

Downs, Robert B., ed. <u>The First Freedom</u>. Chicago: ALA,
    1960.

Gelhorn, Walter. "Restraints on Book Reading." Downs 20-40.

O'Neill, Terry, ed. <u>Censorship--Opposing Viewpoints</u>. St.
    Paul: Greenhaven, 1985.

Pincus, Fred L. "The Left Must Guard American Values."
    O'Neill 163-166.

Rogers, Donald J. <u>Banned! Book Censorship in the Schools</u>.
    New York: Julian, 1988.

Sheinfeld, Lois. "The First Amendment Forbids Censorship."
    O'Neill 203-207.

Sweet, William. "Schoolbook Controversies." <u>Editorial
    Research Reports</u>. Ed. Hoyt Gimlin. Vol. 2. Washington,
    D.C.: Congressional, 1982. 673-692.

Thomas, Carl. "Radical Left Censorship Undermines
    Education." O'Neill 158-162.

Wittenburg, Philip. <u>The Protection of Literary Property</u>.
    Boston: Writer, 1978.

Literary Paper

The Problem of Motherhood
in Defoe's <u>Moll Flanders</u> and <u>Roxana</u>

Sara Rinehart
English Literature 203
Professor Perkins
May 25, 19--

Rinehart 1

The Problem of Motherhood

in Defoe's <u>Moll Flanders</u> and <u>Roxana</u>

The similarities and contrasts between Daniel Defoe's heroines Moll Flanders and Roxana have been described by many critics. Although the two women's affairs with numerous men have been examined carefully, their relationships with their children have attracted little critical attention. Moll and Roxana between them bear twenty-four children, but only two--Moll's son Humphry and Roxana's daughter Susan--are even named. The lack of details about the children is partly explained by the fact that both Moll and Roxana are telling only their own stories, not those of the people around them. This tendency of Moll and Roxana to concentrate on themselves and virtually to ignore their children has caused critics to label the two women as "unnatural mothers." In fact, Defoe uses the acceptance or rejection of motherhood as a final step in the redemption or ultimate fall of Moll Flanders and Roxana.

Of the two characters, Moll has the worst childhood and possibly the better excuse for being a poor mother. The daughter of a Newgate convict who is shipped abroad, Moll is left "in bad hands" at the age of about six months (34). Moll herself suggests that she might have turned out better if England had had orphanages:

> I had . . . been left a poor desolate girl
> without friends, without clothes, without help
> or helper in the world . . . by which I was not
> only exposed to very great distresses . . . but
> brought into a course of life which was not only
> scandalous in itself, but which in its ordinary

course tended to the swift destruction both of
soul and body. (33-34)

After the "bad hands" and some time with gypsies,
Moll is lodged with her first surrogate mother, who
genuinely cares for her: "she loved me very well" (35).
Such care should have averted some of the emotional shock
of being born and abandoned in a prison. However, after
her nurse's death, Moll is "turned out of doors to the
wide world" (41) and loses her resolution to be a
gentlewoman and earn her own living:

> The fright of my condition had made such an
> impression upon me, that I did not want now to
> be a gentlewoman, but was very willing to be a
> servant, and that any kind of servant they
> thought fit to have me be. (41)

Moll has the good fortune of being hired by a family
to be an upstairs servant. As such, she is always with the
daughters of the family and has "all the advantages of
education that I could have had if I had been as much a
gentlewoman as they were" (42). Unfortunately, she also
becomes the mistress of the older son, who promises,
should she become pregnant, "I'll take care of you and
provide for you, and the child too" (51). Moll wants to
believe that the oldest son means to marry her and ". . .
protect me from all the world" (54).

Moll's childhood illusions come to an end when she
realizes that the elder son has no intentions of marrying
her. Miriam Lerenbaum suggests that the illness Moll
suffers as a result marks her transition from child to
adult (106). Yet she fails to make the emotional
transition to adulthood. She is still looking for someone

to offer her stability. The older brother encourages her to marry another man by emphasizing that she will be protected and "come into a safe station" in life (59). It is this appeal that finally makes her accept her first husband:

> My imagination of being turned out to the world a mere cast-off whore . . . with little to provide for myself, with no friend, no acquaintance in the whole world, out of that town. . . . All this terrified me to the last degree. . . . (74)

In stark contrast to Moll's early beginnings, Roxana's childhood appears marked by good fortune and advantage. Her parents are "People of better Fashion" living in excellent circumstances:

> I wanted neither Wit, Beauty, or Money. In this Manner I set out into the World, having all the Advantages that any Young Woman cou'd desire, to recommend me to others, and form a Prospect of happy Living to myself. (6-7)

Yet there is a flaw in this ideal picture. Roxana's mother dies young and cannot advise her on the transition from childhood to adulthood. Her father turns out to be little help as well and is against her marriage, at age fifteen, to an older man.

After marriage Roxana's illusions of a happy life, like Moll's, are quickly dashed, and she is confronted by circumstances that force adulthood on her. After her father's death and the failure of her husband's business, she and her five children are left at the mercy of their relations. Like Moll, Roxana is suddenly thrust into the hard, cold world without adequate resources: "to think of one single Woman not bred to Work, and at a Loss where to get Employment, to get the Bread of five Children, that was not possible" (15). Although Roxana is physically and socially an adult, she is emotionally unequipped to manage her own life. She needs a mother or a keeper in order to survive.

As the stories of the two women unfold, Defoe develops this theme of the girl-woman searching for someone to take care of her. Moll continually reenacts her attempts to gain stability and protection from two sources: surrogate mothers and husband-keepers. The fact that she has children of her own does not seem to affect this search; her children all but disappear from the story soon after they are born. Moll's surrogate mothers include a string of landladies and companions that appear between husbands or keepers. They take charge of her life briefly, then transfer their charge to some man. Each time Moll believes she has found stability, only to have some act of fate intervene. In one instance she unknowingly marries her brother, thus coming to know her natural mother as her mother-in-law. When Moll discovers the secret, she leaves the marriage in horror; but it is her mother, not Moll herself, who attempts to arrange Moll's future:

> she promised to make me easy in my
> circumstances, as far as she was able, and to
> leave me what she could . . . I should not be
> left destitute, but be able to stand on my own
> feet. (109)

Of all the surrogate mothers who enter Moll's life,

her "governess" comes closest to fulfilling her need for stability. Robert A. Erickson suggests that the governess is Moll's "spiritual mother" (81) and points out that she seems to give birth to Moll by nursing her through an illness (80). Moll tries to get the governess to assume full responsibility for her life; "I agreed to put myself into her hands" (167-8). Instead, the governess pushes Moll to accept that responsibility herself and to become independent. Turning Moll away from a life of thievery, she does what she can to help the young woman grow up.

The task is not an easy one, as Defoe makes clear. Moll has made a career of marrying men as a form of protection, only to have the relationship end time after time. Although Moll says "a woman should never be kept for a mistress that had money to keep herself" (78), she really has no intention of keeping herself. "I was resolved now to be married or nothing, and to be well married or not at all," as she puts it (77). Her next four relationships follow the same pattern of courtship, marriage or liaison, dissolution of the relationship, and being cast out into the world alone. Although her marriage to Jemmy breaks the pattern somewhat--she ends up support- ing him--in the end he deserts her and she is left alone, friendless and pregnant.

Moll is unable to accept motherhood throughout her childbearing years. After her first husband's death, her two children are "taken happily off my hands by my husband's father and mother" (76). Her child by her second husband is dismissed in one sentence: "I had no child (I had had one by my gentleman draper, but it was buried)" (80-81). Moll has three children by her Bath lover, but only one survives. This surviving son assumes importance to her only when she realizes the boy can help her to persuade the Bath gentleman to give her money. When the gentleman volunteers to take care of the child if she wishes, Moll quickly accepts his offer (132). Her comment that "It was death to me to part with the child" is not particularly believable given the fact that she has already given up three children. Of her last two children by the banker, only one of them is ever heard from again, a little boy who is cared for by Moll's governess (195).

Her lack of "natural" maternal concern for her children in comparison with her concern for herself is also evident in her treatment of the children she had when married to her brother. When the news of Moll's true relationship to her husband comes out, she is clearly more concerned about the effect on herself than on her children. Although the children "would be ruined, too, having no legal claim to any of his effects," she is more devastated by the thought of seeing her husband "in the arms of another wife in a few months, and . . . myself the most miserable creature alive" (108-109). After Moll's mother figures out what she should do, the children mysteriously drop out of sight.

Moll's attitude and feelings about motherhood are nowhere more dramatically shown than in her relationship to her son by Jemmy. After she and Jemmy part, Moll must assume complete responsibility for the child. Even though she has money, the weight and anxiety of this responsibility makes her ill. While her son is on her hands, the burden is an "inexpressible misfortune" (172) and her "great and main difficulty" (173). Once the boy is taken off her hands, she can get on with her life again:

> And thus my great care was over, after a manner,
> which though it did not at all satisfy my mind,
> yet was the most convenient for me, as my
> affairs then stood, of any that could be thought
> of at that time. (177)

Moll's comments at this point provide the greatest insight into her as both mother and child herself. She deplores mothers who give away their children, yet she has done essentially the same thing with six of her own. Her subsequent words are even more revealing:

> We are born into the world helpless, and
> incapable either to supply our own wants or so
> much as make them known . . . without help we
> must perish; and this requires not only an
> assisting hand, whether of the mother or
> somebody else, but there are two things
> necessary in that assisting hand, that is, care
> and skill . . . . I question not but that these
> are partly the reasons why affection was placed
> by nature in the hearts of mothers to their
> children . . . (174)

Moll's words are both an indictment and a pardon of herself and her natural mother. Moll has not been able to assume responsibility for herself or her children, instead abandoning them to others as she was abandoned. Up to this point, neither she nor her mother possess the requisite "care and skill" to be good mothers; they have both left their children to the care of someone else.

Roxana's concern with her children's well-being does not take the form of action until the very last part of Defoe's novel. Like Moll, Roxana throughout her life has

moved through a series of surrogate mothers and
husband-keepers who take care of her. Although Roxana does
not forget her children, neither does she raise them. Each
affair she undertakes is supposed to better her circumstances, but she does not relieve her children once she is
financially able to do so. In fact, at the end she used
her notoriety and its ill effects on the children as an
excuse not to acknowledge them. Roxana refuses to accept
responsibility for anyone else as long as she can find
someone willing to take on that task for her.

Roxana finds two surrogate mothers during her adult
life: Amy and a Quaker woman. Amy, like the Quaker woman
after her, allows Roxana to lead two lives at once: she
can carry on business while in retirement, run households
and errands in two counties, and finally play mother to
children without ever having to see them. Amy takes care
of all the dirty work. Roxana can leave her five children
completely in Amy's care (19). Likewise, the Quaker woman,
who acts primarily during Amy's absences, relieves Roxana
of the responsibility for domestic duties: "in the affairs
of receiving Money, Interests, Rents, and the like . . .
she was as faithful as Amy cou'd be, and as diligent"
(326). With these two surrogate mothers in charge, Roxana
can do as she pleases.

Roxana's relationships with men, like her
relationships with surrogate mothers, parallel Moll's in
many respects, but with one important difference. While
Moll searches for stability and safety in her
relationships, Roxana looks for financial gain (166).
Although her liaisons with the landlord and the prince are
affectionate, more importantly, they are lucrative. Both

men lavish money, jewels, and property on her and even write her into their wills. The one man she does feel more affection for, a merchant, she refuses to marry until he is able to promise a purchased title of nobility to go along with the title of wife.

Roxana's various marriages and liaisons produce a total of twelve children. She professes great concern for them, but once they are out of her hands, she does not attempt to get them back. At first this is because she cannot afford to keep them; but as her financial conditions improve, she does nothing to recover her children. Her first five children are abandoned to relatives when she is in her early twenties. She does not attempt to find out about them until twenty to thirty years later, and then she sends Amy to inquire about them in her stead. Roxana's two sons by the prince are cared for by him; there is no evidence in the book that Roxana ever tries to see the children. Not even her son by the Dutch merchant, a man for whom she had real affection, escapes these negative feelings. The boy is put to nurse; she does not care to see him:

> I had shown a general Neglect of the Child,
> thro' all the gay Years of my London Revels;
> except that I sent Amy to look upon it now and
> then . . . as for me, I scarce saw it four times
> in the first four Years of its Life, and often
> wish'd it wou'd go quietly out of the World. (263)

When the boy is later legitimized, Roxana refers to him as "the merchant's son" and not as her own (329).

Moll and Roxana, although they are able to ignore their children while they are children, are forced to come to terms with them once they are grown. Resolving their relationships with their children becomes for each of them the final test toward accepting their adult roles. The two women resolve the problem in quite different ways.

Moll's reunion with her son Humphrey is in some respects a direct result of her governess's efforts to get her to do "something" to restore her life. Moll has turned to thievery to survive and ends up in Newgate jail. Jemmy reenters her life, awakening her maternal feelings and leading to a conversion of Moll to a "Christian" life. After her own soul is changed, she saves Jemmy and they sail to America where she meets her son Humphrey. The emotion she experiences is overwhelming:

> I thought all my entrails burned within me, that
> my very bowels moved, and I knew not what to do,
> as I now know not how to express these agonies!
> . . . I stood gazing and trembling, and looking
> after him as long as I could see him . . . .
> (299)

Even though her desire to meet her son is partially motivated by her desire to receive her inheritance from her mother, Moll is strong enough to accept her grown son when he comes to her seeking the mother he never knew:

> I can neither express nor describe the joy that
> touched my very soul when I found, for it was
> easy to discover that part, that he came not as
> a stranger, but as a son to a mother, and indeed
> as a son who had never before known what a
> mother of his own was . . . . (309)

Moll's acknowledgement of her son ensures her further good fortune, as Defoe makes clear in the remainder of the book. Her acceptance of adult responsibility is linked to her moral and worldly prosperity.

The final relationship between Roxana and her daughter Susan, however, is strikingly different. Moll has accepted responsibility for her own life and left behind her pattern of dependent relationships before she accepts her son. Roxana, on the other hand, is confronted by Susan while her dependent patterns remain unbroken. Roxana retires with her Quaker woman, her second surrogate mother, without leaving the care of her first. She has not assumed responsibility for her own life and is unprepared to make herself known to anyone, such as her children, who may be dependent on her.

Roxana's motivation for seeking out her children is never clear. She admits that it has "the Face of doing good" (188, emphasis mine): this is not the same as actually being good. Although two of her children are content with Amy's management, Susan wants Roxana to acknowledge her motherly responsibilities. Roxana's horror of this responsibility, combined with some realization that she ought to come to terms with it, is played out when she meets her daughter:

> I was bound to come so near my Girl, as to kiss her, which I wou'd not have done, had it been possible to have avoided it; but there was no room to escape.
>
> . . . No Pen can describe, no Words can express . . . the strange Impression which this thing made upon my Spirits; I felt something shoot thro' my Blood; my Heart flutter'd; my Head flash'd, and was dizzy, and all within me . . .

>   turn'd about, and much ado I had, not to abandon
>   myself to an Excess of Passion at the first
>   Sight of her, much more when my lips touch'd her
>   Face. . . . (277)

The intensity of emotion parallels that of Moll when she first sees Humphrey. However, while Moll is moved to acknowledge her son and embrace her role as mother, Roxana is moved to avoid all further contact with her daughter. She even fantasizes her daughter's death as a way to keep from seeing her again: "had she died by any ordinary Distemper, I shou'd have shed but very few Tears for her . . ." (302). Given a choice between acknowledging her daughter and her adult roles or continuing to be childlike, Roxana's choice is clear: Amy, the surrogate mother, wins over Susan the daughter.

Roxana's rejection of Susan and later rejection of her other daughter is linked directly by Roxana to her subsequent fate:

>   I fell into a dreadful Course of Calamities, and
>   Amy also; the very Reverse of our former Good
>   Days; the Blast of Heaven seem'd to follow the
>   Injury done the poor Girl, by us both; and I was
>   brought so low again, that my Repentance seem'd
>   to be only the Consequence of my Misery, as my
>   Misery was of my Crime. (329-30)

As Moll's assumption of her roles of adult and mother brings her greater prosperity and a "sincere penitence" (317), Roxana's rejection of those roles blasts her in this world and potentially in the next.

Defoe has constructed two satisfying endings to his novels. Moll takes hold of herself and her life, first through thievery, then through redemption. Her acceptance of her role as natural mother to at least one of her children is another step toward spiritual healing. Her trust in grace will take her much of the rest of the way. Conversely, _Roxana_ is truly the story of vice punished. The "Fortunate Mistress" is at the end neither fortunate nor--yet--mistress of herself. Roxana remains an unnatural daughter and mother rather than a fully adult, mature human being. Defoe has used the role of mother to show the spiritual flowering of Moll and spiritual withering of Roxana.

Rinehart 14

Works Cited

Defoe, Daniel. <u>The Fortunes and Misfortunes of the Famous</u>
<u>Moll Flanders</u>. London: Penguin, 1978.

---. <u>Roxana: The Fortunate Mistress</u>. London: Oxford UP,
1964.

Erickson, Robert A. "Moll's Fate: 'Mother Midnight' and
<u>Moll Flanders</u>." <u>Studies in Philology</u> 76 (1979): 75-
100.

Lerenbaum, Miriam. "Moll Flanders: A Woman on Her Own
Account." <u>The Authority of Experience: Essays in</u>
<u>Feminist Criticism</u>. Eds. Arlyn Diamond and Lee R.
Edwards. Amherst: U of Massachusetts P, 1977. 101-17.

Rinehart 15

Works Consulted

Birdsall, Virginia Ogden. <u>Defoe's Perpetual Seekers: A
    Study of the Major Fiction</u>. London: Associated U
    Presses, 1985.

Castle, Terry J. "'Amy, who knew my Disease': A
    Psychosexual Pattern in Defoe's <u>Roxana</u>." <u>ELH: Journal
    of English Literary History</u> 46 (1979): 81-96.

Chaber, Lois A. "Matriarchal Mirror: Women and Capital in
    <u>Moll Flanders</u>." <u>PMLA</u> 97 (1982): 212-26.

Marshall, Dorothy. <u>English People in the Eighteenth
    Century</u>. London: Longmans, Green, 1978.

Richetti, John J. "The Portrayal of Women in Restoration
    and Eighteenth-Century English Literature." <u>What
    Manner of Woman: Essays on English and American Life
    and Literature</u>. Ed. Marlene Springer. New York: New
    York UP, 1977. 65-97.

Shinagel, Michael. "The Maternal Theme in <u>Moll Flanders</u>:
    Craft and Character." <u>Cornell Library Journal</u> 7
    (1969): 3-23.

Stoler, John A. <u>Daniel Defoe: An Annotated Bibliography of
    Modern Criticism, 1900-1980</u>. New York: Garland, 1984.

INDEX